1004226211

		DATE DUE		

BIBLIOGRAPHY ON PSYCHOLOGICAL TESTS USED IN RESEARCH AND PRACTICE IN SPORT AND EXERCISE PSYCHOLOGY

BIBLIOGRAPHY ON PSYCHOLOGICAL TESTS USED IN RESEARCH AND PRACTICE IN SPORT AND EXERCISE PSYCHOLOGY

Arnold LeUnes

Mellen Studies in Psychology
Volume 7

The Edwin Mellen Press
Lewiston•Queenston•Lampeter

Library of Congress Cataloging-in-Publication Data

LeUnes, Arnold D.
   Bibliography on psychological tests used in research and practice in sport and exercise
psychology / Arnold LeUnes.
      p. cm. -- [Mellen studies in psychology ; v. 7]
   Includes indexes.
   ISBN-0-7734-7001-8
   1. Sports--Psychological aspects--Bibliography. 2. Psychological tests--Bibliography.
   I. Title. [II. Series.]

   Z7514.P79 L48 2002
   [GV706.4+]
   016.796'01--dc21

                                                                        2002069304

This is volume 7 in the continuing series
Mellen Studies in Psychology
Volume 7 ISBN 0-7734-7001-8
MSPs Series ISBN 0-7734-7529-X

A CIP catalog record for this book is available from the British Library.

         The Edwin Mellen Press   The Edwin Mellen Press
                Box 450   Box 67
          Lewiston, New York   Queenston, Ontario
           USA 14092-0450   CANADA L0S 1L0

                       The Edwin Mellen Press, Ltd.
                       Lampeter, Ceredigion, Wales
                       UNITED KINGDOM SA48 8LT

                  Printed in the United States of America

Dedication. This book is dedicated to my father, George John LeUnes, and my mother, Marion Katherine Chamberlain Hunt. My father, a Type A personality by any assessment, taught me many things, and perhaps none of the lessons were more important than the notion that any task worth doing is worth doing well. To him, a solid work ethic was of paramount importance, and I think I "inherited" some of it from him. This ethic has been put to a real test during the four years I have spent creating this citations project.

As for my mother, she taught me that being a Type B personality is acceptable. Her lessons in having fun, being flexible, and not taking oneself too seriously have served me well in life as well as in the conduct and completion of this work.

Table of Contents

Commendatory Preface

It is my privilege to write the commendatory preface for the work of my colleague and collaborator, Professor Arnold LeUnes. I have know Dr. LeUnes for twenty-seven years, and we have collaborate on seven refereed articles and a successful text entitled Sport Psychology which is published by Brooks/Cole and is now in its third edition. Dr. LeUnes is the author of 22 of the 26 chapters in the latest edition of the book, and the intelligence, creativity, and work ethic he brought to bear there is reflected in the present citations project. He is convinced that the bibliography will fill a real vacuum in the psychological assessment area within sport and exercise psychology, and I am sure that he is correct in that assumption. Locating useful psychological assessment inventories, becoming familiar with their psychometric strengths and weaknesses, and locating and assimilating the essential related references is a large undertaking. That undertaking has been made less arduous by the compilation amassed over the past four years by Dr. LeUnes and his students. It is a pleasure to recommend this work to the researchers, practitioners, and undergraduate and graduate students in sport and exercise psychology.

Jack R. Nation, Ph.D
Professor of Psychology
Texas A&M University
College Station, TX 77843-4235

Foreword

The creation of this bibliography really began almost twenty years ago with the creation of a brief list of citations related to the Profile of Mood States, a popular assessment device both within and external to sport and exercise psychology. My thought was that compiling bibliographies would be a good way to introduce undergraduate students to the research process. Being meticulous, attending to detail, and learning to search high and low in the library were all required if these works were to be reasonably complete. Also, familiarity with a variety of computer search engines was required of the students, thus familiarizing them with those mechanisms for conducting research. In the process, I became fascinated with the utility these things provided me in working with other students and professionals. On occasion, some of the students in my sport psychology classes would undertake the creation of a bibliography on a favorite topic. As time passed, it became clear that it would be feasible to take the existing bibliographies and expand them considerably, hence the creation of the present more voluminous work.

It has been a long process but a rewarding one, now that the task has been completed. Psychological assessment is a big part of sport and exercise psychology, and hopefully this volume will be useful to professionals and students in the various research and practice settings.

iii
Acknowledgments

Over the years, a large number of students have contributed their time, intelligence, and diligence to making this compilation possible. I would like to thank undergraduate Psychology majors Jolee Burger, Shannon Champion, Jessica Garner, Sue Ann Hayward, Kristi Hilburn, and Shellie Permenter for their capable assistance over the past four years. Also, a large number of graduate student in Sport Management assisted with the project, and I am grateful for their efforts. Among them were Misty Anderson, Stefanie Andrus, Margaret (Peggy) Bowersox, Holly Cliett, Jonathan Cornwell, George Cunningham, Lydia Dubuisson, Michael Hobson, Paul Keiper, Scott Lazenby, Farah Mensik, Todd Moore, Brian Nowell, Michael Sagas, Meredith Sholars, Noah Stein, Jeremy Stoehner, and Mark Wood. Psychology graduate students were also involved with the project from time to time, and a special thanks goes out to two of them, Suzanne Daiss and Alicia Egeberg-Snow. Working with all of these young people and seeing them grow, graduate, and go out into the "real world" has been a spectacular adventure for me. Thanks to all of you!

INTRODUCTION

The purpose of this collection of citations is to assist researchers, practitioners, and students in sport and exercise psychology in the conduct of their applied and/or research efforts. As anyone involved in these endeavors can attest, amassing the relevant literature on a topic is often an arduous task. Computer searches are one method for accomplishing this task, but are seldom thorough. Another time-honored method involves the tedious process of poring over volumes in the library. The virtue of the present work is that it simplifies the task of locating references for sport researchers, practitioners, and undergraduate and graduate students in the sports sciences.

The impetus for this collection was provided through a series of bibliographies published in the 1980s and 1990s on the Profile of Mood States (POMS), a popular psychometric instrument used in sport and exercise psychology research. The first POMS bibliography was published in 1986, has been updated on three occasions since, and has grown over the years to nearly 400 references (Daiss & LeUnes, 1986; LeUnes & Egeberg, 1988; LeUnes, Hayward, & Daiss, 1988; Snow & LeUnes, 1994, LeUnes & Burger, 1998, LeUnes, 2000). Given the success of the POMS bibliographies, a decision was made to encompass a broader array of psychological tests that have been used in sport and exercise psychology research, hence the present collection.

There are four key components to this book. One is a listing of relevant psychological assessment devices that have been used and are currently in use in sport and exercise psychology research and practice. Second, there is a list of citations by sport. As an example of the utility of such a listing, let us say that a researcher is conducting an investigation involving the sport of softball. He or she could then consult the List of Sports (Chapter Twenty-One) and find 31 citations in which psychometric instruments have been utilized. The same can be said for 64 other sport and exercise areas, though the number of references varies greatly from sport to sport. Also, an additional 18 categories have been created that are not about a particular sport, but have considerable relevance to sport and exercise psychology. Two examples of these 18 categories are "injury" and "steroids/other drugs." Clearly, these inclusions are not sports in and of themselves but they are most certainly relevant to sport and exercise psychology, hence their inclusion.

Third, there is a List of Authors (Chapter Twenty-Two). Let us say, for sake of example, that the reader is specifically interested in the work of Dr. Trent Petrie. A quick scan of the authors list would reveal each of Dr. Petrie's 32 citations in which psychological assessment devices have been utilized.

Finally, the compilation is completed with a brief section on social desirability responding, a topic of considerable interest to sport and exercise psychologists. One of the continuing points of contention concerning psychometric instruments is their varying susceptibility to responses from subjects who might be answering some or all test items in a socially desirable manner as opposed to a completely honest one, hence the inclusion of the citations to the Marlowe-Crowne Scale of Social Desirability.

In summary, there are citations for 65 different sports as well as 18 sport-related categories, and an author index of over 3,000 contributors to the sport and exercise psychology literature.

The compilation process for this volume began with a decision on how best to proceed in terms of working through a considerable literature that was initiated in some cases over 50 years ago. It was decided that the task would be undertaken on four not unrelated fronts. First of all, reading the available literature from a host of journals that publish articles about sport and exercise psychology was initiated. Based on this protracted review process, the 73 psychometric instruments contained in this volume were isolated for further coverage.

The second step was to institute a backtracking process that started with the most contemporary article on a particular instrument and ended with citations from the year in which the assessment device was published. Obviously, no articles could be written about a test that did not yet exist. In cases where many articles were written involving an unusually popular instrument, the backtracking process was indeed arduous. To stay current and thorough, every month or two for the past three years, the table of contents of countless journals were read with an eye for isolating articles in which psychometric instruments were used. When it seemed obvious or likely that an article dealt with a psychometric instrument, the abstract was then read to determine if such was actually the case. From there, the methods sections of each article was scrutinized to determine what psychological tests were employed, the name or names of the authors, and what sport or sports were being studied.

The third approach to data collection involved conducting periodic computer searches from ERIC, Sportdiscus, Web of Science, and Psycinfo. These useful search engines provided many additional leads on relevant publications, though the incompleteness of these mechanisms as a means of finding references was striking.

Finally, several authors were emailed and asked to provide an up-to-date list of their publications. It was assumed that these authors would indeed be authoritative sources, and they were. In a couple of instances, however, some articles had been found that authors did not even have on their own vitas.

Once all of the preceding avenues for amassing references were exhausted, the process of typing in all the relevant citations was begun. First of all, a list of psychological assessment devices was created by category of traits or characteristics measured. This list, of course, is found in the Table of Contents. Four major types of assessment devices were noted, and they are: Measures of Enduring Traits, Measures of Temporary States, Sport-Specific Measures, and Measures of Response Tendencies. As stated earlier, 73 different tests are subsumed under one of these four headings.

As the reader will see, at the end of each of the 2287 references is a citation concerning the sample on which a particular test was used. In some cases, the decision about what to parenthetically include was easy, such as in cases where only softball players were studied. In other instances, the authors cited samples of multiple sports, sometimes as many as ten or fifteen different ones. In these instances, we used the term "Various Sports" to represent them. At times, the author's description of subjects was ambiguous, such as studies of exercise in which the students were from college classrooms or physical education settings. In these cases, such terms as "College Students" or "Physical Education Class(es)" were used. Other inclusions of this sort are "Psychometric" and "Review Article." "Psychometric" is used to indicate citations that may not necessarily pertain to sport or exercise per se, but are included because they deal with important psychometric issues, things such as validity, reliability, norms, and item analysis. As for "Review Articles", these citations did not involve the administration of psychometric instruments but instead summarized a relevant body of literature. These sorts of inclusions are important in that they provide grounding for other assessment studies.

Clearly, any system of classification is possessed of arbitrariness, and this one is no exception. When all was said and done, however, it was determined that 65 different sport categories and 18 sport-related categories had been the subject of citations, and they can be found in the Chapter Twenty-one, the List of Sports. Once the preceding classification was accomplished, a listing of citations by author was compiled and this listing can be found in chapter Twenty-two appropriately entitled List of Authors.

One final note concerning authors and sports merits attention. There are several cases in which a particular research study utilized several different assessment devices. In those cases, the authors and the sports have been cited two or three times. That is to say, an author may have five numerical designations beside his or her name, but actually be the author of only two or three separate studies. Obviously, the same thing can be said for the sport listing. Softball, for instance, may have 31 citations but not be the subject of quite that many separate investigations.

It is only fair to say that I have done the majority of the research on this project. However, in several instances, undergraduate and graduate students made important contributions to the volume. Accordingly, they have been awarded what amounts to chapter authorships. These student authorships are scattered throughout the volume where warranted, and are testimony to the diligence, patience, and ability to attend to minute details of these men and women.

It is hoped that researchers, practitioners, and students have been provided with a valuable resource with which to build a research project or a treatment program. No claim is made that the literature on psychological tests in sport and exercise psychology has been exhausted here. It can honestly be stated, however, that every thing possible has been done over the past several years to exhaust the literature. The reader will, of course, find some things that have been overlooked, but the omissions did not occur for lack of effort.

By the time this work is available to the readership, new citations will have been published. It will then be incumbent on the reader to conduct his or her own updating to acquire the most recent literature. It is anticipated that this compilation will be updated in a few years, and readers are urged to submit overlooked or new citations to the author, thus providing valuable input for the the next edition.

SECTION ONE

MEASURES OF ENDURING TRAITS

Enduring traits are thought by personality theorists to have been developed, fostered, and firmly established over a period of many years. As a result, they are thought to be most descriptive of the true person. To put it another way, the enduring traits may be thought of as a snapshot of the "real you." In this section, the citations will involve measures of aggression, authoritarianism and machiavellianism, burnout, eating disorders, locus of control, omnibus personality inventories measuring a wide assortment of traits, optimism and pessimism, self-concept and related constructs, sensation seeking, and sex role orientation Perhaps one could find fault with the inclusion of burnout and eating disorders in this section. However, given the relationship of long-standing enduring traits such as perfectionism, control, and anxiety to the development of these disorders, a decision was made to list them here.

CHAPTER ONE

AGGRESSION

Buss-Perry Aggression Questionnaire

1.   Archer, J., Kilpatrick, G., & Bramwell, R. (1995). Comparison of two aggression inventories. **Aggressive Behavior, 21**, 371-380. (Psychometric)

2.   Bryant, F. B., & Smith, B.D. (2001). Refining the architecture of aggression: A measurement model for the Buss-Perry Aggression Questionnaire. **Journal of Research in Personality, 35**, 138-167. (Psychometric)

3.   Bushman, B. J., & Wells, G. L. (1998). Trait aggressiveness and hockey penalties: Predicting hot tempers on the ice. **Journal of Applied Psychology, 83**, 969-974. (Ice Hockey)

4.   Buss, A. H., & Perry, M. (1992). The Aggression Questionnaire. **Journal of Personality and Social Psychology, 63**, 452-459. (Psychometric)

5.   Buss, A. H., & Warren, W. L. (2000). **The Aggression Questionnaire manual**. Los Angeles, CA: Western Psychological Services. (Test Manual)

6.   Dill, K. E., Anderson, C. A., Anderson, K. B., & Deuser, W. E. (1997). Effects of aggressive personality on social expectations and social perceptions. **Journal of Research in Personality, 31**, 272-292.(Psychometric)

7.   Harris, J. A. (1995). Confirmatory factor analysis of the Aggression Questionnaire. **Behavior Research and Therapy, 33**, 991-993. (Psychometric)

8.   Harris, J. A. (1997). A further evaluation of the Aggression Questionnaire: Issues of validity and reliability. **Behavior Research and Therapy, 35**, 1047-1053. (Psychometric)

9.   Nakano, K. (2001). Psychometric evaluation on the Japanese adaptation of the Aggression Questionnaire. **Behaviour Research and Therapy, 39**, 853-858. (Psychometric)

10. Wann, D. L., Fahl, C. L., Erdmann, J. B., & Littleton, J. D. (1999). Relationship between identification with the role of sport fan and trait aggression. **Perceptual and Motor Skills, 88**, 1296-1298. (Sports Fans)

11. Williams, T. W., Boyd, J. C., Cascardi, M. A., & Poythress, N. (1996). Factor structure and convergent validity of the Aggression Questionnaire in an offender population. **Psychological Assessment, 8**, 398-403. (Psychometric)

CHAPTER TWO
AUTHORITARIANISM/MACHIAVELLIANISM

California F-Scale

12.   Dowell, L., Badgett, J., & Chevrette, J. (1968). Motor skills achievement and authoritarian dimensions. **Perceptual and Motor Skills, 27**, 469-470. (Psychometric)

13.   Laughlin, N. T., & McGlynn, G. H. (1983). The relationship between teacher and student (A) preferences for task – or relationship – motivated instruction and (B) degree of authoritarianism and (C) student evaluations of teacher effectiveness. **International Journal of Sport Psychology, 14**, 27-40. (Physical Education Class(es)

14.   LeUnes, A., & Nation, J. R. (1982). Saturday's heroes: A psychological portrait of college football players. **Journal of Sport Behavior, 5**, 139-149. (Football)

15.   Nation, J. R., & LeUnes, A. (1983). A personality profile of the black athlete in college football. **Psychology, 20**, 1-3. (Football)

16.   Nation, J. R., & LeUnes, A. (1983). Personality characteristics of intercollegiate football players as determined by position, classification, and redshirt status. **Journal of Sport Behavior, 6**, 92-102. (Football)

17.   Riddick, C. C. (1984). Comparative psychological profiles of three groups of female collegians: Competitive swimmers, recreational swimmers, and inactive swimmers. **Journal of Sport Behavior, 7**, 160-174. (Swimming)

Machiavellianism Scale

18.   Bem, S. L. (1977). On the utility of alternative procedures for assessing psychological androgyny. **Journal of Consulting and Clinical Psychology, 45**, 196-205. (Psychometric)

19. Browne, J. (1977). Machiavellianism: A study involving physical education and recreation students. **Australian Journal for Health, Physical Education and Recreation, 76,** 44-48. (Physical Education class(es)

20. Russell, G. W. (1974). Machiavellianism, locus of control, aggression, performance and precautionary behavior in ice hockey. **Human Relations, 27,** 825-837. (Ice Hockey)

21. Zenker, S. I., & Wolfgang, A. K. (1982). Relationship of Machiavellianism and locus of control to preferences for leisure activity by college men and women. **Psychological Reports, 50,** 583-586. (Leisure Activity)

CHAPTER THREE

BURNOUT

Maslach Burnout Inventory (MBI)

22.   Byrne, B. M. (1993). The Maslach Burnout Inventory: Testing the factorial validity and invariance across elementary, intermediate, and secondary teachers. **Journal of Occupational & Organizational Psychology, 66,** 197-212. (Psychometric)

23.   Capel, S. A., Sisley, B. L., & Desertrain, G. S. (1987). The relationship of role conflict and role ambiguity to burnout in high school basketball coaches. **Journal of Sport Psychology, 9,** 106-117. (Basketball, Coaching)

24.   Dale, J., & Weinberg, R. S. (1989). The relationship between coaches' leadership style and burnout. **The Sport Psychologist, 3,** 1-13. (Coaching)

25.   Danylchuk, K. E. (1993). The presence of occupational burnout and its correlates in university physical education personnel. **Journal of Sport Management, 7,** 107-121. (Physical Education Class(es)

26.   Flor, K. K. (1996). The relationship between personality hardiness, stress, and burnout in selected college athletes. **International Institute for Sport & Human Performance.** (Various Sports)

27.   Green, D. E., & Walkey, F. H. (1988). A confirmation of the 3-factor structure of the Maslach Burnout Inventory. **Educational and Psychological Measurement, 48,** 579-585. (Psychometric)

28.   Haggerty, T. J. (1982). **An assessment of the degree of burnout in Canadian university coaches: A national survey.** Toronto: York University. (Coaching)

29.   Hendrix, A. E., Acevedo, E. O., & Hebert, E. (2000). An examination of stress and burnout in certified athletic trainers at division I-A universities. **Journal of Athletic Training, 35,** 139-144. (Athletic Training)

30.   Hoeksema, J. H., Guy, J. D., Brown, C. K., & Brady, J. L. (1993). The relationship between psychotherapist burnout and satisfaction with leisure activities. **Psychotherapy in Private Practice, 12,** 51-57. (Leisure Activity)

31.   Hunt, K. R., & Miller, S. R. (1994). Comparison levels of perceived stress and burnout among college basketball and tennis coaches. In W.K. Simpson, A. LeUnes, & J.S. Picou (Eds.), **Applied Research in Coaching and Athletics Annual, 1994.Boston: American Press** (198-222). (Basketball, Coaching, Tennis)

32.   Kelley, B. C., Eklund, R. C., & Ritter-Taylor, M. (1999). Stress and burnout among collegiate tennis coaches. **Journal of Sport & Exercise Psychology, 21,** 113-130. (Coaching, Tennis)

33.   Koustelios, A. D., Kellis, S., & Bagiatis, K. (1997). The role of family variables on football coaches' burnout. **Coaching and Sport Science Journal, 2,** 41-45. (Coaching, Football)

34.   Koustelios, A. D., Kellis, S., & Bagiatis, K. (1999). Job satisfaction and burnout in a sport setting: A multiple regression analysis. **European Journal for Sport Management, 61,** 31-39. (Sport Employees)

35.   Martin, J. J., Kelley, B. C., & Eklund, R. C. (1999). A model of stress and burnout in male high school athletic directors. **Journal of Sport & Exercise Psychology, 21,** 280-294. (Athletic Directors)

36.   Pastore, D. L., & Judd, M. R. (1993). Gender differences in burnout among coaches of women's athletic teams at 2-year colleges. **Sociology of Sport Journal, 10,** 205-212. (Coaching)

37.   Quigley, T., Slack, T., & Smith, G. (1987). Burnout in secondary-school teacher coaches. **Alberta Journal of Educational Research, 33,** 260-274. (Coaching)

38.   Quigley, T., Slack, T., & Smith, G. (1989). The levels and possible causes of burnout in secondary school teacher-coaches. **CAPHER Journal, 55,** 20-25. (Coaching)

39.   Raedeke, T. D., Granzyk, T. L., & Warren, A. (2000). Why coaches experience burnout: A commitment perspective. **Journal of Sport & Exercise Psychology, 22**, 85-105. (Coaching)

40.   Rainey, D. W. (1995). Stress, burnout, and intention to terminate among umpires. **Journal of Sport Behavior, 18**, 312-323. (Sports Officials)

41.   Rainey, D. W. (1999). Sources of stress, burnout, and intention to terminate among basketball referees. **Journal of Sport Behavior, 22**, 578-590. (Basketball, Sports Officials)

42.   Schaufeli, W. B., & van Dierendock, D. (1993). The construct validity of two burnout measures. **Journal of Organizational Behavior, 14**, 631-647. (Psychometric)

43.   Schaufeli, W. B., Daamen, J., & van Mierlo, H. (1994). Burnout among Dutch teachers: An MBI validation study. **Educational and Psychological Measurement, 54**, 803-812. (Psychometric)

44.   Schaufeli, W. B., & van Dierendonck, D. (1993). The construct validity of two burnout measures. **Journal of Organizational Behavior, 14**, 631-647. (Psychometric)

45.   Taris, T. W., Schreurs, P. J. G., & Schaufeli, W. B. (1999). Construct validity of the Maslach Burnout Inventory-General Survey: A two-sample examination of its factor structure and correlates. **Work and Stress, 13**, 223-237. (Psychometric)

46.   Taylor, A. H., Daniel, J. V., Leith, L., & Burke, R. J. (1990). Perceived stress, psychological burnout and paths to turnover intentions among sport officials. **Journal of Applied Sport Psychology, 2**, 84-97. (Sports Officials)

47.   Vealey, R. S., Armstrong, L., & Comar, W. (1998). Influence of perceived coaching behaviors on burnout and competitive anxiety in female college athletes. **Journal of Applied Sport Pychology, 10**, 297-318. (Coaching, Various Sports)

48.   Vealey, R. S., Udry, E. M., Zimmerman, V., & Soliday, J. (1992).
Intrapersonal and situational predictors of coaching burnout. **Journal of Sport &**
Exercise Psychology, 14, 40-58. (Coaching)

49.   Walkey, F. H., & Green, D. E. (1992). An exhaustive examination of the
replicable factor structure of the Maslach Burnout Inventory. **Educational and**
Psychological Measurement, 52, 309-323. (Psychometric)

50.   Wilson, V. E., & Bird, E. I. (1988). Burnout in coaching – part two:
Results from survey of national coaches. **Sports Science Perspective on**
Research and Technology in Sport, 8, 1-6. (Coaching)

CHAPTER FOUR
EATING DISORDERS

The Bulimia Test (BULIT)

51.   Diehl, N., Johnson, C. E., Rogers, R. L., & Petrie, T. A. (1998). Social physique anxiety and disorder eating: What's the connection? **Addictive Behaviors, 23**, 1-6. (College Students)

52.   Kashubeck-West, S., Mintz, L. B., & Saunders, K. T. (2001). Assessment of eating disorders in women. **The Counseling Psychologist, 29**, 662-694. (Review Article)

53.   Petrie, T. A. (1993). Disordered eating in female collegiate gymnasts: Prevalence and personal-attitudinal correlates. **Journal of Sport & Exercise Psychology, 15**, 424-436. (Gymnastics)

54.   Petrie, T. A., & Stoever, S. (1993). The incidence of bulimia nervosa and pathogenic weight control in female collegiate gymnasts. **Research Quarterly for Exericise and Sport, 64**, 238-241. (Gymnastics)

55.   Smith, M. C., & Thelen, M. H. (1984). Development and validation of a test for bulimia. **Journal of Consulting and Clinical Psychology, 52**, 863-872. (Psychometric)

56.   Thelen, M. H., Farmer, J., Wonderlich, S., & Smith, M. C. (1991). A revision of the bulimia test: The BULIT-R. **Psychological Assessment: A Journal of Consulting and Clinical Psychology, 3**,119-124. (Psychometric)

Eating Attitudes Test (EAT)

57.   Al-Subaie, A., Al-Shamari, S., Bamgboye, E., Al-Sabhan, K., Al-Shehri, S., & Bannah, A. R. (1996). Validity of the Arabic version of the Eating Attitudes Test. **International Journal of Eating Disorders, 20**, 321-324. (Psychometric)

58. Beals, K., & Manore, M. (1994). The prevalence and consequences of subclinical eating disorders in female athletes. **International Journal of Sport Nutrition, 4**, 175-185. (Review Article)

59. Brooks-Gunn, J., Burrow, C., & Warren, M. P. (1988). Attitudes toward eating and body weight in different groups of female adolescent athletes. **International Journal of Eating Disorders, 7**, 749-757. (Various Sports)

60. Brooks-Gunn, J., Warren, M. P., & Hamilton, L. H. (1987). The relation of eating problems and amenorrhea in ballet dancers. **Medicine and Science in Sports and Exercise, 19**, 41-44. (Dance)

61. Diehl, N., Johnson, C. E., Rogers, R. L., & Petrie, T. A. (1998). Social physique anxiety and disordered eating? What's the connection? **Addictive Behaviors, 23**, 1-6. (College Students)

62. Enns, M. P., Drewnowski, A., & Grinker, J. A. (1987). Body composition, body size estimation, and attitudes toward eating in male college athletes. **Psychosomatic Medicine, 49**, 56-64. (Skiing, Swimming, Wrestling)

63. Estok, P. J., & Rudy, E. B. (1996). The relationship between eating disorders and running in women. **Research in Nursing and Health, 19**, 377-387. (Running)

64. Evers, C. L. (1987). Dietary intake and symptoms of anorexia-nervosa in female university dancers. **Journal of the American Dietetic Association, 87**, 66-68. (Dance)

65. Garner, D. M., & Garfinkel, P. E. (1979). Eating Attitudes Test: Index of the symptoms of anorexia nervosa. **Psychological Medicine, 9**, 273-279. (Psychometric)

66. Garner, D. M., & Rosen, L. W. (1991). Eating disorders among athletes: Research and recommendations. **Journal of Applied Sport Science Research, 5**, 100-107. (Review Article)

17

67. Garner, D. M., Olmsted, M. P., Bohr, Y., & Garfinkel, P. E. (1982). The Eating Attitudes Test: Psychometric features and clinical correlates. **Psychological Medicine, 12**, 871-878. (Psychometric)

68. Harris, M. B., & Greco, D. (1990). Weight control and weight concern in competitive female gymnasts. **Journal of Sport & Exercise Psychology, 12**, 427-433. (Gymnastics)

69. Hickson, J. F., & Kish, K. (1989). Eating attitude and nutritional intake of adolescent female gymnasts. **Journal of Applied Sport Science Research, 3**, 48-50. (Gymnastics)

70. Holderness, C. C., Brooks-Gunn, J., & Warren, M. P. (1994). Eating disorders and substance use: A dancing vs a nondancing population. **Medicine and Science in Sports and Exercise, 26**, 297-302. (Dance)

71. Kashubeck-West, S., Mintz, L. B., & Saunders, K. T. (2001). Assessment of eating disorders in women. **The Counseling Psychologist, 29**, 662-694. (Review Article)

72. Kiernan, M., Rodin, J., Brownell, K. D., Wilmore, J. H., & Crandall, C. (1992). Relation of level of exercise, age, and weight-cycling history of weight and eating concerns in male and female runners. **Health Psychology, 11**, 418-421. (Running)

73. Legrange, D., Tibbs, J., & Noakes, T. D. (1994). Implications of a diagnosis of anorexia-nervosa in ballet school. **International Journal of Eating Disorders, 15**, 369-376. (Dance)

74. Nasser, M. (1986). The validity of the Eating Attitudes Test in a nonwestern population. **Acta Psychiatrica Scandinavica, 73**, 109-110. (Psychometric)

75. Nudelman, S., Rosen, J. C., & Leitenberg, H. (1988). Dissimilarities in eating attitudes, body image distortion, depression, and self-esteem between high-intensity male runners and women with bulimia nervosa. **International Journal of Eating Disorders, 7**, 625-633. (Running)

76. Picard, C. L. (1999). The level of competition as a factor for the development of eating disorders in female collegiate athletes. **Journal of Youth and Adolescence, 28**, 583-594. (Various Sports)

77. Raciti, M. C., & Norcross, J. C. (1987). The EAT and EDI: Screening, interrelationships and psychometrics. **International Journal of Eating Disorders, 6**, 579-586. (Psychometric)

78. Rosen, J. C., Silberg, N. T., & Gross, J. (1988). Eating Attitudes Test and Eating Disorders Inventory: Norms of adolescent girls and boys. **Journal of Consulting and Clinical Psychology, 56**, 305-308. (Psychometric)

79. Rucinski, A. (1989). Relationship of body-image and dietary-intake of competitive ice skaters. **Journal of the American Dietetic Association, 89**, 98-100. (Figure Skating/Ice Skating)

80. Slay, H. A., Hayaki, J., Napolitano, M. A., & Brownell, K. D. (1998). Motivations for running and eating attitudes in obligatory versus nonobligatory runners. **International Journal of Eating Disorders, 23**, 267-275. (Running)

81. Stoutjesdyk, D., & Jevne, R. (1993). Eating disorders among high-performance athletes. **Journal of Youth and Adolescence, 22**, 271-282. (Various Sports)

82. Wakui, S., Shimomitsu, T., Odagiri, Y., Ohya, Y., & Katsumura, T. (1999). Eating disorder symptoms, weight loss behaviors and weight-cycling in female college students: Correlates of exercise behavior. **Japanese Journal of Physical Fitness and Sports Medicine, 48**, 607-618. (College Students, Exercise)

83. Warren, B. J., Stanton, A. L., & Blessing, D. L. (1990). Disordered eating patterns in competitive female athletes. **International Journal of Eating Disorders, 9**, 565-569. (Various Sports)

84. Wilkins, J. A., Boland, F. J., & Albinson, J. G. (1991). A comparison of male and female athletes and nonathletes on eating disorders indices: Are athletes protected? **Journal of Sport Behavior, 14**, 129-143. (Various Sports)

85. Yates, A., Shisslak, C. M., Allender, J., & Leehey, K. (1992). Comparing obligatory and nonobligatory runners. **Psychosomatics, 33**, 180-189. (Running)

Eating Disorders Inventory (EDI)

86. Abood, D. A., & Black, D. R. (2000). Health education prevention for eating disorders among college female athletes. **American Journal of Health Behavior, 24**, 209-219. (Various Sports)

87. Anderson, S. L., Zager, K., Hetzler, R. K., Nahakian-Nelms, M., & Syler, G. (1996). Comparison of eating disorder inventory (EDI-2) scores of male bodybuilders to the male college subgroup. **International Journal of Sport Nutrition, 6**, 255-262. (Bodybuilding)

88. Ashley, C. D., Smith, J. F., Robinson, J. B., & Richardson, M. (1996). Disordered eating in female collegiate athletes and collegiate females in an advanced program of study: A preliminary investigation. **International Journal of Sport Nutrition, 6**, 391-401. (Dance, Various Sports)

89. Beals, K., & Manore, M. (1994). The prevalence and consequences of subclinical eating disorders in female athletes. **International Journal of Sport Nutrition, 4**, 175-185. (Review Article)

90. Benson, J. E., Allemann, Y., Theintz, G. E., & Howald, H. (1990). Eating problems and calorie intake levels in Swiss adolescent athletes. **International Journal of Sports Medicine, 11**, 249-252. (Gymnastics, Swimming)

91. Borgen, J. S. (1994). Are male compulsive jogging and female eating disorders parallel states? **Norsk Tidsskrift for Idrettsmedisin, 3**, 6. (Running)

92. Brooks, C., Taylor, R. D., Hardy, C. A., & Lass, T. (2000). Proneness to eating disorders: Weightlifters compared to exercisers. **Perceptual and Motor Skills, 90**, 906. (Exercise, Weightlifting)

93.   Cox, L. M., Lantz, C. D., & Mayhew, J. L. (1997). The role of social physique anxiety and other variables in predicting eating behaviors in college students. **International Journal of Sports Nutrition, 7**, 310-317. (College Students)

94.   Davis, C. (1990). Body image and weight preoccupation: A comparison between exercising and nonexercising women. **Appetite, 15**, 13-21. (Exercise)

95.   Davis, C. (1990). Weight and diet preoccupation: The role of exercise. **Personality and Individual Differences, 11**, 823-827. (Exercise)

96.   Davis, C. (1992). Body image, dieting behaviours, and personality factors: A study of high-performance female athletes. **International Journal of Sport Psychology, 23**, 179-192. (Various Sports)

97.   Davis, C., & Cowles, M. (1989). A comparison of weight and diet concerns and personality factors among female athletes and nonathletes. **Journal of Psychosomatic Research, 33**, 527-536. (Various Sports)

98.   Davis, C., & Katzman, M. A. (1998). Chinese men and women in the United States and Hong Kong: Body and self-esteem ratings as a prelude to dieting and exercise. **International Journal of Eating Disorders, 23**, 99-102. (Exercise)

99.   Davis, C., & Strachan, S. (2001). Elite female athletes with eating disorders: A study of psychopathological characteristics. **Journal of Sport & Exercise Psychology, 23**, 245-253. (Dance, Various Sports)

100.   Eberly, C. C., & Eberly, B. W. (1985). A review of the Eating Disorder Inventory. **Journal of Counseling and Development, 64**, 285. (Review Article)

101.   Favaro, A., Caregaro, L., Burlina, A. B., & Santonastaso, P. (2000). Tryptophan levels, excessive exercise, and nutritional status in anorexia nervosa. **Psychosomatic Medicine, 62**, (Exercise)

102.   Fogelholm, M., & Hiilloskorpi, H. (1999). Weight and diet concerns in Finnish female and male athletes. **Medicine and Science in Sports and Exercise, 31**, 229-235. (Dance, Various Sports)

103.   Frederick, C. M., & Morrison, C. S. (1998). A mediational model of social physique anxiety and eating disordered behaviors. **Perceptual and Motor Skills, 86**, 139-145. (College Students)

104.   Fulkerson, J. A., Keel, P. K., Leon, G. R., & Dorr, T. (1999). Eating-disordered behaviors and personality characteristics of high school athletes and nonathletes. **International Journal of Eating Disorders, 26**, 73-79. (Various Sports)

105.   Garner, D. M. (1991). **Eating Disorders Inventory-2 professional manual**. Odessa, FL: Psychological Assessment Resources. (Test Manual)

106.   Garner, D. M., & Garfinkel, P. E. (1979). Eating Attitude Test: Index of the symptoms of anorexia-nervosa. **Psychological Medicine, 9**, 273-279. (Review Article)

107.   Garner, D. M., & Olmsted, M. P. (1983). **Manual for the Eating Disorders Inventory (EDI)**. Lutz, FL: Psychological Assessment Resources. (Test Manual)

108.   Garner, D. M., & Rosen, L. W. (1991). Eating disorders among athletes: Research and recommendations. **Journal of Applied Sport Science Research, 5**, 1001-1007. (Review Article)

109.   Garner, D. M., Olmsted, M. P., & Polivy, J. (1983). The development and validation of a multidimensional eating disorder inventory for anorexia and bulimia. **International Journal of Eating Disorders, 2**, 15-34. (Psychometric)

110.   Garner, D. M., Garfinkel, P. E., Rockert, W., & Olmsted, M. (1987). A prospective study of eating disturbance in the ballet. **Psychotherapy and Psychosomatics, 48**, 170-175. (Dance)

111.   Garner, D. M., Olmsted, M. P., Polivy, J., & Garfinkel, P. E. (1984). Comparison between weight-preoccupied women and anorexia nervosa. **Psychosomatic Medicine, 46**, 255-266. (Dance)

112.   Haase, A. M., Prapavessis, H., & Owens, R. G. (1999). Perfectionism and eating attitudes in competitive rowers: Moderating effects of body mass, weight classification and gender. **Psychology and Health, 14**, 643-657. (Rowing)

113.   Hamilton, L. H., Brooks-Gunn, J., Warren, M. P., & Hamilton, W. G. (1988). The role of selectivity in the pathogenesis of eating problems in ballet dancers. **Medicine and Science in Sports and Exercise, 20**, 560-565. (Dance)

114.   Harris, M. B., & Greco, D. (1990). Weight control and weight concern in competitive female gymnasts. **Journal of Sport & Exercise Psychology, 12**, 427-433. (Gymnastics)

115.   Holderness, C. C., Brooks-Gunn, J., & Warren, M. P. (1994). Eating disorders and substance use: A dancing versus a nondancing population. **Medicine and Science in Sports and Exercise, 26**, 297-302. (Dance)

116.   Joiner, T. E., & Heatherton, T. F. (1998). First- and second-order factor structure of the Eating Disorders Inventory. **International Journal of Eating Disorders, 23**, 189-198. (Psychometric)

117.   Kashubeck-West, S., Mintz, L. B., & Saunders, K. T. (2001). Assessment of eating disorders in women. **The Counseling Psychologist, 29**, 662-694. (Review Article)

118.   Kiernan, M., Rodin, J., Brownell, K. D., Wilmore, J. H., & Crandall, C. (1992). Relation of level of exercise, age, and weight-cycling history to weight and eating concerns in male and female runners. **Health Psychology, 11**, 418-421. (Running)

119.   Kirchner, E. M., Lewis, R. D., & O'Connor, P. J. (1995). Bone mineral density and ditary intake of female college gymnasts. **Medicine and Science in Sports and Exercise, 27**, 543-549. (Gymnastics)

120.   Klock, S. C., & DeSouza, M. J. (1995). Eating disorder characteristics and psychiatric symptomatology of eumenorrheic and amenorrheic runners. **International Journal of Eating Disorders, 17**, 161-166. (Running)

121. Krane, V., Stiles-Shipley, J. A., Waldron, J., & Michalenok, J. (2001). Relationships among body satisfaction, social physique anxiety, and eating behaviors in female athletes and exercisers. **Journal of Sport Behavior, 24**, 247-264. (Exercise, Various Sports)

122. Kurtzman, F. D., Yager, J., Landsverk, J., Wiesmeier, E., & Bodurka, D. C. (1989). Eating disorders among selected female student populations at UCLA. **Journal of the American Dietetic Association, 89**, 45-50. (Dance, Various Sports)

123. Leon, G. R. (1991). Eating disorders in female athletes. **Sports Medicine, 12**, 219-227. (Review Article)

124. Marshall, J. D., & Harber, V. J. (1996). Body dissatisfaction and drive for thinness in high performance hockey athletes. **International Journal of Sports Medicine, 17**, 541-544. (Ice Hockey)

125. Martin, K. A., & Hausenblas, H. A. (1998). Psychological commitment to exercise and eating disorders symptomatology among female aerobic instructors. **The Sport Psychologist, 12**, 180-190. (Exercise)

126. Nudelman, S., Rosen, J. C., & Leitenberg, H. (1988). Dissimilarities in eating attitudes, body image distortion, depression, and self-esteem between high-intensity male runners and women with bulimia nervosa. **International Journal of Eating Disorders, 7**, 625-633. (Running)

127. O'Connor, P. J., Lewis, R. D., & Kirchner, E. M. (1995). Bone mineral density and dietary intake of female collegiate gymnasts. **Medicine and Science in Sports and Exercise, 27**, 543-549. (Gymnastics)

128. O'Connor, P. J., Lewis, R. D., & Kirchner, E. M. (1995). Eating disorder symptoms in female college gymnasts. **Medicine and Science in Sports and Exercise, 27**, 550-555. (Gymnastics)

129. Olson, M. S., Williford, H. N., Richards, L. A., Brown, J. A., & Pugh, S. F. (1996). Self-reports on the Eating Disorders Inventory by female aerobic instructors. **Perceptual and Motor Skills, 82,** 1051-1058. (Exercise, Marathon, Running, Weightlifting)

130. Pasman, L., & Thompson, J. K. (1988). Body image and eating disturbance in obligatory runners, obligatory weightlifters, and sedentary individuals. **International Journal of Eating Disorders, 7,** 759-769. (Running, Weightlifting)

131. Petrie, T. A. (1996). Differences between male and female college lean sport athletes, nonlean sport athletes, and nonathletes on behavioral and psychological indices of eating disorders. **Journal of Applied Sport Psychology, 8,** 218-230. (Various Sports)

132. Picard, C. L. (1999). The level of competition as a factor for the development of eating disorders in female collegiate athletes. **Journal of Youth and Adolescence, 28,** 583-594. (Various Sports)

133. Raciti, M. C., & Norcross, J. C. (1987). The EAT and EDI: Screening, interrelationships, and psychometrics. **International Journal of Eating Disorders, 6,** 579-586. (Psychometric)

134. Reel, J. J., & Gill, D. L. (1996). Psychosocial factors related to eating disorders among high school and college female cheerleaders. **The Sport Psychologist, 10,** 195-206. (Cheerleading)

135. Richert, A. J., & Hummers, J. A. (1986). Patterns of physical activity in college students at possible risk for eating disorders. **International Journal of Eating Disorders, 7,** 757-763. (Exercise)

136. Rippon, C., Nash, J., Myburgh, K. H., & Noakes, T. D. (1988). Abnormal eating attitude test scores predict menstrual dysfunction in lean females. **International Journal of Eating Disorders, 7,** 617-624. (Dance, Marathon)

137.   Rosen, J. C., Silberg, N. T., & Gross, J. (1988). Eating Attitudes Test and Eating Disorders Inventory: Norms for adolescent girls and boys. **Journal of Consulting and Clinical Psychology, 56**, 305-308. (Psychometric)

138.   Ryujin, D. H., Breaux, C., & Marks, A. D. (1999). Symptoms of eating disorders among female distance runners: Can the inconsistencies be unraveled? **Women and Health, 30**, 71-83. (Running)

139.   Sands, R., Tricker, J., Sherman, C., Armatas, C., & Maschette, W. (1977). Disordered eating patterns, body image, self-esteem, and physical activity in preadolescent school children. **International Journal of Eating Disorders, 21**, 159-166. (Exercise)

140.   Siegel, A. J., Stewart, E. L., & Barone, B. (1990). Body image assessment and eating attitudes in marathon runners: Inverse findings to patients with anorexia nervosa. **Annals of Sports Medicine, 5**, 65-70. (Marathon)

141.   Skowron, E. A., & Friedlander, M. L. (1994). Psychological separation, self-control, and weight preoccupation among elite women athletes. **Journal of Counseling and Development, 72**, 310-315. (Swimming)

142.   Smolak, L., Murnen, S. K., & Ruble, A. E. (2000). Female athletes and eating problems: A meta-analysis. **International Journal of Eating Disorders, 27**, 371-380. (Psychometric)

143.   Sundgot-Borgen, J. (1994). Eating disorders in female athletes. **Sports Medicine, 17**, 176-188. (Review Article)

144.   Sundgot-Borgen, J. (1994). Risk and trigger factors for the development of eating disorders in female elite athletes. **Medicine and Science in Sports and Exercise, 26**, 414-419. (Various Sports)

145.   Sundgot-Borgen, J. & Corbin, C. B. (1987). Eating disorders among female athletes. **Physician and Sportsmedicine, 15**(2), 88-95. (Various Sports)

146.   Syzmanski, L. A., & Chrisler, J. C. (1990/1991). Eating disorders, gender role, and athletic activity. **Psychology: A Journal of Human Behavior, 27/28**, 20-27. (Various Sports)

147.   Taub, D. E., & Blinde, E. M. (1994). Disordered eating among adolescent female athletes: Influence of athletic participation and sport team membership. **Adolescence, 27**, 833-848. (Various Sports)

148.   Taylor, G. M., & Ste-Marie, D. M. (2001). Eating disorders symptoms in Canadian pair and dance figure skaters. **International Journal of Sport Psychology, 32**, 21-28. (Figure Skating/Ice Skating)

149.   Thiel, A., Gottfried, H., & Hesse, F. W. (1993). Subclinical eating disorders in male athletes: A study of the low-weight category in rowers and wrestlers. **Acta Psychiatrica Scandinavica, 88**, 259-265. (Rowing, Wrestling)

150.   Walberg, J. L., & Johnston, C. S. (1991). Menstrual function and eating behavior in female recreational weight lifters and competitive body builders. **Medicine and Science in Sports and Exercise, 23**, 30-36. (Bodybuilding, Weightlifting)

151.   Warren, B. J., Stanton, A. L., & Blessing, D. L. (1990). Disordered eating patterns in competitive female athletes. **International Journal of Eating Disorders, 9**, 565-569. (Various Sports)

152.   Wear, R. W., & Pratz, O. (1987). Test-retest reliability of the Eating Disorders Inventory. **International Journal of Eating Disorders, 6**, 767-769. (Psychometric)

153.   Weight, L. M., & Noakes, T. D. (1987). Is running an analog of anorexia?: A survey of the incidence of eating disorders in female distance runners. **Medicine and Science in Sports and Exercise, 19**, 213-217. (Running)

154.   Welch, G., Hall, A., & Walkey, F. H. (1988). The factor structure of the Eating Disorders Inventory. **Journal of Clinical Psychology, 44**, 51-56. (Dance, Psychometric)

155.   Wilkins, J. A., Boland, F. J., & Albinson, J. G. (1991). A comparison of male and female athletes and nonathletes on eating disorders indices: Are athletes protected? **Journal of Sport Behavior, 14**, 129-143. (Various Sports)

CHAPTER FIVE
LOCUS OF CONTROL

Health Locus of Control Scale (HLOC)

156.   Brandon, J. E. & Loftin, J. M. (1991). Relationship of fitness to depression, state and trait anxiety, internal health locus of control, and self-control. **Perceptual and Motor Skills, 73**, 563-568. (Cycling)

157.   Carter, J. A., Lee, A. M., & Greenockle, K. M. (1987). Locus of control, fitness values, success expectations and performance in a fitness class. **Perceptual and Motor Skills, 65**, 777-778. (Exercise)

158.   Chen, C. Y., Neufeld, P. S., Feely, C. A., & Skinner, C. S. (1999). Factors influencing compliance with home exercise programs among patients with upper-extremity impairment. **American Journal of Occupational Therapy, 53**, 171-180. (Exercise)

159.   Chen, W. W. (1995). Enhancement of health locus of control through biofeedback training. **Perceptual and Motor Skills, 80**, 395-398. (Biofeedback)

160.   Cooper, D., & Fraboni, M. A. (1988). Toward a more valid and reliable Health Locus of Control Scale. **Journal of Clinical Psychology, 44**, 536-540. (Psychometric)

161.   Dishman, R. K., & Gettman, L. R. (1980). Psychobiologic influences on exercise adherence. **Journal of Sport Psychology, 2**, 295-310. (Endurance Training)

162.   Dishman, R. K., & Steinhardt, M. (1990). Health locus of control predicts free-living, but not supervised, physical activity: A test of exercise-specific control and outcome-expectancy hypotheses. **Research Quarterly for Exercise and Sport, 61**, 383-394. (Exercise)

163.   Heiby, E. M., Onorato, V. A. & Sato, R. (1987). Cross-validation of the Self-Motivation Inventory. **Journal of Sport Psychology, 9**, 394-399. (Running)

28

164. Huck, D. M., & Armer, J. M. (1996). Health perceptions and health-promoting behaviors among elderly catholic nuns. **Family and Community Health, 18**, 81-91. (Exercise)

165. Labbe, E. E., & Welsh, M. C. (1993). Children and running: Changes in physical fitness, self-efficacy, and health locus of control. **Journal of Sport Behavior, 16**, 85-97. (Exercise)

166. Labbe, E. E., Delaney, D., Olson, K., & Hickman, H. (1993). Skin-temperature biofeedback training: Cognitive and developmental factors in a nonclinical child population. **Perceptual and Motor Skills, 76**, 955-962. (Biofeedback, Exercise)

167. Labbe, E. E., Welsh, M. C., & Delaney, D. (1988). Effects of consistent aerobic exercise on the psychological functioning of women. **Perceptual and Motor Skills, 67**, 919-925. (Exercise)

168. Labbe, E. E., Welsh, M. C., Coldsmith, B., & Hickman, H. (1991). High school cross country runners: Running commitment, health locus of control and performance. **Journal of Sport Behavior, 14**, 85-92. (Cross Country)

169. O'Connell, J. K., & Price, J. H. (1982). Health locus of control of physical fitness program participants. **Perceptual and Motor Skills, 55**, 925-926. (Exercise)

170. Oldridge, N. B., & Streiner, D. L. (1990). The health belief model: Predicting compliance and dropout in cardiac rehabilitation. **Medicine and Science in Sports and Exercise, 22**, 678-683. (Exercise)

171. Pistacchio, T., Weinberg, R. S., & Jackson, A. (1989). The development of a psychobiologic profile of individuals who experience and those who do not experience exercise related mood enhancement. **Journal of Sport Behavior, 12**, 151-166. (Exercise)

172. Rabinowitz, S., Melamed, S. E., Weisberg, E., Tal, D., & Ribak, J. (1992). Personal determinants of leisure-time exercise activities. **Perceptual and Motor Skills, 75**, 779-784. (Exercise)

173. Slenker, S. E., Price, J. H., & O'Connell, J. K. (1985). Health locus of control of joggers and nonexercisers. **Perceptual and Motor Skills, 61**, 323-328. (Running)

174. Strawbridge, W. J., Camacho, T. C., Cohen, R. D., & Kaplan, G. A. (1993). Gender differences in factors associated with change in physical functioning in old age: A 6-year longitudinal study. **The Gerontologist, 33**, 603-609. (Exercise)

175. Wilson, D. K., Williams, Z. L., Arheart, K., Bryant, E. S., & Alpert, B. (1994). Race and sex differences in health locus of control beliefs and cardiovascular reactivity. **Journal of Pediatric Psychology, 19**, 769-778. (Exercise)

Internal-External Locus of Control Scale (I-E Scale)

176. Aguglia, E. & Sapienza, S. (1984). Locus of control according to Rotter's S.R.I. in volleyball players. **International Journal of Sport Psychology, 15**, 250-258. (Volleyball)

177. Bem, S. L. (1977). On the utility of alternative procedures for assessing psychological androgyny. **Journal of Consulting and Clinical Psychology, 45**, 196-205. (Psychometric)

178. Bezjak, J. E., & Lee, J. W. (1990). Relationship of self-efficacy and locus of control constructs in predicting college students' physical fitness behaviors. **Perceptual and Motor Skills, 71**, 499-508. (Exercise)

179. Blau, G. J. (1984). Brief note comparing the Rotter and Levenson measures of locus of control. **Perceptual and Motor Skills, 58**, 173-174. (Psychometric)

180. Bleak, J. L., & Frederick, C. M. (1998). Superstitious behavior in sport: Levels of effectiveness and determinants of use in three collegiate sports. **Journal of Sport Behavior, 21**, 1-15. (Football, Gymnastics, Track and Field)

181.   Brone, R., & Reznikoff, M. (1989). Strength gains, locus of control, and self-description of college football players. **Perceptual and Motor Skills, 69**, 483-493. (Football)

182.   Celestino, R., Tapp, J., & Brumet, M. E. (1979). Locus of control correlated with marathon performance. **Perceptual and Motor Skills, 48**, 1249-1250. (Marathon)

183.   Chapman, C. L., & DeCastro, J. M. (1990). Running addiction: Measurement and associated psychological characteristics. **Journal of Sports Medicine and Physical Fitness, 30**, 283-290. (Running)

184.   Chen, W. W. (1995). Enhancement of health locus of control through biofeedback training. **Perceptual and Motor Skills, 80**, 395-398. (Biofeedback)

185.   Coleman, D., & Iso-Ahola, S. E. (1993). Leisure and health: The role of social support and self-determination. **Journal of Leisure Research, 25**, 111-128. (Review Article)

186.   Colley, A., Roberts, N., & Chipps. A. (1985). Sex-role identity, personality and participation in team and individual sports by males and females. **International Journal of Sport Psychology, 16**, 103-112. (Various Sports)

187.   Dahlhauser, M., & Thomas, M. B. (1979). Visual disembedding and locus of control as variables associated with high school football injuries. **Perceptual and Motor Skills, 49**, 254. (Football, Injury)

188.   Daiss, S., LeUnes, A., & Nation, J. R. (1986). Mood and locus of control of a sample of college and professional football players. **Perceptual and Motor Skills, 63**, 733-734. (Football)

189.   DiGiuseppe, R. A. (1973). Internal-external control of retirement and participation in team, individual, and intramural sports. **Perceptual and Motor Skills, 36**, 33-34. (Intramural Sports, Various Sports)

190.   Doganis, G., Theodorakis, Y., & Bagiatis, K. (1991). Self-esteem and locus of control in adult female fitness program participants. **International Journal of Sport Psychology, 22**, 154-165. (Exercise)

191. Finn, J. A., & Straub, W. F. (1977). Locus of control among Dutch and American women softball players. **The Research Quarterly, 48**, 56-60. (Softball)

192. Friend, J., & LeUnes, A. (1990). Predicting baseball player performance. **Journal of Sport Behavior, 13**, 73-86. (Baseball)

193. Furst, D. M., Tenenbaum, G., & Weingarten, G. (1984). Attribution of causality in sport events: Validation of the Wingate Sport Achievement Responsibility Scale. **Journal of Sport Psychology, 6**, 430-439. (Psychometric)

194. Gilliland, K. (1974). Internal versus external locus of control and the high-level athletic competitor. **Perceptual and Motor Skills, 39**, 38. (Various Sports)

195. Hall, E. G. (1980). Comparison of postperformance state anxiety of internals and externals following failure or success on a simple motor task. **Research Quarterly for Exercise and Sport, 51**, 306-314. (Motor Task)

196. Hall, E. G., & Bunker, L. K. (1979). Locus of control as a mediator of social facilitation effects during motor skill learning. **Journal of Sport Psychology, 1**, 332-335. (Motor Task)

197. Hall, E. G., Church, G. E., & Stone, M. (1980). Relationship of birth order to selected personality characteristics of nationally ranked Olympic weight lifters. **Perceptual and Motor Skills, 51**, 971-976. (Weightlifting)

198. Hanson, S. J., McCullagh, P., & Tonymon, P. (1992). The relationship of personality characteristics, life stress, and coping resources to athletic injury. **Journal of Sport & Exercise Psychology, 14**, 262-272. (Decathlon, Heptathlon, Injury, Track and Field)

199. Hassmen, P., & Koivula, N. (1996). Ratings of perceived exertion by women with internal or external locus of control. **Journal of General Psychology, 123**, 297-307. (Motor Task)

200. Jackson, A., Richardson, P. A., Weinberg, R. S., & Yukelson, D. (1983). Interpersonal attraction and leadership within collegiate sport teams. **Journal of Sport Behavior, 6**, 28-36. (Baseball, Soccer)

201.   Kleiber, D. A. (1979). Fate control and leisure attitudes. **Leisure Sciences,** **2,** 239-248. (Leisure Activity)

202.   Kleiber, D. A., & Crandall, R. (1981). Leisure and work ethics and locus of control. **Leisure Sciences, 4,** 477-485. (Leisure Activity)

203.   Kleiber, D. A., & Hemmer, J. D. (1981). Sex differences in the relationship of locus control and recreational sport participation. **Sex Roles, 7,** 801-810. (Leisure Activity, Various Sports)

204.   Kohl, R. M., & Shea, C. H. (1988). Perceived exertion: Influences of locus of control and expected work intensity and duration. **Journal of Human Movement Studies, 15,** 255-272. (Motor Task)

205.   Kumar, A., Pathak, N., & Thakur, G. P. (1985). Death anxiety and locus of control in individual, team and non-athletes. **International Journal of Sport Psychology, 16,** 280-288. (Various Sports)

206.   Lefcourt, H. M. (1992). Durability and impact of the locus of control construct. **Psychological Bulletin, 112,** 411-414. (Review Article)

207.   Lefcourt, H. M. (1966). Internal versus external control of reinforcement. **Psychological Bulletin, 65,** 206-220. (Review Article)

208.   Lindbloom, G., & Faw, T. T. (1982). Three measures of locus of control: What do they measure? **Journal of Personality Assessment, 46,** 70-71. (Psychometric)

209.   Lynn, R. W., Phelan, J. G., & Kiker, V. L. (1969). Beliefs in internal-external control of reinforcement and participation in group and individual sports. **Perceptual and Motor Skills, 29,** 551-553. (Basketball, Gymnastics)

210.   McKelvie, J. S., & Huband, E. D. (1980). Locus of control and anxiety in college athletes and non-athletes. **Perceptual and Motor Skills, 50,** 819-822. (Various Sports)

211.   Ntoumanis, N., & Jones, J. G. (1998). Interpretation of competitive trait anxiety symptoms as a function of locus of control beliefs. **International Journal of Sport Psychology, 29,** 99-114. (Cricket, Ice Hockey, Swimming)

212. Perri, S. & Templer, D. I. (1984). The effects of an aerobic exercise program on psychological variables in older adults. **International Journal of Aging & Human Development, 20**, 167-172. (Exercise)

213. Prapavessis, H., & Carron, A. V. (1988). Learned helplessness in sport. **The Sport Psychologist, 2**, 189-201. (Tennis)

214. Rushall, B. S., & Sherman, C. A. (1987). A definition and measurement of pressure in sport. **Journal of Applied Research in Coaching and Athletics, 2**, 1-23. (Psychometric)

215. Sargunaraj, D., & Kumaraiah, V. (1991). The reliability of translations of STAI, CSAQ, EPI, and I-E Scale. **Journal of Personality and Clinical Studies, 7**, 99-101. (Psychometric)

216. Scheer, J. K., & Ansorge, C. J. (1979). Influence due to expectations of judges: A function of internal-external locus of control. **Journal of Sport Psychology, 1**, 53-58. (Gymnastics)

217. Schrader, M. P., & Wann, D. L. (1999). High-risk recreation: The relationship between participant characteristics and degree of involvement. **Journal of Sport Behavior, 22**, 426-441. (Various Sports)

218. Smith, H. L., & Dechter, A. (1991). No shift in locus of control among women in the 1970's. **Journal of Personality and Social Psychology, 60**, 638-640. (Psychometric)

219. Sonstroem, R. J., & Walker, M. I. (1973). Relationship of attitudes and locus of control to exercise and physical fitness. **Perceptual and Motor Skills, 36**, 1031-1034. (Running)

220. Taylor, J. (1987). A review of validity issues in sport psychological research: Types, problems, solutions. **Journal of Sport Behavior, 10**, 1-13. (Psychometric)

221. Valliant, P. M., Simpson-Housley, P., & McKelvie, J. S. (1981). Personality in athletic and non-athletic college groups. **Perceptual and Motor Skills, 52**, 963-966. (Various Sports)

222. Walkey, F. H. (1979). Internal control, powerful others, and chance: A confirmation of Levenson's factor structure. **Journal of Personality Assessment, 43**, 532-535. (Psychometric)

223. Ward, E. A. (1994). Construct validity of need for achievement and locus of control scales. **Educational and Psychological Measurement, 54**, 983-992. (Psychometric)

224. Weigand, D. A., & Broadhurst, C. J. (1998). The relationship among perceived competence, intrinsic motivation, and control perceptions in youth soccer. **International Journal of Sport Psychology, 29**, 324-338. (Soccer)

225. Yates, A., Shisslak, C. M., Allender, J., Crago, M., & Leehey, K. (1992). Comparing obligatory and nonobligatory runners. **Psychosomatics, 33**, 180-189. (Running)

226. Zenker, S. I., & Wolfgang, A. K. (1982). Relationship of machiavellianism and locus of control to preferences for leisure activity by college men and women. **Psychological Reports, 50**, 583-586. (Leisure Activity)

227. Zientek, C. E. C., & Breakwell, G. M., (1991). Attributional schema of players before and after knowledge of game outcome. **Journal of Sport Behavior, 14**, 211-222. (Field Hockey)

228. Zimet, G. D. (1979). Locus of control and biofeedback: A review of literature. **Perceptual and Motor Skills, 49**, 871-877. (Biofeedback, Review Article)

Levenson's Locus of Control Scale (IPC Scale)

229. Betts, W. (1982). Relation of locus of control to aspiration level and to competitive anxiety. **Psychological Reports, 51**, 71-76. (Physical Education Class(es)

230. Blau, G. J. (1984). Brief note comparing the Rotter and Levenson measures of locus of control. **Perceptual and Motor Skills, 58**, 173-174. (Psychometric)

231. Brewer, B. W., & Petrie, T. A. (1995). A comparison between injured and uninjured football players on selected psychosocial variables. **The Academic Athletic Journal,** Spring, 11-18. (Football)

232. Feher, P., Meyers, M. C., & Skelly, W. A. (1998). Psychological profile of rock climbers: State and trait attributes. **Journal of Sport Behavior, 21,** 167-180. (Rock Climbing)

233. Friend, J., & LeUnes, A. (1990). Predicting baseball player performance. **Journal of Sport Behavior, 13,** 73-86. (Baseball)

234. Granito, V. J., & Carlton, E. B. (1993). Relationship between locus of control and satisfaction with intercollegiate volleyball teams at different levels of competition. **Journal of Sport Behavior, 16,** 221-228. (Volleyball)

235. Iannos, M., & Tiggemann, M. (1997). Personality and the excessive exerciser. **Personality and Individual Differences, 22,** 775-778. (Exercise)

236. LeUnes, A., & Nation, J. R. (1982). Saturday's heroes: A psychological portrait of college football players. **Journal of Sport Behavior, 5,** 139-149. (Football)

237. Lindbloom, G., & Faw, T. T. (1982). Three measures of locus of control: What do they measure? **Journal of Personality Assessment, 46,** 70-71. (Psychometric)

238. Long, B. C., & Haney, C. J. (1986). Enhancing physical activity in sedentary women: Information, locus of control, and attitudes. **Journal of Sport Psychology, 8,** 8-24. (Exercise)

239. McCready, M. L., & Long, B. C. (1985). Locus of control, attitudes toward physical activity, and exercise adherence. **Journal of Sport Psychology, 7,** 346-359. (Exercise)

240. Nagy, S., & Frazier, S. E. 1988). The impact of exercise on locus of control, self-esteem, and mood states. **Journal of Social Behavior and Personality, 3,** 263-268. (Exercise)

241. Persson, C. V. (1988). **The adaptation and validation of a sport-specific measure of locus of control.** (Microform Publications), University of Oregon: College of Human Development and Performance. (Various Sports)

242. Rushall, B. S., & Sherman, C. A. (1987). A definition and measurement of pressure in sport. **Journal of Applied Research in Coaching and Athletics, 2**, 1-23. (Psychometric)

243. Shapiro, J. E., & Lawson, H. A. (1982). Locus of control: A neglected measure for affective development in physical education. **Physical Educator, 39,** 126-130. (Review Article)

244. Trafton, T. A., Meyers, M. C., & Skelly, W. A. (1997). Psychological characteristics of the telemark skier. **Journal of Sport Behavior, 20,** 465-476. (Skiing)

245. VanRaalte, J. L., Brewer, B. W., Nemeroff, C. J., & Linder D. E. (1991). Chance orientation and superstitious behavior on the putting green. **Journal of Sport Behavior, 14,** 41-50. (Golf)

246. Walkey, F. H. (1979). Internal control, powerful others, and chance: A confirmation of Levenson's factor structure. **Journal of Personality Assessment, 43**, 532-535. (Psychometric)

247. Ward, E. A. (1994). Construct validity of need for achievement and locus of control scales. **Educational and Psychological Measurement, 54,** 983-992. (Psychometric)

248. Whitehead, J. R., & Corbin, C. B. (1988). Multidimensional scales for the measurement of locus of control of reinforcements for physical fitness behaviors. **Research Quarterly for Exercise and Sport, 59,** 108-117. (Exercise)

Nowicki - Strickland Locus of Control Scale for Children

249. Adame, D. D., Radell, S. A., & Johnson, T. C. (1991). Physical fitness, body image, and locus of control in college women dancers and nondancers. **Perceptual and Motor Skills, 72**, 91-95. (Dance)

250. Anshel, M. H. (1979). Effect of age, sex, and type of feedback on motor performance and locus of control. **Research Quarterly, 50**, 305-317. (Motor Task)

251. Cole, S. P. (1989). Physical fitness, body image, and locus of control in college freshman men and women. **Perceptual and Motor Skills, 68**, 400-402. (Exercise)

252. Fagan, W., Sherrill, C., & French, R. (1995). Locus of control of quad rugby players and able-bodied men. **Clinical Kinesiology, 49**, 53-57. (Rugby)

253. Foon, A. E. (1989). Sports participation among adolescent females: Effects on self-esteem, affiliation patterns and locus of control. **Journal of Human Movement Studies, 16**, 225-231. (Various Sports)

254. Goldberg, B., & Shephard, R. J. (1982). Personality profiles of disabled individuals in relation to physical activity patterns. **Journal of Sports Medicine and Physical Fitness, 22**, 477-484. (Exercise)

255. Goodman, S. H., & Waters, L. K. (1987). Convergent validity of five locus of control scales. **Educational and Psychological Measurement. 47**, 743-747. (Psychometric)

256. Jambor, E. A., & Rudisill, M. E. (1992). The relationship between children's locus of control and sport choices. **Journal of Human Movement Studies, 22**, 35-48. (Youth)

257. Kerr, G. A. & Goss, J. D. (1997). Personal control in elite gymnasts: The relationships between locus of control, self-esteem, and trait anxiety. **Journal of Sport Behavior, 20**, 69-82. (Gymnastics)

258. Kerr, G. A., & Minden, H. A. (1988). Psychological factors related to the occurrence of athletic injuries. **Journal of Sport & Exercise Psychology, 10**, 167-173. (Gymnastics, Injury)

259. Lambert, S. M., Moore, D. W. , & Dixon, R. S. (1999). Gymnastics in training: The differential effects of self- and coach-set goals as a function of locus of control. **Journal of Applied Sport Psychology, 11**, 72-82. (Gymnastics)

260. Langsner, S. J., & Anderson, S. C. (1987). Outdoor challenge education and self-esteem and locus of control of children with behavior disorders. **Adapted Physical Activity Quarterly, 4**, 237-246. (Leisure Activity)

261. Lindbloom, G., & Faw, T. T. (1982). Three measures of locus of control: What do they measure? **Journal of Personality Assessment, 46**, 70-71. (Psychometric)

262. Lufi, D., Porat, Y., & Tenenbaum, G. (1986). Psychological predictors of competitive performance in young gymnasts. **Perceptual and Motor Skills, 63**, 59-64. (Gymnastics)

263. Morris, A. F., Vaccaro, P., & Clarke, D. H. (1979). Psychological characteristics of age-group competitive swimmers. **Perceptual and Motor Skills, 48**, 1265-1266. (Swimming)

264. Nowicki, S., & Strickland, B. R. (1973). A locus of control scale for children. **Journal of Consulting and Clinical Psychology, 40**, 148-154. (Psychometric)

265. Porat, Y., Lufi, D., & Tenenbaum, G. (1989). Psychological components contribute to select young female gymnasts. **International Journal of Sport Psychology, 20**, 279-286. (Gymnastics)

266. Simons, C. W., & Birkimer, J. C. (1988). An exploration of factors predicting the effects of aerobic conditioning on mood state. **Journal of Psychosomatic Research, 32**, 63-75. (Exercise)

267. Watters, D. A., Thomas, B. H., & Streiner, D. L. (1990). Factor analysis of the Nowicki-Strickland Locus of Control Scale: Why replication is so difficult. **Educational and Psychological Measurement, 50**, 515-523. (Psychometric)

268. Wolf, T. M., Sklov, M. C., Hunter, S. M., & Berenson, G. S. (1982). Factor analytic study of the children's Nowicki-Strickland Locus of Control Scale. **Educational and Psychological Measurement, 42**, 333-337. (Psychometric)

CHAPTER SIX
OMNIBUS PERSONALITY MEASURES

Edwards Personal Preference Schedule (EPPS)

269.   Adams, A. J., & Stone, T. H. (1977). Satisfaction of need for achievement in work and leisure time activities. **Journal of Vocational Behavior, 11**, 174-181. (Leisure Activity)

270.   Balasz, E. K. (1975). Psycho-social study of outstanding female athletes. **Research Quarterly, 46**, 267-273. (Various Sports)

271.   Balasz, E., & Nickerson, E. (1976). Personality needs profile of some outstanding female athletes. **Journal of Clinical Psychology, 32**, 15-49. (Various Sports)

272.   Chen, H. (1988). A personality trait analysis of the elite athletes of the Republic of China for the 24th Olympic Games in Seoul. **Asian Journal of Physical Education, 10**, 54-72. (Various Sports)

273.   Davis, C., & Cowles, M. (1989). A comparison of weight and diet concerns and personality factors among female athletes and non-athletes. **Journal of Psychosomatic Research, 33**, 527-536. (Various Sports)

274.   Dayries, J. L., & Grimm, R. L. (1970). Personality traits of women athletes as measured by the Personal Preference Schedule. **Perceptual and Motor Skills, 30**, 229-230. (Various Sports)

275.   Edwards, A. L. (1959). **Edwards Personal Preference Schedule**. New York: Psychological Corporation. (Test Manual)

276.   Fletcher, R. (1971). Differences between civilian and corps intramural participants in selected personality characteristics. **Psychology, 8**, 41-42. (Intramural Sports, Various Sports)

277.   Gravelle, L., Searle, R., & St. Jean, P. (1982). Personality profiles of the Canadian women's national volleyball team. **Volleyball Technical Journal, 7**, 13-17. (Volleyball)

278.   Harrison, P., & Jones, B. J. (1975). Research and women in sports: Closing the gap. **Physical Educator, 32**, 84-88. (Various Sports)

279.   Johnsgard, K., & Ogilvie, B. C. (1968). The competitive racing driver. **Journal of Sports Medicine, 8**, 87-95. (Automobile Racing)

280.   Johnsgard, K., Ogilvie, B. C., & Merritt, K. (1975). The stress seekers: A psychological study of sports parachutists, racing drivers, and football players. **Journal of Sports Medicine, 15**, 158-169. (Automobile Racing, Football, Skydiving)

281.   Johnsgard, K. (1977). Personality and performance: A psychological study of amateur sport car racing. **Journal of Sports Medicine and Physical Fitness, 17**, 97-104. (Automobile Racing)

282.   Ogilvie, B. C. (1968). Psychological consistencies within the personality of high-level competitors. **Journal of the American Medical Association, 205**, 156-162. (Swimming)

283.   Scheer, J. K., Ansorge, C. J., & Howard, J. H. (1983). Judging bias induced by viewing contrived videotapes: A function of selected psychological variables. **Journal of Sport Psychology, 5**, 427-437. (Gymnastics)

284.   Singer, R. N. (1969). Personality differences between and within baseball and tennis players. **Research Quarterly, 40**, 582-588. (Baseball, Tennis)

285.   Stoner, S., & Bandy, M. A. (1977). Personality traits of females who participate in intercollegiate competition and nonparticipants. **Perceptual and Motor Skills, 45**, 332-334. (College Students)

286.   Thirer, J., & Greer, D. L. (1981). Personality characteristics associated with beginning, intermediate, and competitive bodybuilders. **Journal of Sport Behavior, 4**, 3-11. (Bodybuilding)

287.   Thirer, J., Knowlton, R., Sawka, M., & Chang, T. J. (1978). Relationship of psychophysiological characteristics to perceived exertion and levels of anxiety on competitive swimmers. **Journal of Sport Behavior, 1**, 169-173. (Swimming)

288. Thorpe, J. A. (1958). Study of personality variables among successful women students and teachers of physical education. **Research Quarterly, 29**, 83-92. (Physical Education Class(es)

289. Wendt, D. T., & Patterson, T. W. (1974). Personality characteristics of women in intercollegiate competition. **Perceptual and Motor Skills, 38**, 861-862. (Various Sports)

290. Widdop, J. H., & Widdop, V. A. (1975). Comparison of the personality traits of female teacher education and physical education students. **Research Quarterly, 46**, 274-281. (Physical Education Class(es)

291. Williams, J. M., Hoepner, B. J., Moody, D. L., & Ogilvie, B. C. (1970). Personality traits of champion level female fencers. **Research Quarterly, 41**, 446-453. (Fencing)

Eysenck Personality Inventory/Eysenck Personality Questionnaire (EPI/EPQ)

292. Arai, Y., & Hisamichi, S. (1998). Self-reported exercise frequency and personality: A population-based study in Japan. **Perceptual and Motor Skills, 83**, 1371-1375. (Exercise)

293. Bamber, D., & Cockerill, I. M. (2000). The pathological status of exercise dependence. **British Journal of Sports Medicine, 34**, 125-132. (Exercise)

294. Beaumaster, E. J., Knowles, J. B., & MacLean, A. W. (1978). The sleep of skydivers: A study of stress. **Society for Psychophysiological Research, 15**, 209-213. (Skydiving)

295. Berger, B. G. & Owen, D. R. (1992). Mood alteration with yoga and swimming: Aerobic exercise may not be necessary. **Perceptual and Motor Skills, 75**, 1331-1343. (Swimming, Yoga)

296. Berger, B. G., Grove, J. R., Prapavessis, H., & Butki, B. D. (1997). Relationship of swimming distance, expectancy, and performance to mood states of competitive athletics. **Perceptual and Motor Skills, 84**, 1199-1210. (Swimming)

297. Biasiotto, J., Ferrando, E., & Ritter, E. (1987). Psychological profiles of U.S.P.F. female powerlifters. **Powerlifting USA, 11(5)**, 17. (Weightlifting)

298. Breivik, G., Roth, W. T., & Jorgensen, P. E. (1998). Personality, psychological states and heart rate in non-expert parachutists. **Personality and Individual Differences, 25**, 365-380. (Skydiving)

299. Briggs, C. A., Sandstrom, E. R., & Nettleton, B. (1979). An approach to prediction of performance using behavioral and physiological variables. **Perceptual and Motor Skills, 49**, 843-848. (Running)

300. Callies, A., Pierce, C., Popkin, M., & Stillner, V. (1983). Predicting successful behavior indicators in an athletic contest. **Military Medicine, 148**, 668-672. (Dog Sled Racing)

301. Caruso, J. C., Witkiewitz, K., Belcourt-Dittloff, A., & Gottlieb, J. D. (2001). Reliability of scores from the Eysenck Personality Questionnaire: A reliability generalization study. **Educational and Psychological Measurement, 61**, 675-689. (Psychometric)

302. Coleman, J. A. (1980). Personality and stress in the shooting sports. **Journal of Psychosomatic Research, 24**, 287-296. (Shooting)

303. Colley, A., Roberts, N., & Chipps. A. (1985). Sex-role identity, personality and partici-pation in team and individual sports by males and females. **International Journal of Sport Psychology, 16**, 103-112. (Various Sports)

304. Corr, P. J., & Gray, J. A. (1996). Structure and validity of the attributional style questionnaire: A cross-sample comparison. **Journal of Psychology, 130**, 645-657. (Psychometric)

305. Dabrowska, H. (1993). Emotional-cognitive mechanisms of functioning of men and women in sports. **Biology of Sport, 10**, 267-273. (Rowing)

306. Daino, A. (1985). Personality traits of adolescent tennis players. **International Journal of Sport Psychology, 16**, 120-125. (Tennis)

307. Davis, C. (1990). Body image and weight preoccupation: A comparison between exercising and nonexercising women. **Appetite, 15**, 13-21. (Exercise)

308. Davis, C. (1990). Weight and diet preoccupation: The role of exercise. **Personality and Individual Differences, 11**, 823-827. (Exercise)

309. Davis, C. (1992). Body image, dieting behaviours, and personality factors: A study of high performance female athletes. **International Journal of Sport Psychology, 23**, 179-192. (Various Sports)

310. Davis, C., & Cowles, M. (1989). A comparison of weight and diet concerns and personality factors among female athletes and nonathletes. **Journal of Psychosomatic Research, 33**, 527-536. (Various Sports)

311. Davis, C., & Mogk, J. P. (1994). Some personality correlates of interest and excellence in sport. **International Journal of Sport Psychology, 25**, 131-143. (Various Sports)

312. Davis, C., Fox, J., Brewer, H., & Ratusny, D. (1995). Motivations to exercise as a function of personality characteristics, age, and gender. **Personality and Individual Differences, 19,**165-174. (Exercise)

313. Egloff, B., & Gruhn, A. J. (1996). Personality and endurance sports. **Personality and Individual Differences, 21**, 223-229. (Running, Triathlon)

314. Eysenck, H. J., Nias, D. B. K., & Cox, D. N. (1982). Sport and personality. **Advances in Behavioral Research and Therapy, 4**, 1-56. (Review Article)

315. Feher, P., Meyers, M. C., & Skelly, W. A. (1998). Psychological profile of rock climbers: State and trait attributes. **Journal of Sport Behavior, 21**, 167-180. (Rock Climbing)

316.   Forrest, S., Lewis, C. A., & Shevlin, M. E. (2000). Examining the factor structure and differential functioning of the Eysenck Personality Questionnaire revised: Abbreviated. **Personality and Individual Differences, 29**, 579-588. (Psychometric)

317.   Francis, L. J., & Katz, Y. J. (1992). The comparability of the short form EPQ-R indices of extraversion, neuroticism, and the lie scale with the EPQ for a sample of 190 student teachers in Israel. **Educational and Psychological Measurement, 5**, 695-700. (Psychometric)

318.   Francis, L. J., & Wilcox, C. (1998). The relationship between Eysenck's personality dimensions and Bem's masculinity and femininity scales revisited. **Personality and Individual Differences, 25**, 683-687. (Psychometric)

319.   Francis, L. J., Jones, S. H., & Kelly, P. (1999). Personality and church attendance among female hockey players. **Social Behavior and Personality, 27**, 519-521. (Field Hockey)

320.   Francis, L. J., Kelly, P., & Jones, S. H. (1998). The personality profile of female students who play hockey. **Irish Journal of Psychology, 19**, 394-399. (Field Hockey)

321.   Frazier, S. E. (1987). Introversion-extroversion measures in elite and nonelite distance runners. **Perceptual and Motor Skills, 64**, 867-872. (Running)

322.   Freedson, P., Mihevic, P., Loucks, A., & Girandola, R. (1983). Physique, body composition, and psychological characteristics of competitive female body builders. **Physician and Sportsmedicine, 11(5)**, 85-93. (Bodybuilding)

323.   Fuchs, C. & Zaichkowsky, L. D. (1983). Psychological characteristics of male and female bodybuilders: The iceberg profile. **Journal of Sport Behavior, 6**, 136-145. (Bodybuilding)

324.   Glicksohn, J., & Abulafia, J. (1998). Embedding sensation seeking within the big three. **Personality and Individual Differences, 25**, 1085-1099. (Psychometric)

45

325. Grouios, G. (1992). On the reduction of reaction time with mental practice. **Journal of Sport Behavior, 15,** 141-157. (Various Sports)

326. Hagberg, J. M., Mullin, J. P., Bahrke, M. S., & Limburg, J. (1979). Physiological profiles and selected psychological characteristics of national class American cyclists. **Journal of Sports Medicine and Physical Fitness, 19,** 341-346. (Cycling)

327. Hassmen, P., Koivula, N., & Hansson, T. (1998). Precompetitive mood states and performance of elite male golfers: Do trait characteristics make a difference? **Perceptual and Motor Skills, 86,** 1443-1457. (Golf)

328. Herrera, E., & Gomezamor, J. (1995). Differences in personality and menstrual variables between physically active and sedentary women. **Personality and Individual Differences, 19,** 389-392. (Exercise)

329. Hills, P., & Argyle, M. (1998). Positive moods derived from leisure and their relationship to happiness and personality. **Personality and Individual Differences, 25,** 523-535. (Leisure Activity)

330. Ikulayo, P. B., & Vipene, J. B. (1996) Dominant personality characteristics of Nigerian female athletes in selected sports. **Journal of the International Council for Health, Physical Education, Recreation, Sport, and Dance, 32,** 58-59. (Field Hockey, Soccer, Table Tennis)

331. Kanters, M. A. (2000). Recreational sport participation as a moderator of college stress. **Journal of the National Intramural and Recreational Sports Association, 24**(2), 10-23. (Intramural Sports)

332. Kerr, J. H. (1980). What makes a climber? Action: **British Journal of Physical Education, 11,** 7-8. (Rock Climbing)

333. Kirkcaldy, B. D. (1980). An analysis of the relationship between psychophysiological variables connected to human performance and the personality variables extraversion and neuroticism. **International Journal of Sport Psychology, 11,** 276-289. (Endurance Training)

334. Kirkcaldy, B. D. (1982). Personality and sex differences related to positions in team sports. **International Journal of Sport Psychology, 13**, 141-153. (Various Sports)

335. Kowal, D. M., Patton, J. F., & Vogel, J. A. (1978). Psychological states and aerobic fitness of male and female recruits before and after basic training. **Aviation, Space, and Environmental Medicine, 49**, 603-606. (Exercise)

336. Laforestrie, R. & Missoum, G. (1983). Sport psychology: Approach to psychological mechanisms linked to the identification of young sports talent and to the optimization of performance. **Bulletin de Psychologie, 37**, 347-357. (Review Article)

337. Lane, M., & Lester, D. (1995). Watching televised sports and personality. **Perceptual and Motor Skills, 81**, 966. (Sports Fans)

338. Layton, C. (1988). The personality of black-belt and nonblack-belt traditional karateka. **Perceptual and Motor Skills, 67**, 218. (Martial Arts)

339. Marusic, A., Musek, J., & Gudjonsson, G. (2001). Injury proneness and personality. **Nordic Journal of Psychiatry, 55**, 157-161. (Injury)

340. Mathers, S., & Walker, M. B. (1999). Extraversion and exercise addiction. **Journal of Psychology, 133**, 125-128. (Exercise)

341. Maxeiner, J. (1982). Extraversion and neuroticism of volleyball players. **Leistungssport, 5**, 415. (Volleyball)

342. Mellors, V., Boyle, G. J., & Roberts, L. (1994). Effects of personality, stress and life-style on hypertension: An Australian twin study. **Personality and Individual Differences, 16**, 967-974. (Exercise)

343. Meyers, M. C., Sterling, J. C., & LeUnes, A. (1988). Psychological characterization of the collegiate rodeo athlete. **Journal of Sport Behavior, 11**, 59-64. (Rodeo)

344. Mikel, K. (1983). Extraversion in adult runners. **Perceptual and Motor Skills, 57**, 141-146. (Running)

345. Mohan, J., Mall, N. N., & Paul, V. P. (1979). Comparative study of extroversion, neuroticism and attitude towards sport of handball players and non-players. **Society for the National Institutes of Physical Education and Sports Journal, 2**, 3-6. (Handball)

346. Morgan, W. P. (1968). Personality characteristics of wrestlers participating in the world championships. **Journal of Sports Medicine and Physical Fitness, 8**, 212-216. (Wrestling)

347. Morgan, W. P., & Costill, D. L. (1972). Psychological characteristics of the marathon runner. **Journal of Sport Medicine, 12**, 42-46. (Marathon)

348. Morgan, W. P., & Johnson, R. W. (1979). Personality characteristics of successful and unsuccessful oarsmen. **International Journal of Sport Psychology, 9**, 119-133. (Rowing)

349. Morgan, W. P., & Pollock, M. L. (1977). Psychologic characterization of the elite distance runner. **Annals of the New York Academy of Sciences, 301**, 382-403. (Running)

350. Morgan, W. P., O'Connor, P. J., Ellickson, K. A., & Bradley, P. W. (1988). Personality structure, mood states, and performance in elite male distance runners. **International Journal of Sport Psychology, 19**, 247-263. (Running)

351. Morgan, W. P., O'Connor, P. J., Sparling, P. B., & Pate, R. R. (1987). Psychological characterization of the elite female distance runner. **International Journal of Sports Medicine, 8**, 124-131. (Running)

352. Motl, R. W., Berger, B. G., & Leuschen, P. S. (2000). The role of enjoyment in the exercise-performance relationship. **International Journal of Sport Psychology, 31**, 347-363. (Rock Climbing)

353. Newcombe, P. A., & Boyle, G. J. (1995). High school students' sports personalities: Variations across participation level, gender, type of sport, and stresses. **International Journal of Sport Psychology, 26**, 277-294. (Various Sports)

354. Potgieter, J. R. & Venter, R. E. (1995). Relationship between adherence to exercise and scores on extraversion and neuroticism. **Perceptual and Motor Skills, 81**, 520-522. (Exercise)

355. Power, S. L. (1986). Psychological assessment procedures of a track and field national event squad training weekend. In J. Watkins, T. Reilly, & L. Burwitz (Eds.), **Sports science**. New York: E & FN Spon. (Track and Field)

356. Reid, B. M., & Hay, D. (1979). Some behavioral characteristics of rugby and association footballers. **International Journal of Sport Psychology, 10**, 239-251. (Rugby, Soccer)

357. Sargunaraj, D., & Kumaraiah, V. (1991). The reliability of translations of STAI, CSAQ, EPI, and I-E Scale. **Journal of Personality and Clinical Studies, 7**, 99-101. (Psychometric)

358. Shifren, K., Bauserman, R., & Carter, D. B. (1993). Gender-role orientation and physical health: A study among young adults. **Personality and Individual Differences, 29**, 421-432. (Exercise)

359. Stelmack, R. M., & Pivik, R. T. (1996). Extraversion and the effect of exercise on spinal motoneuronal excitability. **Personal and Individual Differences, 21**, 69-76. (Exercise)

360. Szabo, A. (1992). Habitual participation in exercise and personality. **Perceptual and Motor Skills, 74**, 978. (Exercise)

361. Trafton, T. A., Meyers, M. C., & Skelly, W. A. (1997). Psychological characteristics of the telemark skier. **Journal of Sport Behavior, 20**, 465-476. (Skiing)

362. Tremayne, P., & Barry, R. J. (1990). Repression of anxiety and its effects on psychophysiological responses to stimuli in competitive gymnasts. **Journal of Sport & Exercise Psychology, 12**, 333-352. (Gymnastics)

363. Tucker, L. A. (1982). Weight training experience and psychological well-being. **Perceptual and Motor Skills, 55**, 553-554. (Weight Training)

364. Yates, A., Shisslak, C. M., Allender, J., Crago, M., & Leehey, K. (1992). Comparing obligatory and nonobligatory runners. **Psychosomatics, 33**, 180-189. (Running)

365. Yeung, R. R. & Hemsley, D. R. (1996). Effects of personality and acute exercise on mood states. **Personal and Individual Differences, 20**, 545. (Exercise)

366. Yeung, R. R., & Hemsley, D. R. (1997). Exercise behavior in an aerobics class: The impact of personality traits and efficacy cognitions. **Personality and Individual Differences, 23**, 425-431. (Exercise)

Minnesota Multiphasic Personality Inventory (MMPI)

367. Aheng, R., & Qiu, Y. J. (1987). A study of the personality trend of the players in the Chinese first-rate women's volleyball teams. **Information on Psychological Sciences, 3**, 22-27. (Volleyball)

368. Beaumaster, E. J., Knowles, J. B., & MacLean, A. W. (1978). The sleep of skydivers: A study of stress. **Society for Psychophysiological Research, 15**, 209-213. (Skydiving)

369. Blaser, P. & Schilling, G. (1975). Personality tests in sport. **International Journal of Sport Psychology, 7**, 22-35. (Review Article)

370. Booth, E. G. (1957). Personality traits of athletes as measured by the MMPI. **Research Quarterly, 29**, 127-138. (Various Sports)

371. Booth, E. G. (1960). Personality traits of athletes as measured by the MMPI: A rebuttal. **Research Quarterly, 32**, 421-423. (Various Sports)

372. Brown, D. R., Morgan, W. P., & Kihlstrom, J. F. (1989). Comparison of test construction strategies in an attempt to develop an athletic potential scale. **International Journal of Sport Psychology, 20**, 93-113. (Psychometric)

373. Chodzko-Zajko, W. J. & Ismail, A. H. (1984). MMPI interscale relationships in middle-aged males SS before and after an 8-month fitness program. **Journal of Clinical Psychology, 40**, 163-169. (Exercise)

374.   Dahlstrom, W. G. & Welch, G. S. (1960). **An MMPI handbook.** Minneapolis: University of Minnesota Press. (Test Manual)

375.   Delk, J. L. (1973). Some personality characteristics of skydivers. **Life-Threatening Behaviors, 3,** 51-57. (Skydiving)

376.   Dworkin, R. H., Burke, B. W., & Maher, B. A. (1976). Longitudinal study of the genetics of personality. **Journal of Personality and Social Psychology, 34,** 510-518. (Review Article)

377.   Folkins, C. H. & Wieselberg-Bell, N. (1981). Personality profile of ultramarathon runners: A little deviance may go a long way. **Journal of Sport Behavior, 4,** 119-127. (Ultrarunning/Ultramarathon)

378.   Geron, E., Furst, D. M., & Rotstein, P. (1986). Personality of athletes participating in various sports. **International Journal of Sport Psychology, 17,** 120-135. (Various Sports)

379.   Handal, P. J. (1973). Development of social desirability and acquiescence controlled repression sensitization scale and some preliminary validity data. **Journal of Clinical Psychology, 39,** 486-487. (Psychometric)

380.   Hauck, E. R., & Blumenthal, J. A. (1992). Obsessive and compulsive traits in athletes. **Sports Medicine, 14,** 215-227. (Review Article)

381.   Hunt, D. (1969). A cross racial comparison of personality traits between athletes and non athletes. **Research Quarterly, 40,** 704-707. (Various Sports)

382.   Johnsgard, K. A. (1977). Personality and performance: A psychological study of amateur sport car racing. **Journal of Sports Medicine and Physical Fitness, 17,** 97-104. (Automobile Racing)

383.   Johnsgard, K. A., & Ogilvie, B. C. (1968). The competitive racing driver. **Journal of Sports Medicine, 8,** 87-95. (Automobile Racing)

384.   Johnsgard, K. A., Ogilvie, B. C., & Merritt, K. (1975). The stress seekers: A psychological study of sports parachutists, racing drivers, and football players. **Journal of Sports Medicine, 15,** 158-169. (Automobile Racing, Football, Skydiving)

385. Johnson, T. & Morgan, W. P. (1981). Personality characteristics of college athletes in different sports. **Scandinavian Journal of Sport Science, 3,** 41-49. (Various Sports)

386. Kroll W., Loy, J., Hosek, V., & Vanek, M. (1973). Multivariate analysis of the personality profiles of championship Czechoslovakian athletes. **International Journal of Sport Psychology, 4,** 131-147. (Various Sports)

387. Landers, D. M. (1970). Psychological femininity and the prospective physical educator. **Research Quarterly, 41,** 164-170. (Physical Education Class(es)

388. Laplace, J. P. (1954). Personality and its relationship to success in professional baseball. **Research Quarterly, 25,** 313-319. (Baseball)

389. Morgan, W. P., & Johnson, R. W. (1978). Personality characteristics of successful and unsuccessful oarsmen. **International Journal of Sport Psychology, 11,** 119-133. (Rowing)

390. Notarnicola, G. (1988). Psychopedagogic availability: On a group of sports psychologists faced with an erroneous performance. **Movimento, 4,** 197-198. (Review Article)

391. Ogilvie, B. C. (1968). Psychological consistencies within the personality of high-level competitors. **Journal of the American Medical Association, 205,** 156-162. (Swimming)

392. Ogilvie, B. C. & Pool, C. C. (1974). Aerobatics pilots: Why do they fly that way? **Physician and Sportsmedicine, 2**(11), 63-65. (Aerobatics)

393. Parker, R. M., Lambert, M. J., & Burlingame, G. M. (1994). Psychological features of female runners presenting with pathological weight control behaviors. **Journal of Sport & Exercise Psychology, 16,** 119-134. (Running)

394. Penny, G. D. & Rust, J. O. (1980). Effect of a walking-jogging program on personality characteristics of middle-aged females. **Journal of Sports Medicine and Physical Fitness, 20,** 221-226. (Exercise)

395. Peterson, S. L., Weber, J. C., & Trousdale, W. W. (1967). Personality traits of women in team sports vs women in individual sports. **Research Quarterly, 38**, 686-690. (Various Sports)

396. Rasch, P. J., Hunt, M. B., & Robertson, P. G. (1959). The Booth Scale as a predictor of competitive behavior of college wrestlers. **Research Quarterly, 31**, 117-118. (Wrestling)

397. Schurr, K. T., Ashley, M., & Joy, K. (1977). A multivariate analysis of male athlete characteristics: Sport type and success. **Multivariate Experimental Clinical Research, 3**, 53-68. (Various Sports)

398. Sharp, M. W. & Reilley, R. R. (1975). Relationship of aerobic physical fitness to selected personality traits. **Journal of Clinical Psychology, 31**, 428-430. (Exercise)

399. Slusher, H. (1964). Personality and intelligence characteristics of selected high school athletes and non-athletes. **Research Quarterly, 35**, 539-545. (Various Sports)

400. Smoley, B. A. (1976). Relationship between sports and aggression. In Craig, T. T. (Ed.), **Humanistic and mental health aspects of sports, exercise and recreation** (pp. 49-54). Chicago: American Medical Association. (Review Article)

401. Tamorri, S., Benzi, M., Pugliese, M., & Polani, D. (1987). The hunter's personality as conceptualized by the MMPI. **Movimento, 3**, 94-97. (Leisure Activity)

402. Taylor, L. D. (1997). MMPI-2 and ballet majors. **Personality and Individual Differences, 22**, 521-526. (Dance)

403. Templer, D. I. & Daus, A. T. (1979). Athlete adjustment prediction scale: Determination of feasibility. **Journal of Sport Medicine and Physical Fitness, 19**, 413-416. (Psychometric)

404. Trulson, M. E. (1987). Martial arts training: A novel "cure" for juvenile delinquency. **Human Relations, 39**, 1131-1140. (Martial Arts)

405. Walker, M. B., & Hailey, B. J. (1987). Physical fitness levels and psychological states versus traits. **Perceptual and Motor Skills, 64,** 12-25. (Exercise)

406. Wang, Y. (1986). **Personality characteristics of college athletes as measured by the Minnesota Multiphasic Personality Inventory (MMPI).** Microform Publications, University of Oregon, Eugene, Ore. (Test Manual)

407. Williams, R. L. & Youssef, Z. I. (1971). Stereotypes of football players as a function of positions. **Journal of Sports Medicine, 3,** 7-11. (Football)

408. Yates, A., Shisslak, C. M., Allender, J., Crago, M., & Leehey, K. (1992). Comparing obligatory to nonobligatory runners. **Psychosomatics, 33,** 180-189. (Running)

Myers-Briggs Type Indicator (MBTI)

409. Cashel, C., Lane, S., & Montgomery, D. (1998). The relationship of Jungian typology to leisure interests. **Journal of Applied Recreation Research, 23,** 91-106. (Leisure Activity)

410. Ellen, A., Ruble V., & Schurr, K. T. (1985). Myers-Briggs type inventory and demographic characteristics of students attending and not attending a college basketball game. **Journal of Sport Behavior, 8,** 181-194. (Basketball)

411. Furnham, A. (1990). The fakability of the 16PF, the Myers-Briggs and Firo-B personality measures. **Personality and Individual Differences, 11,** 711-716. (Psychometric)

412. Helmes, E., Harris, J. A., & Fraboni, M. A. (1996). Social desirability in the Myers-Briggs Type Indicator. **International Journal of Psychology, 31,** 84117. (Psychometric)

413. Meyers, K., & Ullyot, J. (1994). Archetypology and Jungian typology in elite women runners. **Psyche and Sports,** 149-161. (Running)

414. Murray, J. B. (1990). Review of research on the Myers-Briggs Type Indicator. **Perceptual and Motor Skills, 70,** 1187-1202. (Review Article)

415.   Nisbet, J., Ruble, V., Schurr, K. T., & Wallace, D. (1984). Myers-Briggs type inventory characteristics of more and less successful players on an American football team. **Journal of Sport Behavior, 7,** 47-57. (Football)

416.   Pittenger, D. J. (1993). The utility of the Myers-Briggs Type Indicator. **Review of Educational Research, 63,** 467-488. (Review Article)

417.   Saggino, A., Cooper, C., & Kline, P. (2001). A confirmatory factor analysis of the Myers-Briggs Type Indicator. **Personality and Individual Differences, 30,** 3-9. (Psychometric)

Personality Big Five-----NEO-PI/NEO-FFI

418.   Caldwell-Andrews, A., Baer, R. A., & Berry, D. T. R. (2000). Effects of response sets on NEO-PI-R scores and their relations to external criteria. **Journal of Personality Assessment, 74,** 472-488 (Psychometric)

419.   Courneya, K. S., & Hellsten, L. M. (1998). Personality correlates of exercise behavior, motives, barriers and preferences: An application of the five-factor model. **Personality and Individual Differences, 24,** 625-633. (Exercise)

420.   Hayes, T. (1996). How do athletic status and disability status affect the five-factor model on personality? **Human Performance, 9,** (121-140. (Review Article)

421.   Hsiao, E. T., & Thayer, R. E. (1998). Exercising for mood regulation: The importance of experience. **Personality and Individual Differences, 24,** 829-836. (Exercise)

422.   Piedmont, R. L., Hill, D. C., & Blanco, S. (1999). Predicting athletic performance using the five-factor measure of personality. **Personality and Individual Differences, 27,** 769-777. (Soccer)

423.   Saggino, A. (2000). The Big Three or the Big Five? A replication study. **Personality and Individual Differences, 28,** 879-886. (Psychometric)

424. Scandell, D. J. (2000). Development and validation of validity scales for the NEO-Five Factor Inventory. **Personality and Individual Differences, 29**, 1153-1162. (Psychometric)

425. Viswesvaran, C., & Ones, D. S. (1999). Meta-analyses of fakability estimates: Implications for personality measurement. **Educational and Psychological Measurement, 59**, 197-210. (Psychometric)

16 Personality Factor Questionnaire (16PF)

426. Abdelkader, M. S., & Adams, I. C. (1987). A personality comparison of British and Egyptian female physical education students. **Journal of Human Movement Studies, 13**, 189-195. (Physical Education Class(es)

427. Amusa, L. O., & Udoh, C. O. (1984). Multivariate personality profile analysis of athletes and nonathletes. **Snipes Journal, 7**, 12-18. (Various Sports)

428. Barker, M., Wyatt, T. J., Johnson, R. L., Stone, M. H., O'Bryant, H. S., Poe, C., & Kent, M. (1993). Performance factors, psychological assessment, physical characteristics, and football playing ability. **Journal of Strength and Conditioning Research, 7**, 224-233. (Football)

429. Bolton, B. (1980). Comments on "Comments on the reliability of a personality questionnaire used in physical education and sport research." **Psychological Reports, 46**, 1133-1134. (Psychometric)

430. Bolton, B., & Renfrow, N. E. (1979). Personality characteristics associated with aerobic exercise in adult females. **Journal of Personality Assessment, 43**, 504-508. (Exercise)

431. Breivik, G. (1996). Personality, sensation seeking and risk taking among Everest climbers. **International Journal of Sport Psychology, 27**, 308-320. (Mountain Climbing)

432. Brown, E. Y., & Shaw, C. N. (1975). Effects of a stressor on a specific motor task on individuals displaying selected personality factors. **Research Quarterly, 46**, 71-77. (Motor Task)

433. Bushan, S., & Agarwal, V. (1978). Personality characteristics of high and low achieving Indian sports persons. **International Journal of Sport Psychology, 9**, 191-198. (Badminton, Table Tennis)

434. Carr, R. J. (1973). Personality test scores (16 PF) of female P. E. students. **British Journal of Physical Education, 4**, 25-26. (Physical Education Class(es)

435. Cattell, R. B., & Cattell, H. E. P. (1995). Personality structure and the new fifth edition of the 16PF. **Educational and Psychological Measurement, 55**, 926-937. (Review Article)

436. Cattell, R. B., Eber, H. W., & Tatsuoka M. M. (1970). **Handbook for the 16 Personality Factor Questionnaire.** Champaign, IL: Institute for Personality and Ability Testing. (Test Manual)

437. Cattell, R. B., Saunders, D. R., & Stice, G. F. (1950). **Sixteen Personality Factor Questionnaire.** Champaign, IL: Institute for Personality and Ability Testing. (Test Manual)

438. Cheng, H., & Wu, Y. D. (1987). Comparison of the personality traits of judo coaches and athletes. **Asian Journal of Physical Education, 9**, 23-37. (Martial Arts)

439. Clay, J. T. (1974). Personality traits of female intercollegiate athletes and female intercollegiate athletic coaches. **s.n., s.l.**, 129. (Various Sports)

440. Cober, L. J. (1972). A personality factor study of participants in high risk sports. **s.n., s.l.**, 83. (Mountain Climbing, Scuba, Skydiving)

441. Cockerill, I. M. (1968). Personality and golfing ability. **Research Papers in Physical Education, 6**, 18-22. (Golf)

442. Conforto, C., & Marcenaro, M. (1979). Psychometric and psychodynamic investigation of the personality of tennis players. **International Journal of Sport Psychology, 10**, 217-230. (Tennis)

443. Cooper, L. (1969). Athletics, activity and personality. **Research Quarterly, 40**, 17-22. (Various Sports)

444. Cramer, S. R., Nieman, D. C., & Lee, J. W. (1990). The effects of moderate exercise training on personality traits in women. **Annals of Sports Medicine, 5**, 120-132. (Exercise)

445. Curtin, R. S. (1977). A study of self-perception, personality traits, and player perceptions, of selected male high school basketball coaches. **s.n., s.l.**, 193. (Basketball)

446. Dallman, G. W. (1973). Analysis of the differences between selected personality traits of successful and unsuccessful coaches in football, wrestling, and basketball. **s.n., s.l.**, 52. (Basketball, Football, Wrestling)

447. Darden, E. (1972). Sixteen personality factor profiles of competitive bodybuilders and weightlifters. **Research Quarterly, 43**, 142-147. (Bodybuilding, Weightlifting)

448. Daus, A. T., Wilson, J., & Freeman, W. M. (1986). Psychological testing as an auxiliary means of selecting successful college and professional football players. **Journal of Sports Medicine, 26**, 274-278. (Football)

449. Davey, C. P. (1981). Personality, motivation, arousal, and psychological preparation for sport. **Sports Coach, 5**, 13-19. (Various Sports)

450. Davey, C. P. (1977). Personality and motivation of Australian women athletes. **Australian Journal of Sports Medicine, 9**, 69-71. (Various Sports)

451. Diamond, P., Brisson, G. R., Candas, B., & Peronnet, F. (1989). Trait anxiety, submaximal physical exercise and blood androgens. **European Journal of Applied Physiology and Occupational Physiology, 58**, 699-704. (Exercise)

452. Dolphin, C., O'Brien, M., Cahill, N., & Cullen, J. (1980). Personality factors and some physiological correlates in athletes. **Journal of Psychosomatic Research, 24**, 281-285. (Archery, Cross Country, Martial Arts, Rowing)

453. Evans, V., & Quarterman, J. (1983). Personality characteristics of successful and unsuccessful black female basketball players. **International Journal of Sport Psychology, 14**, 105-115. (Basketball)

454. Farge, E. J., Hartung, G. H., & Borland, C. M. (1979). Runners and meditators: A comparison of personality profiles. **Journal of Personality Assessment, 43**, 501-503. (Running)

455. Figone, A. J. (1976). Differences in personality traits between baseball players at three selected levels of competition. **s.n., s.l.**, 236. (Baseball)

456. Garland, D. J., & Barry, J. R. (1990). Personality and leader behaviors in collegiate football: A multidimensional approach to performance. **Journal of Research in Personality, 24**, 355-370. (Football)

457. Gibson, B. J. (1975). A review of the theories of Cattell and Murray. In G. G. Watson, & L. Murray (Eds.), **Psycho-social elements of play, games, and recreation-1975** (pp. 66-74). Perth, Australia: University of Western Australia, Department of Physical Education. (Review Article)

458. Gondola, J. C., & Wughalter, E. (1991). The personality characteristics of internationally ranked female tennis players as measured by the Cattell 16 PF. **Perceptual and Motor Skills, 73**, 987-992. (Tennis)

459. Gruber, J. J. (1978). Comments on the reliability of a personality questionnaire used in physical education and sport research. **International Journal of Sport Psychology, 9**, 111-118. (Psychometric)

460. Gruber, J. J., & Perkins, S. (1978). Personality traits of women physical education majors and non-majors at various levels of athletic competition. **International Journal of Sport Psychology, 9**, 40-52. (Various Sports)

461. Hammer, W. H., & Tutko, T. A. (1974). Validation of the Athletic Motivation Inventory. **International Journal of Sport Psychology, 5**, 3-12. (Psychometric)

462. Hammersley, C. H., & Kastrinos, G. (1993). Vocational profiles of certified therapeutic specialists based on the 16PF. **Therapeutic Recreation Journal, 27**, 186-199. (Leisure Activity)

463. Hardy, C. J., & Silva, J. M. (1986). The relationship between selected psychological traits and fear of success in senior elite level wrestlers. **Canadian Journal of Applied Sport Sciences, 11**, 205-210. (Wrestling)

464. Harrison, P., & Jones, B. J. (1975). Research and women in sports: Closing the gap. **Physical Educator, 32**, 84-88. (Various Sports)

465. Hauck, E. R., & Blumenthal, J. A. (1992). Obsessive and compulsive traits in athletes. **Sports Medicine 14**, 215-227. (Review Article)

466. Heinrichs, R. D. (1975). Personality traits of selected collegiate golfers. **s.n., s.l.**, 88. (Golf)

467. Hendry, L. B. (1968). Assessment of personality traits in the coach-swimmer relationship, and a preliminary examination of the father-figure stereotype. **Research Quarterly, 39**, 543-551. (Swimming)

468. Howard, J. H., Cunningham, D. A., & Rechnitzer, P. A. (1987). Personality and fitness decline in middle-aged men. **International Journal of Sport Psychology, 18**, 100-111. (Exercise)

469. Ikulayo, P. B., & Vipene, J. B. (1996). Dominant personality characteristics of Nigerian female athletes in selected sports. **Journal of the International Council for Health, Physical Education, Recreation, Sport, and Dance, 32**, 58-59. (Field Hockey, Soccer, Table Tennis)

470. Ismail, A. H., & Young, R. J. (1977). Effects of chronic exercise on the personality of adults. **Annals of the New York Academy of Sciences, 301**, 958-967. (Exercise)

471. Jerome, W. C., & Valliant, P. M. (1983). Comparison of personalities between marathon runners and cross-country skiers. **Perceptual and Motor Skills, 56**, 35-38. (Skiing, Marathon)

472. Joesting, J., & Whitehead, G. I. (1976). Comparison of woman's studies students with female golf star athletes on the 16 PF. **Perceptual and Motor Skills, 42**, 477-478. (Golf)

473. Johnsgard, K. A. (1977). Personality and performance: A psychological study of amateur sport car racing. **Journal of Sports Medicine and Physical Fitness, 17,** 97-104. (Automobile Racing)

474. Johnsgard, K. A., & Ogilvie, B. C. (1968). The competitive racing driver. **Journal of Sports Medicine, 8,** 87-95. (Automobile Racing)

475. Johnsgard, K. A., Ogilvie, B. C., & Merritt, K. (1975). The stress seekers: A psychological study of sports parachutists, racing drivers, and football players. **Journal of Sports Medicine, 15,** 158-169. (Automobile Racing, Football, Skydiving)

476. Kerr, J. H. (1980). What makes a climber? **British Journal of Physical Education, 11,** 7-8. (Mountain Climbing)

477. King, J. P., & Chi, P. S. K. (1979). Social structure, sex roles, and personality: Comparison of male/female athletes/nonathletes. In J. H. Goldstein (Ed.), **Sports, games, and play: Social and psychological viewpoints-1979** (pp. 115-148). Hillsdale, N. J.: Lawrence Erlbaum Associates. (Review Article)

478. King, J. P., & Peter, S. K. (1974). Personality and the athletic social structure: A case study. **Human Relations, 27,** 179-193. (Basketball, Cross Country, Football, Swimming, Track and Field)

479. Kroll, W. (1967). Sixteen personality factor profiles of collegiate wrestlers. **Research Quarterly, 38,** 49-57. (Wrestling)

480. Kroll, W., Loy, J., Hosek, V., & Vanek, M. (1973). Multivariate analysis of the personality profiles of championship Czechoslovakian athletes. **International Journal of Sport Psychology, 4,** 131-147. (Various Sports)

481. Kroll, W., & Petersen, K. H. (1965). Personality factor profiles of collegiate football teams. **Research Quarterly, 36,** 433-440. (Football)

482. Kurian, M., Caterino, L. C., & Kulhavy, R. W. (1993). Personality characteristics and duration of ATA Taekwondo training. **Perceptual and Motor Skills, 76,** 363-366. (Martial Arts) 483.

483   Langer, P. (1966). Varsity football performance. **Perceptual and Motor Skills, 23**, 1191- 1199. (Football)

484.   Lowe, B. (1971). The aesthetic sensitivity of athletes. **s.n., s.l.**, 129. (Various Sports)

485.   Maciejczyk, J., & Terelak, J. (1986). Dependence between Type A behavior pattern and personality features. **Biology of Sport, 3**, 215-226. (Review Article)

486.   Magni, G., Rupolo, G., Leo, D. D., Rampazzo, M., & Simini, G. (1985). Aspects of the psychology and personality of high altitude mountain climbers. **International Journal of Sport Psychology, 16**, 12-19. (Mountain Climbing)

487.   Malloy, G. N. (1979). Some personality characteristics of Australian male and female athletes. **Australian Journal of Sports Medicine, 11**, 33-36. (Rowing)

488.   Malumphy. T. M. (1968). Personality of women athletes in intercollegiate competition. **Research Quarterly, 39**, 610-620. (Various Sports)

489.   McCarthy, E. F. (1973). A comparison of the personality characteristics of highly successful, moderately successful, and unsuccessful high school basketball coaches as measured by the Cattell Sixteen Personality Factor Questionnaire. **s.n., s.l.**, 1973. (Basketball)

490.   McHugh, M. M. (1970). Personality traits of varsity lettermen of Illinois State University. **s.n., s.l.**, 79. (Various Sports)

491.   Morris, D. L. (1975). A socio-psychological study of highly skilled women field hockey players. **International Journal of Sport Psychology, 6**, 134-147. (Field Hockey)

492.   Nelson, D. O. (1966). Leadership in sports. **Research Quarterly, 37**, 268-275. (Basketball)

493.   Nieman, D. C., & George, D. M. (1987). Personality traits that correlate with success in distance running. **Journal of Sports Medicine and Physical Fitness, 27**, 345-356. (Running)

494. Novotny, L., & Petrak, B. (1983). Characteristics of juniors and schoolboys-ice hockey players. **International Journal of Sport Psychology, 14**, 15-26. (Ice Hockey)

495. Ogilvie, B. C. (1968). Psychological consistencies within the personality of high-level competitors. **Journal of American Medical Association, 205**, 156-162. (Swimming)

496. Pestonjee, D. M., Singh, R. B., Singh, A. P., & Singh, U. B. (1981). Personality and physical abilities: An empirical investigation. **International Journal of Sport Psychology, 12**, 39-51. (Various Sports)

497. Peterson, S. L., Weber, J. C., & Trousdale, W. (1967). Personality traits of women in team sports vs. women in individual sports. **Research Quarterly, 38**, 686-690. (Various Sports)

498. Phillips, D. A., Carlisle, C. S., Hautala, R., & Larson, R. (1985). Personality traits and teacher-student behaviors in physical education. **Journal of Educational Psychology, 77**, 408-416. (Physical Education Class(es)

499. Power, S. L. (1986). Psychological assessment procedures of a track and field national event squad training weekend. In J. Watkins, T. Reilly, & L. Burwitz (Eds.), **Sports science**. New York: E & FN Spon. (Track and Field)

500. Pyecha, J. (1970). Comparative effects of judo and selected physical education activities on male university freshman personality traits. **Research Quarterly, 41**, 425-431. (Martial Arts, Various Sports)

501. Renfrow, N. E., & Bolton, B. (1979). Personality characteristics associated with aerobic exercise in adult males. **Journal of Personality Assessment, 43**, 261-266. (Running)

502. Renneckar, C. A. (1970). Personality traits of selected women intercollegiate athletes. **s.n., s.l.**, 80. (Various Sports)

503. Ruffer, W. A. (1975). Two studies of personality: Male graduate students in physical education. **Perceptual and Motor Skills, 41**, 187-191. (Physical Education Class(es)

504.   Rushall, B. S. (1970). An investigation of the relationship between personality variables and performance categories in swimmers. **International Journal of Sport Psychology, 1**, 93-104. (Swimming)

505.   Rushall, B. S. (1972). Three studies relating personality variables to football performance. **International Journal of Sport Psychology, 3**, 12-24. (Football)

506.   Ryn, Z. (1988). Psychopathology in mountaineering: Mental disturbances under high-altitude stress. **International Journal of Sports Medicine, 9**, 163-169. (Mountain Climbing)

507.   Salokun, S. O., & Toriola, A. L. (1985). Personality characteristics of sprinters, basketball, soccer, and field hockey players. **Journal of Sports Medicine and Physical Fitness, 25**, 222-226. (Basketball, Field Hockey, Soccer, Track and Field)

508.   Schandel, J. (1965). Psychological differences between athletes and nonparticipants in athletics at three educational levels. **Research Quarterly, 36**, 52-67. (Various Sports)

509.   Secunda, M. D., Blau, B. I., McGuire, J. M., & Burroughs, W. A. (1986). Psychobiomotor assessment of football-playing ability. **International Journal of Sport Psychology, 17**, 215-233. (Football)

510.   Silva, J. M., Shultz, B. B., Haslam, R.W., Martin, T. P., & Murray, D. F. (1985). Discriminating characteristics of contestants at the United States Olympic wrestling trials. **International Journal of Sports Psychology, 16**, 79-102. (Wrestling)

511.   Sinclair, E. D. (1968). Personality and rugby football. **Research Papers in Physical Education, 6**, 23-28. (Rugby)

512.   Singer, R. N. (1969). Personality differences between and within baseball and tennis players. **Research Quarterly, 40**, 582-588. (Baseball, Tennis)

513.   Slusher, H. S. (1964). Personality and intelligence characteristics of selected high school athletes and nonathletes. **Research Quarterly, 35**, 539-545. (Baseball, Basketball, Football, Swimming, Wrestling)

514.   Straub, W. F. (1971). Personality traits of college football players who participated at different levels of competition. **International Journal of Sport Psychology, 2**, 33-41. (Football)

515.   Straub, W. F., & Davis, S. W. (1971). Personality traits of college football players who participated at different levels of competition. **Medicine and Science in Sports, 3**, 39-43. (Football)

516.   Thakur, G. P., & Ojha, M. (1981). Personality differences of Indian table-tennis, badminton, and football players on primary source traits in the 16 PF. **International Journal of Sport Psychology, 12**, 196-203. (Badminton, Football, Table Tennis)

517.   Thomas, G. C., & Sinclair, G. D. (1977). Relationship between personality and performance of Canadian women intercollegiate basketball players. **Proceedings of the Nineth Canadian Psycho-Motor Learning and Sport Psychology Symposium** (pp. 205-214). Banff, Alberta. (Basketball)

518.   Tucker, L. A. (1987). Mental health and physical fitness. **Journal of Human Movement Studies, 13**, 267-273. (Exercise)

519.   Walker, M. B., & Hailey, B. J. (1987). Physical fitness levels and psychological states versus traits. **Perceptual and Motor Skills, 64**, 12-25. (Exercise)

520.   Wall, K. A. (1975). A cross-cultural comparison of personality traits of selected athletes in open or closed skilled sports. **s.n., s.l.**, 137. (Various Sports)

521.   Ward, R. G., Morrow, J. R., Omizo, M. M., & Michael, W. B. (1979). The prediction of performance of Olympic athletes in discus, hammer, javelin, and shotput from measures of personality characteristics. **Educational and Psychological Measurement, 39**, 197-201. (Track and Field)

522. Werner, A. C. (1960). Physical education and the development of leadership characteristics of cadets at the U.S. Military Academy. **Proceedings of NCPEAM, 65**, 100-104. (Exercise)

523. Werner, A. C., & Gottheil, E. (1966). Personality development and participation in college athletics. **Research Quarterly, 37**, 126-131. (Various Sports)

524. Williams, J. M., Hoepner, B. J., Moody, D. L., & Ogilvie, B. C. (1970). Personality traits of champion level female fencers. **Research Quarterly, 41**, 446-453. (Fencing)

525. Williams, L. R. T. (1978). Personality differences and achievement level in sport. **Australian Journal of Science and Medicine in Sport, 17**, 28-30. (Various Sports)

526. Williams, L. R. T. (1985). Prediction of high-level rowing ability. **Journal of Sports Medicine, 18**, 11-17. (Rowing)

527. Williams, L. R. T., & Parkin, W. A. (1980). Personality factor profiles of three hockey groups. **International Journal of Sport Psychology, 11**, 113-120. (Field Hockey)

528. Wilson, V. E., & Minden, H. A. (1979). Canadian approach to sport psychology. In P. Klavora, & J. V. Daniel (Eds.), **Coach, athlete, and the sport psychologist-1979** (pp. 272-284). Champaign, IL: Human Kinetics. (Gymnastics)

529. Young, R. J., & Ismail, A. H. (1978). Ability of biochemical and personality variables in discriminating between high and low physical fitness levels. **Journal of Psychosomatic Research, 22**, 193-199. (Exercise)

CHAPTER SEVEN

OPTIMISM/PESSIMISM

Life Orientation Test (LOT)

530.   Andersson, G. (1996). The benefits of optimism: A meta-analytic review of the Life Orientation Test. **Personality and Individual Differences, 21**, 719-725. (Psychometric)

531.   Braathen, E. T., & Svebak, S. (1994). EMG response patterns and motivational styles as predictors of performance and discontinuation in explosive and endurance sports among talented teenage athletes. **Personality and Individual Differences, 17**, 545-556. (Various Sports)

532.   Burke, K. L., Joyner, A. B., Czech, D. R., & Wilson, M. J. (2000). An investigation of concurrent validity between two optimism/pessimism questionnaires: The Life Orientation Test-Revised and the Optimism/Pessimism Scale. **Current Psychology, 19**, 129-136. (Psychometric)

533.   Chang, L., & McBride-Chang, C. (1996). The factor structure of the Life Orientation Test. **Educational and Psychological Measurement, 56**, 325-329. (Psychometric)

534.   Ford, I. W., Eklund, R. C., & Gordon, S. (2001). An examination of psychological variables moderating the relationship between life stress and injury time-loss among athletes of a high standard. **Journal of Sports Science, 18**, 301-312. (Injury, Various Sports)

535.   Hellandsig, E. T. (1998). Motivational predictors of high performance and discontinuation in different types of sports among talented teenage athletes. **International Journal of Sport Psychology, 29**, 27-44. (Various Sports)

536.   Hjelle, L., Belongia, C., & Nesser, J. (1996). Psychometric properties of the Life Orientation Test and Attributional Style Questionnaire. **Psychological Reports, 78**, 507-515. (Psychometric)

537. Kaissidis-Rodafinos, A., & Anshel, M. H. (2000). Psychological predictors of coping responses among Greek basketball referees. **Journal of Social Psychology, 140**, 329-344. (Basketball, Sports Officials)

538. Marshall, G. N., Wortman, C. B., Kusulas, J. W., Hervig, L. K., & Vickers, R. R. (1992). Distinguishing optimism from pessimism: Relations to fundamental dimensions of mood and personality. **Journal of Personality and Social Psychology, 62**, 1067-1074. (Psychometric)

539. Scheier, M. F., & Carver, C. S. (1987). Dispositional optimism and physical well-being: The influence of generalized expectancies on health. **Journal of Personality, 55**, 169-210. (Exercise)

CHAPTER EIGHT

SELF-CONCEPT/SELF-ESTEEM/SELF-ACTUALIZATION

Personal Orientation Inventory (POI)

540.   Butterfield, G., & Woods, R. (1980). Self-actualization and improvement in tennis skills at summer camps for adolescents. **Adolescence, 15,** 429-434. (Tennis)

541.   Gilstrap, T., & Sherrill, C. (1989). Personality profiles of elite blind female athletes. **Palaestra, 6,** 21-23, 31-34. (Disabled Athletes)

542.   Ilardi, R., & May, W. (1968). A reliability study of Shostrom's Personal Orientation Inventory. **Journal of Humanistic Psychology, 8,** 68-72. (Psychometric)

543.   Leclerc, G., Lefrancois, R., Dube, M., Hebert, R., & Gaulin, P. (1998). The self-actualization concept: A content validation. **Journal of Social Behavior and Personality, 13,** (Psychometric)

544.   Leclerc, G., Lefrancois, R., Dube, M., Hebert, R., & Gaulin, P. (1999). Criterion validity of a new measure of self-concept. **Psychological Reports, 85,** 1167-1176. (Psychometric)

545.   Lefrancois, R., Leclerc, G., Dube, M., Hebert, R., & Gaulin, P. (1997). The development and validation of a self-report measure of self-actualization. **Social Behavior and Personality, 25,** 353-365. (Psychometric)

546.   Lefrancois, R., Leclerc, G., Dube, M., Hebert, R., & Gaulin, P. (1998). Reliability of a new measure of self-actualization. **Psychological Reports, 82,** 875-878. (Psychometric)

547.   McClure, B. A., Holladay, K. L., & Foster, C. D. (1988). Effect of a personal growth group on self-actualization of female gymnasts. **Perceptual and Motor Skills, 66,** 165-166. (Gymnastics)

548.   Ridgway, M. E., & Boyd, R. L. (1994). Self-actualization of able-bodied and wheelchair male college students. **Brazilian International Journal of Adapted Physical Education Research, 1**, 1-17. (Various Sports)

549.   Schindler, T. M., & Waters, M. (1986). Athletic involvement and aspects of self-actualization. **Journal of Sport Behavior, 9**, 59-69. (Various Sports)

550.   Sherrill, C., & Rainbolt, W. (1988). Self-actualization profiles of male able-bodied and elite cerebral palsied athletes. **Adapted Physical Activity Quarterly, 5**, 108-119. (Disabled Athletes)

551.   Sherrill, C., Silliman, L., Gench, B., & Hinson, M. (1990). Self-actualization of elite wheelchair athletes. **Paraplegia, 28**, 252-260. (Disabled Athletes)

552.   Sherrill, C., Gilstrap, T., Richir, K., Gench, B., & Hinson, M. (1988). Use of the Personal Orientation Inventory with disabled athletes. **Perceptual and Motor Skills, 67**, 263-266. (Disabled Athletes)

553.   Sherrill, C., Gench, B., Hinson, M, Gilstrap, T., Richir, K., & Mastro, J. V. (1990). Self-actualization of elite blind athletes: An exploratory study. **Journal of Visual Impairment and Blindness, 84**, 55-60. (Disabled Athletes)

554.   Silliman, L. M., & Sherrill, C. (1989). Self-actualization of wheelchair athletes. **Clinical Kinesiology, 43**, 77-82. (Disabled Athletes)

555.   Tosi, D., & Lindamood, C. (1975). The measurement of self-actualization: A critical review of the Personal Orientation Inventory. **Journal of Personality Assessment, 39**, 215-223. (Psychometric)

556.   Weiss, A. S. (1987). Shostrom Personal Orientation Inventory: Arguments against its basic validity. **Personality and Individual Differences, 8**, 895-903. (Psychometric)

557.   Wise, G., & Davis, J. (1975). The Personal Orientation Inventory: Internal consistency, stability, and sex differences. **Psychological Reports, 36**, 847-855. (Psychometric)

558.   Young, R. A., & Crandall, R. (1984). Wilderness use and self-actualization. **Journal of Leisure Research, 16**, 149-160. (Leisure Activity)

Piers-Harris Children's Self-Concept Scale

559.   Guyot, G. W., Fairchild, L., & Hill, M. (1981). Physical fitness, sport participation, body build, and self concept of elementary school children. **International Journal of Sport Psychology, 12**, 105-116. (Exercise)

560.   Hatfield, B. D., Vaccaro, P., & Benedict, G. J. (1985). Self-concept responses of children to participation in an 8-week precision jump rope program. **Perceptual and Motor Skills, 61**, 1275-1279. (Exercise)

561.   Henderson, D., & Abrams, P. (1983). A comparison of selected dimensions of the self-concept of three self-concept tests for pre-school children. **Early Child Development & Care, 13**, 1-16. (Exercise).

562.   Puckett, J. R., & Ford, H. T. (1981). Self-concept scores and participation in recreation-league team sports. **Perceptual and Motor Skills, 52**, 249-250. (Various Sports)

563.   Richardson, P. A., Weinberg, R. S., Bruya, L., Baun, W., Jackson, A., Caton, I., & Bruya, L. (1980). Physical and psychological characteristics of young children in sports: A descriptive profile. **Physical Educator, 37**, 187-191. (Exercise)

564.   Strauss, R.S., Rodzilsky, D., Burack, G., & Colin, M. (2001). Psychosocial correlates of physical activity in healthy children. **Archives of Pediatrics & Adolescent Medicine, 155**, 897-902. (Exercise)

565.   Wright, J., & Cowden, J. E. (1986). Changes in self-concept and cardiovascular endurance of mentally retarded youths in a Special Olympics swim training program. **Adapted Physical Activity Quarterly, 3**, 177-183. (Disabled Athletes)

Rosenberg Self-Esteem Scale

566. Abood, D. A., & Black, D. R. (2000). Health education prevention for eating disorders among college female athletes. **American Journal of Health Behavior, 24**, 209-219. (Various Sports)

567. Amber, D., Cockerill, I. M., & Carroll, D. (2000). The pathological status of exercise dependence. **British Journal of Sports Medicine, 34**, 125-132. (Exercise)

568. Berry, T. R., & Howe, B. L. (2000). Risk factors for disordered eating in female university athletes. **Journal of Sport Behavior, 23**, 207-218. (Basketball, Field Hockey, Rowing, Soccer, Swimming)

569. Bosscher, R. J. (1993). Running and mixed physical exercises with depressed psychiatric patients. **International Journal of Sport Psychology, 24**, 170-184. (Exercise, Running)

570. Brewer, B. W., & Petrie, T. A. (1995). A comparison between injured and uninjured football players on selected psychosocial variables. **The Academic Athletic Journal**, Spring, (Football)

571. Bridle, M. J. (1984). Comparison of the Tennessee Self-Concept Scale and the Rosenberg Self-Esteem Scale **Occupational Therapy Journal of Research, 4**, 51-52. (Psychometric)

572. Butcher, J. (1989). Adolescent girls' sex role development: Relationship with sports participation, self-esteem, and age at menarche. **Sex Roles, 20**, 575-593. (Various Sports)

573. Diehl, N., Johnson, C. E., Rogers, R. L., & Petrie, T. A. (1998). Social physique anxiety and disordered eating: What's the connection? **Addictive Behaviors, 23**, 1-6. (College Students)

574. Ferring, D., & Filipp, S. H. (1996). Measurement of self-esteem: Findings on reliability, validity, and stability of the Rosenberg Scale. **Diagnostica, 42**, 284-292. (Psychometric)

575.   Fisher, M., Juszcsak, L., & Friedman, S. B. (1996). Sports participation in an urban high school: Academic and psychological correlates. **Journal of Adolescent Health, 18**, 329-334. (Physical Education Class(es), Steroids/Drugs, Various Sports)

576.   Ford, I. W., Eklund, R. C., & Gordon, S. (2001). An examination of psychological variables moderating the relationship between life stress and injury time-loss among athletes of a high standard. **Journal of Sports Science, 18**, 301-312. (Injury, Various Sports)

577.   Goldsmith, R. E. (1986). Dimensionality of the Rosenberg Self-Esteem Scale. **Journal of Social Behavior and Personality, 1**, 253-264, (Psychometric)

578.   Hagborg, W. J. (1993). The Rosenberg Self-Esteem Scale and Harter Self-Perception Profile for Adolescents: A concurrent validity study. **Psychology in the Schools, 30**, 132-136. (Psychometric, Youth)

579.   Hulley, A.J., & Hill, A.J. (2001). Eating disorders and health in elite women distance runners. **International Journal of Eating Disorders, 30**, 312-317. (Running)

580.   Kaissidis-Rodafinos, A., & Anshel, M. H. (2000). Psychological predictors of coping responses among Greek basketball referees. **Journal of Social Psychology, 140**, (Basketball, Sports Officials)

581.   Motl, R. W., & Conroy, D. E. (1999). Validity and factorial invariance of the Social Physique Anxiety Scale. **Medicine and Science in Sports and Exercise, 32**, 1007-1017. (Physical Education Class(es), Psychometric)

582.   Nudelman, S., Rosen, J. C., & Leitenberg, H. (1988). Dissimilarities in eating attitudes, body image distortion, depression, and self-esteem between high-intensity male runners and women with bulimia nervosa. **International Journal of Eating Disorders, 7**, 625-633. (Running)

583.   Paccagnella, M., & Grove, J. R. (2001). Attitudes towards high achievers in sport: An adaptation of Feather's tall poppy scale. **Journal of Science and Medicine in Sport, 4**, 310-323. (College Students)

584.   Park, C. J. (2000). Self-esteem as a mediator of the relationship between Tae Kwon Do training and aggression. **International Council for Health, Physical Education, Recreation, Sport and Dance Journal, 36**(3*)*, 35-37. (Martial Arts)

585.   Petrie, T. A. (1993). Disordered eating in female collegiate gymnasts: Prevalence and personality/attitudinal correlates. **Journal of Sport & Exercise Psychology, 15**, 424-436. (Gymnastics)

586.   Prapavessis, H., & Grove, J. R. (1998). Self-handicapping and self-esteem. **Journal of Applied Sport Psychology, 10**, 175-184. (Golf)

587.   Shevlin, M. E., Bunting, B. P., & Lewis, C. A. (1995). Confirmatory factor analysis of the Rosenberg Self-Esteem Scale. **Psychological Reports, 76**, 707-710. (Psychometric)

588.   Wilkins, J. A., Boland, F. J., & Albinson, J. G. (1991). A comparison of male and female athletes and nonathletes on eating disorders indices: Are athletes protected? **Journal of Sport Behavior, 14**, 129-143. (Various Sports)

Tennessee Self-Concept Scale (TSCS)

589.   Balogun, J. A. (1986). Muscular strength as a predictor of personality in adult females. **Journal of Sports Medicine and Physical Fitness, 26,** 377-383. (Weight Training)

590.   Balogun, J. A. (1987). The interrelationships between measures of physical-fitness and self-concept. **Journal of Human Movement Studies, 13**, 255-265. (Exercise)

591.   Berryman-Miller, S. (1988). Dance/movement: Effects on elderly self-concept. **Journal of Physical Education , Recreation and Dance, 59**, 42-46. (Dance)

592.   Bertinetti, J. F. & Fabry, J. (1977). An investigation of the construct validity of the Tennessee Self-Concept Scale. **Journal of Clinical Psychology, 33**, 416-418. (Review Article)

593. Bishop, S. L., Walling, D. P. & Walker, B. A. (1997). The emperor's clothes: Assessing the validity of scores on the Tennessee Self-Concept Scale. **Educational and Psychological Measurement, 57,** 150-163. (Review Article)

594. Blackman, L., Hunter, G., Hilyer, J. & Harrison, P. (1988). The effects of dance team participation on female adolescent physical fitness and self-concept. **Adolescence, 23,** 437-448. (Dance)

595. Brazell-Roberts, J. V. & Thomas L. E. (1990). Pumping iron and self-esteem. Starting a weight-training program. **Swimming Technique, 26,** 21-23. (Weight Training)

596. Brazell-Roberts, J. V. & Thomas, L. E. (1989). Effects of weight training frequency on the self-concept of college females. **Journal of Applied Sport Science Research, 3,** 40-43. (Weight Training)

597. Bridle, M. J. (1984). Comparison of the Tennessee Self-Concept Scale and the Rosenberg Self-Esteem Scale. **Occupational Therapy Journal of Research, 4,** 51-52. (Psychometric)

598. Brock, B. J. (1988). Effect of therapeutic horseback riding on physically disabled adults. **Therapeutic Recreation Journal, 22,** 34-43. (Disabled Athletes, Equestrian Sport)

599. Brown, E. Y., Morrow, J. R. & Livingston, S. M. (1982). Self-concept changes in women as a result of training. **Journal of Sport Psychology, 4,** 354-363. (Exercise)

600. Dekel, Y., Kudar, K. & Tenenbaum, G. (1994). An exploratory study on the relationship between postural deformation and body-image and self-concept in adolescents: The mediating role of physical activity. **Review of the Hungarian University of Physical Education, 32,** 24-33. (Exercise)

601. Dekel, Y., Tenenbaum, G. & Kudar, K. (1996). An exploratory study on the relationship between postural deformities and body-image and self-esteem in adolescents: The mediating role of physical activity. **International Journal of Sport Psychology, 27,** 183-196. (Exercise)

602. DiLorenzo, T. M., Bargman, E. P., Stucky-Ropp, R., Brassington, G. S., Frensch, P. A., & LaFontaine, T. (1999). Long-term effects of aerobic exercise on psychological outcomes. **Preventive Medicine, 28,** 75-85. (Exercise)

603. Eickhoff, J., Thorland, W. & Ansorge, C. J. (1983). Selected physiological and psychological effects of aerobic dancing among young adult women. **Journal of Sports Medicine and Physical Fitness, 23,** 273-280. (Dance).

604. Ezeilo, B. N. (1982). Cross-cultural utility of the Tennessee Self-Concept Scale. **Psychological Reports, 51,** 897-898. (Review Article).

605. Finkenburg, M. E. (1990). Effect of participation in taekwondo on college women's self-concept. **Perceptual and Motor Skills, 71,** 891-894. (Martial Arts)

606. Finkenberg, M. E. & Teper, L. (1991). Self-concept profiles of competitive bodybuilders. **Perceptual and Motor Skills, 72,** 1039-1043. (Bodybuilding).

607. Finkenberg, M. E., Shows, D. & DiNucci, J. M. (1994). Participation in adventure-based activities and self-concepts of college men and women. **Perceptual and Motor Skills, 78,** 1119-1122. (Adventure Activities).

608. Gellen, M. I., & Hoffman, R. A. (1984). Analysis of the subscales of the Tennessee Self-Concept Scale. **Measurement and Evaluation in Counseling and Development, 17,** 51-55. (Review Article)

609. Hammer, W. M., & Tutko, T. A. (1974). Validation of the Athletic Motivation Inventory. **International Journal of Sport Psychology, 5,** 3-12. (Psychometric)

610. Hoffman, R. A. & Gellen, M. I. (1983). The Tennessee Self-Concept Scale: A revisit. **Psychological Reports, 53,** 1199-1204. (Review Article).

611. Howard, W. L. & Reardon, J. P. (1986). Changes in the self concept and athletic performance of weight lifters through a cognitive-hypnotic approach: An empirical study. **American Journal of Clinical Hypnosis, 28,** 248-257. (Weightlifting)

612. Kalliopuska, M. (1989). Empathy, self-esteem and creativity among junior ballet dancers. **Perceptual and Motor Skills, 69**, 1227-1234. (Dance)

613. Lambert, M. J. (1986). Self concept and injury frequency among female college field hockey players. **Athletic Training, 21**, 220-224. (Field Hockey, Injury)

614. Lambert, M. J., Segger, J. F., Staley, J. S., Spencer, B. & Nelson, D. (1978). Reported self-concept and self-actualizing value changes as a function of academic classes with wilderness experience. **Perceptual and Motor Skills, 46**, 1035-1040. (Leisure Activity)

615. Leddy, M. H., Lambert, M. J., & Ogles, B. M. (1994). Psychological consequences of athletic injury among high-level competitors. **Research Quarterly for Exercise and Sport, 65**, (Injury, Various Sports)

616. Marsh, H. W. & Richards, G. E. (1988). Tennessee Self Concept Scale: Reliability, internal structure and construct validity. **Journal of Personality and Social Psychology, 55**, 612-624. (Review Article)

617. McGuire, B. & Tinsley, H. E. (1981). A contribution to the construct validity of the Tennessee Self-Concept Scale: A confirmatory factor analysis. **Applied Psychological Measurement, 5**, 449-457. (Review Article)

618. Olu, S. S. (1991). Perceived somatotype as related to self-concept in Nigerian adolescent high school students. **Journal of Sports Medicine and Physical Fitness, 31**, 611-617. (Physical Education Class(es)

619. Patrick, G. D. (1986). The effects of wheelchair competition on self-concept and acceptance of disability in novice athletes. **Therapeutic Recreational Journal, 20**, 61-71. (Disabled Athletes)

620. Plummer, O. K. & Koh, Y. O. (1987). Effect of "aerobics" on self-concepts of college women. **Perceptual and Motor Skills, 65**, 271-275. (Exercise)

621. Porat, Y., Lufi, D. & Tenenbaum, G. (1989). Psychological components contribute to select young female gymnasts. **International Journal of Sport Psychology, 20**, 279-286. (Gymnastics)

622. Pound, R. E., Hansen, J. C., & Putnam, B. A. (1977). An empirical analysis of theTennessee Self-Concept Scale. **Educational and Psychological Measurement, 37**, 545-551. (Review Article)

623. Salokun, S. O. (1990). Comparison of Nigerian high school male athletes and nonathletes on self-concept. **Perceptual and Motor Skills, 70**, 865-866. (Various Sports)

624. Sanders, R. L. (1981). Coaching style and the athlete's self-concept. **Athletic Journal, 61**, 66-67. (Basketball, Coaching)

625. Schumaker, J. F., Small, L. & Wood, J. (1986). Self-concept, academic achievement, and athletic participation. **Perceptual and Motor Skills, 62**, 387-390. (Various Sports)

626. Sharpley, C. F. & Hattie J. A. (1983). Cross-cultural and sex differences on the Tennessee Self-Concept Scale: A challenge to Fitts' original data. **Journal of Clinical Psychology, 39**, 717-721. (Review Article)

627. Short, M. A., DiCarlo, S., Steffee, W. P. & Pavlov, K. (1984). Effects of physical conditioning on self-concept of adult obese males. **Physical Therapy, 64**, 194-198. (Exercise)

628. Stein, P. N. & Motta, R. W. (1992). Effects of aerobic and nonaerobic exercise on depression and self-concept. **Perceptual and Motor Skills, 74**, 79-89. (Swimming, Weight Training)

629. Super, J. T., & Block, J. R. (1992). Self-concept and need for achievement of men with physical disabilities. **Journal of General Psychology, 119**, 73-80. (Disabled Athletes)

630. Trujillo, C. M. (1983). The effect of weight training and running exercise intervention programs on the self-esteem of college women. **International Journal of Sport Psychology, 14**, 162-173. (Running, Weight Training)

631.   Tucker, L. A. (1982). Effect of weight-training program on the self-concepts of college males. **Perceptual and Motor Skills, 54,** 1055-1061. (Weight Training)

632.   Tucker, L. A. (1983). Weight training: A tool for the improvement of self and body concepts of males. **Journal of Human Movement Studies, 9,** 31-37. (Weight Training)

633.   Tucker, L. A. (1984). Trait psychology and performance: A credulous viewpoint. **Journal of Human Movement Studies, 10,** 53-62. (Weight Training)

634.   Vincent, F. (1976). Comparison of self-concept of college women athletes and physical education majors. **Research Quarterly, 47,** 218-225. (Various Sports)

635.   Walsh, J. A., Wilson, G. L. & McLellarn, R. W. (1989). A confirmatory factor analysis of the Tennessee Self-Concept Scale. **Criminal Justice and Behavior, 16,** 465-472. (Review Article)

636.   White, S. A. & Zientek, C. E. C. (1991). Verbal persuasion and self-concept: An exploratory analysis in special Olympians. **Clinical Kinesiology, 45,** 9-13. (Disabled Athletes)

637.   Wilfley, D., & Kunce, J. (1986). Differential physical and psychological effects of exercise. **Journal of Counseling Psychology, 33,** 337-342. (Exercise)

638.   Young, M. L. (1981). Comparison of self-concepts of women high school and college tournament basketball players. **Research Quarterly for Exercise and Sport, 52,** 286-290. (Basketball)

639.   Young, M. L. (1985). Estimation of fitness and physical ability, physical performance, and self-concept among adolescent females. **Journal of Sports Medicine and Physical Fitness, 25,** 144-150. (Exercise)

640.   Young, M. L. & Cohen, D. A. (1979). Self-concept and injuries among female college tournament basketball players. **American Corrective Therapy Journal, 33,** 139-142. (Basketball)

641.   Young, M. L. & Cohen, D. A. (1981). Self-concept and injuries among female high school basketball players. **Journal of Sports Medicine and Physical Fitness, 21,** 55-61. (Basketball)

CHAPTER NINE
SENSATION SEEKING

Sensation Seeking Scale (SSS)

642. Arnett, J. (1994). Sensation seeking - A new conceptualization and a new scale. **Personality and Individual Differences, 16**, 289-296. (Psychometric)

643. Bouter, L. M., Knipschild, P. G., Feij, J. A., & Volovics, A. (1988). Sensation seeking and injury risk in downhill skiing. **Personality and Individual Differences, 9**, 667-673. (Injury, Skiing)

644. Braathen, E. T., & Svebak, S. (1994). EMG response patterns and motivational styles as predictors of performance and discontinuation in explosive and endurance sports among talented teenage athletes. **Personality and Individual Differences, 17**, 545-556. (Various Sports)

645. Breivik, G. (1996). Personality, sensation seeking and risk taking among Everest climbers. **International Journal of Sport Psychology, 27**, 308-320. (Mountain Climbing)

646. Breivik, G., Roth, W. T., & Jorgensen, P. E. (1998). Personality, psychological states and heart rate in non-expert parachutists. **Personality and Individual Differences, 25**, 365-380. (Skydiving)

647. Campbell, J. B., Tyrrell, D., & Zingaro, M. (1993). Sensation seeking among whitewater canoe and kayak paddlers. **Personality and Individual Differences, 14**, 488-491. (Rowing)

648. Chirivella, E. C., & Martinez, L. M. (1994). The sensation of risk and motivational tendencies in sports: An empirical study. **Personality and Individual Differences, 16**, (Martial Arts, Parasailing, Tennis)

649. Cronin, C. (1991). Sensation seeking among mountain climbers. **Personality and Individual Differences, 12**, 653-654. (Mountain Climbing)

650. Davis, C., & Mogk, J. P. (1994). Some personality correlates of interest and excellence in sport. **International Journal of Sport Psychology, 25,** 131-143. (Various Sports)

651. Franken, R. E., Hill, R., & Kierstead, J. (1994). Sport interest as predicted by the personality measures of competitiveness, mastery, instrumentality, expressivity, and sensation seeking. **Personality and Individual Differences, 17,** 467-476. (Various Sports)

652. Freixanet, M. G. (1991). Personality profile of subjects engaged in high physical risk sports. **Personality and Individual Differences, 12,** 1087-1093. (Mountain Climbing)

653. Gilchrist, H., Povey, R., Dickinson, A., & Povey, R. (1995). The Sensation Seeking Scale Its use in a study of the characteristics of people choosing adventure holidays. **Personality and Individual Differences, 19,** 513-516. (Adventure Activities, Leisure Activity)

654. Glicksohn, J., & Abulafia, J. (1998). Embedding sensation seeking within the big three. **Personality and Individual Differences, 25,** 1085-1099. (Psychometric)

655. Gundersheim, J. (1987). Sensation seeking in male and female athletes and nonathletes. **International Journal of Sport Psychology, 18,** 87-99. (Various Sports)

656. Hartman, M. L., & Rawson, H. E. (1992). Differences in and correlates of sensation seeking in male and female athletes and nonathletes. **Personality and Individual Differences, 13,** 805-812. (Various Sports)

657. Haynes, C. A., Miles, J. N. V., & Clements, K. (2000). A confirmatory factor analysis of two models of sensation seeking. **Personality and Individual Differences, 29,** 823-839. (Psychometric)

658.   Hellandsig, E. T. (1998). Motivational predictors of high performance and discontinuation in different types of sports among talented teenage athletes. **International Journal of Sport Psychology, 29**, 27-44. (Risk Sports, Various Sports)

659.   Heyman, S. R., & Ross, K. G. (1980). Psychological variables affecting SCUBA performance. In C. H. Nadeau, W. R., Halliwell, K. M. Newell, & G. C. Roberts (Eds.), **Psychology of sport and motor behavior**. Champaign, IL: Human Kinetics. (Scuba)

660.   Horvath, P., & Zuckerman, M. (1993). Sensation seeking, risk appraisal, and risky behaviour. **Personality and Individual Differences, 14**, 41-52. (College Students)

661.   Hymbaugh, K., & Garrett, J. (1974). Sensation seeking among skydivers. **Perceptual and Motor Skills, 38**, 118. (Skydiving)

662.   Jack, S. J., & Ronan, K. R. (1998). Sensation seeking among high- and low-risk sports participants. **Personality and Individual Differences, 25**, 1063-1083. (Automobile Racing, Exercise, Golf, Hang Gliding, Marathon, Mountain Climbing, Skydiving, Swimming)

663.   Kerr, J. H. (1991). Arousal-seeking in risk sport participants. **Personality and Individual Differences, 12**, 613-616. (Various Sports)

664.   Kerr, J. H., & Svebak, S. (1989). Motivational aspects of preference for and participation in risk and safe sports. **Personality and Individual Differences, 10**, 797-800. (Various Sports)

665.   Levenson, M. R. (1990). Risk taking and personality. **Journal of Personality and Social Psychology, 58**, 1073-1080. (Rock Climbing)

666.   Madsen, D. B., Das, A. K., Bogen, I., & Grossman, E. E. (1987). A short Sensation Seeking Scale. **Psychological Reports, 60**, 1179-1184. (Psychometric)

667.   Malkin, M. J. & Rabinowitz, E. (1998). Sensation seeking and high-risk recreation. **Parks and Recreation, 33**, 34-45. (Risk Sport)

668.	McCutcheon, L. (1980). Running and sensation seeking. **North Virginia Community College Journal**, Fall, 11. (Running)

669.	Michel, G., Mouren-Simeoni, M. C., Perez-Diaz, F., Falissard, B., Carton, S., & Jouvent, R. (1999). Construction and validation of a sensation seeking scale for adolescents. **Personality and Individual Differences, 26**, 159-174. (Psychometric, Risk Sports)

670.	O'Sullivan, D. M., Zuckerman, M., & Kraft, M. (1998). Personality characteristics of male and female participants in team sports. **Personality and Individual Differences, 25**, 119-128. (Various Sports)

671.	Potgieter, J. R., & Bisschoff, F. (1990). Sensation seeking among medium- and low-risk sports participants. **Perceptual and Motor Skills, 71**, 1203-1206. (Rugby, Running)

672.	Rainey, D. W., Amunategui, F., Agocs, H., & Larick, J. (1992) Sensation seeking and competitive trait anxiety among college rodeo athletes. **Journal of Sport Behavior, 15**, 307-317. (Baseball, Hang Gliding, Rodeo, Wrestling)

673.	Robinson, D. W. (1985). Stress seeking: Selected behavioral characteristics of elite rock climbers. **Journal of Sport Psychology, 7**, 400-404. (Rock Climbing)

674.	Rossi, B., & Cereatti, L. (1993). The sensation seeking in mountain athletes as assessed by Zuckerman's Sensation Seeking Scale. **International Journal of Sport Psychology, 24**, 417-431. (Rock Climbing, Skiing)

675.	Rowland, G.L., Franken, R.E., & Harrison, K. (1986). Sensation seeking and participation in sporting activities. **Journal of Sport Psychology, 8**, 212-220. (Physical Education Class(es))

676.	Rowland, G. L., & Franken, R. E. (1986). The four dimensions of sensation seeking: A confirmatory factor analysis. **Personality and Individual Differences, 2**, 237-240. (Psychometric)

677.   Schrader, M.P., & Wann, D.L. (1999). High-risk recreation: The relationship between participant characteristics and degree of involvement. **Journal of Sport Behavior, 22,** 426-441. (Various Sports)

678.   Schroth, M. L. (1995). A comparison of sensation seeking among different groups of athletes and nonathletes. **Personality and Individual Differences, 18,** 219-222. (Various Sports)

679.   Slanger, E., & Rudestam, K. E. (1997). Motivation and disinhibition in high risk sports: Sensation seeking and self-efficacy. **Journal of Research in Personality,** 31, 355-374. (Rock Climbing, Skiing)

680.   Stacy, A. W., Newcomb, M. D., & Bentler, P. M. (1991). Social psychological influences on sensation-seeking from adolescence to adulthood. **Personality and Social Psychology Bulletin, 17,** 701-708. (Psychometric)

681.   Straub, W. F. (1982). Sensation seeking among high and low-risk male athletes. **Journal of Sport Psychology, 4,** 246-253. (Automobile Racing, Hang Gliding)

682.   Torki, M. A (1993). Dimensions of sensation seeking scale form VI: Cross-cultural comparison. **Perceptual and Motor Skills, 76,** 567-570. (Exercise)

683.   Trimpop, R. M., Kerr, J. H., & Kirkcaldy, B. D. (1999). Comparing personality constructs of risk-taking behavior. **Personality and Individual Differences, 26,** 237-254. (Psychometric)

684.   Wagner, A. M., & Houlihan, D. D. (1994). Sensation seeking and trait anxiety in hang-glider pilots and golfers. **Personality and Individual Differences, 16,** 975-977. (Golf, Hang Gliding)

685.   Weiner, S. (1984). Sensation seeking, fear, and anxiety in a group of high avocational risk takers. **Dissertation Abstracts International, 45,** 1064. (Hang Gliding)

686. Zaleski, Z. (1984). Sensation-seeking and risk taking behaviour. **Personality and Individual Differences, 5,** 607-608. (Automobile Racing, Mountain Climbing)

687. Zarevski, P., Marusic, I., Zolotic, S., Bunjevac, T., & Vukosav, Z. (1998). Contribution of Arnett's inventory of sensation seeking and Zuckerman's sensation seeking scale to the differentiation of athletes engaged in high and low risk sports. **Personality and Individual Differences, 25,** 763-768. (Caving, Hang Gliding, Mountain Climbing, Scuba, Skydiving)

688. Zuckerman, M. (1979). **Sensation seeking: Beyond the optimal level of arousal.** Hillsdale, NJ: Erlbaum. (Test Manual)

689. Zuckerman, M. (1983). Sensation seeking and sports. **Personality and Individual Differences, 4,** 285-292. (Review Article)

690. Zuckerman, M. (1990). The psychophysiology of sensation seeking. **Journal of Personality, 58,** 313-345. (Review Article)

691. Zuckerman, M. (1996). Item revisions in the Sensation Seeking Scale Form V (SSS-V). **Personality and Individual Differences, 20,** 515. (Psychometric)

692. Zuckerman, M., & Link, K. (1968). Construct validity for the sensation seeking scale. **Journal of Consulting and Clinical Psychology, 32,** 420-426. (Psychometric)

CHAPTER TEN
SEX ROLE ORIENTATION

Bem Sex-Role Inventory (BSRI)

693.   Andersen, M. B., & Williams, J. W. (1987). Gender role and sport competition anxiety: A re-examination. **Research Quarterly, 58**, 52-56. (Various Sports)

694.   Antill, J. K., & Cunningham, J. D. (1982). Comparative factor analysis of the Personal Attributes Questionnaire and the Bem Sex Role Inventory. **Social Behavior and Personality, 10**, 163-172. (Psychometric)

695.   Bem, S. L. (1974). The measurement of psychological androgyny. **Educational and Psychological Measurement, 42**, 155-162. (Psychometric)

696.   Bem, S. L. (1977). On the utility of alternative procedures for assessing psychological androgyny. **Journal of Consulting and Clinical Psychology, 45**, 196-205. (Psychometric)

697.   Brown, R. M., Hall, L. R., Holtzer, R., Brown, S. L., & Brown, N. L. (1997). Gender and video game performance. **Sex Roles, 36**, 793-812. (Motor Task)

698.   Burke, K. L. (1986). Comparison of psychological androgyny within a sample of female college athletes who participate in sports traditionally appropriate and traditionally inappropriate for competition by females. **Perceptual and Motor Skills, 63**, 779-782. (Basketball, Softball, Swimming, Tennis)

699.   Butcher, J. (1985). Longitudinal analysis of adolescent girls' participation in physical activity. **Sociology of Sport Journal, 2**, 132-143. (Physical Activity)

700.   Butcher, J. (1989). Adolescent girls' sex role development: Relationship with sports participation, self-esteem, and age at menarche. **Sex Roles, 20**, 575-593. (Various Sports)

701.   Campbell, T., Gillaspy, J. A., & Thompson, B. (1997). The factor structure of the Bem Sex- Role Inventory (BSRI): Confirmatory analysis of long and short forms. **Educational and Psychological Measurement, 57**, 118-124. (Psychometric)

702.   Caron, S. L., Carter, D. B., & Brightman, L. A. (1985). Sex-role orientation and attitudes towards women: Differences among college athletes and nonathletes. **Perceptual and Motor Skills, 61**, 803-806. (Various Sports)

703.   Chalip, L., Villiger, J., & Duignan, P. (1980). Sex-role identity in a select sample of women field hockey players. **International Journal of Sport Psychology,** 11, 240-258. (Field Hockey)

704.   Colley, A., Roberts, N., & Chipps, A. (1985). Sex-role identity and participation in team and individual sports by males and females. **International Journal of Sport Psychology, 18**, 103-112. (Various Sports)

705.   Colley, A., Griffith, D., Landers, D. M., & Jaggli, N. (1996). Childhood play and adolescent leisure preferences: Associations with gender typing and the presence of siblings. **Sex Roles, 35**, 233-245. (Leisure Activity)

706.   Colley, A., Nash, J., O'Donnel, L. A., & Restorick, L. (1987). Attitudes to the female sex role and typing of physical activities. **International Journal of Sport Psychology, 18**, 19-29. (Exercise)

707.   Delignieres, D., Marcellini, A., Brisswalter, J., & Legros, P. (1994). Self perception of fitness and personality-traits. **Perceptual and Motor Skills, 78**, 843-851. (Exercise)

708.   Edwards, S. W., Gordin, R. G., & Henschen, K. P. (1984). Sex-role orientations of female NCAA championship gymnasts. **Perceptual and Motor Skills, 58**, 625-626. (Gymnastics)

709.   Frable, D., & Bem, S. L. (1985). If you're gender-schematic, all members of the opposite sex look alike. **Journal of Personality and Social Psychology,** 49, 459-468. (Psychometric)

710. Friedman, E., & Berger, B. G. (1991). Influence of gender, masculinity, and femininity on the effectiveness of three stress reduction techniques: Jogging, relaxation response, and group interaction. **Journal of Applied Sport Psychology, 3**, 61-86. (Exercise)

711. Gackenbach, J. (1982). Collegiate swimmers: Sex differences in self-reports and indices of physiological stress. **Perceptual and Motor Skills, 55**, 555-558. (Swimming)

712. Hallinan, C. J. (1998). Dimensions of gender differentiation and centrality in the employment structure of university recreation centers. **Journal of Sport Behavior, 21** (Leisure Activity)

713. Henschen, K. P., Edwards, S. W., & Mathinos, L. (1982). Achievement motivation and sex-role orientation of high school female track and field athletes versus nonathletes. **Perceptual and Motor Skills, 55**, 183-187. (Track and Field)

714. Holt, C. L. (1998). Assessing the current validity of the Bem Sex-Role Inventory. **Sex Roles, 39**, 929-941. (Psychometric)

715. Houseworth, S., Peplow, K., & Thirer, J. (1989). Influence of sport participation upon sex role orientation of Caucasian males and their attitudes toward women. **Sex Roles, 20**, 317-325. (Various Sports)

716. Jackson, S. A., & Marsh, H. W. (1986). Athletic or antisocial? The female sport experience. **Journal of Sport Psychology, 8**, 198-211. (Weightlifting)

717. Kane, M. J. (1982). The influence of level of sport participation and sex-role orientation on female professionalization of attitudes toward play. **Journal of Sport Psychology, 4**, 290-294. (Basketball, Softball, Volleyball)

718. Koivula, N. (1995). Ratings of gender appropriateness of sports participation: Effects of gender-based schematic processing. **Sex Roles, 33**, 543-557. (Exercise)

719. Koivula, N. (1999). Sport participation: Differences in motivation and actual participation due to gender typing. **Journal of Sport Behavior, 22**, 360-380. (Exercise)

720.   Lantz, C. D., & Schroeder, P. J. (1999). Endorsement of masculine and feminine gender roles: Differences between participation in and identification with the athletic role. **Journal of Sport Behavior, 22,** 545-557. (Various Sports)

721.   Martin, B. A., & Martin, J. H. (1995). Comparing perceived sex role orientation of the ideal male and female athlete to the ideal male and female person. **Journal of Sport Behavior, 18,** 286-301. (Exercise)

722.   Myers, A. M., & Lips, H. M. (1978).Participation in competitive amateur sports as a function of psychological androgyny. **Sex Roles, 4,** 571-578. (Badminton, Handball, Racquetball, Squash)

723.   Myers, A. M., & Sugar, J. (1979). A critical analysis of the scoring of the BSRI: implications for conceptualization. **JSAS Catalog of Selected Documents in Psychology, 9,** 24. (Ms. No. 1833). (Psychometric)

724.   Ostrow, A. C., Jones, D. C., & Spiker, D. D. (1981). Age role expectations and sex role expectations for selected sport activities. **Research Quarterly, 52,** 216-227. (Various Sports)

725.   Owie, I. (1981). Influence of sex-role standards in sport competition anxiety. **International Journal of Sport Psychology, 12,** 289-292. (Exercise)

726.   Pedhazur, E. J., & Tetenbaum, T. J. (1979). Bem Sex-Role Inventory: A theoretical and methodological critique. **Journal of Personality and Social Psychology, 31,** 996-1016. (Psychometric)

727.   Salminen, S.   (1990). Sex role and participation in traditionally inappropriate sports. **Perceptual and Motor Skills, 71,** 1216-1218. (Exercise)

728.   Segal, J. D., & Weinberg, R. S. (1984). Sex, sex role orientation and competitive trait anxiety. **Journal of Sport Behavior, 7,** 153-159. (Exercise)

729.   Shifren, K., Bauserman, R., & Carter, D. B. (1993). Gender role orientation and physical health: A study among young adults. **Sex Roles, 29,** 421-432. (Exercise)

730. Spence, J. T., & Buckner, C. E. (2000). Instrumental and expressive traits, trait stereotypes, and sexist attitudes. **Psychology of Women Quarterly, 24**, 44-62. (Psychometric)

731. Spence, J. T., & Hall, S. (1996). Children's gender-related self-perceptions, activity preferences, and occupational stereotypes: A test of three models of gender constructs. **Sex Roles, 35**, 659-691. (Psychometric)

732. Spence, J. T., & Helmreich, R. L. (1978). **Masculinity and femininity: Their psychological dimensions, correlates, and antecedents**. Austin, TX: University of Texas Press. (Test Manual)

733. Swain, A., & Jones, J. G. (1991). Gender role endorsement and competitive anxiety. **International Journal of Sport Psychology, 22,** 50-65. (Exercise)

734. Syzmanski, L. A., & Chrisler, J. C. (1990/1991). Eating disorders, gender-role, and athletic activity. **Psychology: A Journal of Human Behavior, 27/28**, 20-29. (Various Sports)

735. Tinsley, E. G., Sullivan-Guest, S., & McGuire, J. M. (1984). Feminine sex role and depression in middle-aged women. **Sex Roles, 11**, 25-32. (Psychometric)

736. Trujillo, C. M. (1983). The effect of weight training and running exercise intervention programs on the self-esteem of college women. **International Journal of Sport Psychology, 14**, 162-173. (Running, Weight Training)

737. Uguccioni, S. M., & Ballantyne, R. H. (1980). Comparison of attitudes and sex roles for athletic participants and nonparticipants. **International Journal of Sport Psychology, 11**, 42-48. (Basketball, Swimming)

738. Wark, K. A., & Wittig, A. F. (1979). Sex role and sport competition anxiety. **Journal of Sport Psychology, 1**, 248-250. (Youth)

739. Wittig, A. F. (1984). Sport competition anxiety and sex role. **Sex Roles, 11**, 469-473. (Exercise)

740. Wittig, A. F., Duncan, S. L., & Schurr, K. T. (1987). The relationship of gender, gender-role, endorsement and perceived physical self-efficacy to sport competition anxiety. **Journal of Sport Behavior, 11**, 192-199. (Exercise)

741. Wrisberg, C. A., Draper, M. V., & Everett, J. J. (1988). Sex role orientations of male and female collegiate athletes from selected individual and team sports. **Sex Roles, 19**, 81-90. (Basketball, Swimming, Track and Field, Volleyball)

742. Yates, A., Shisslak, C. M., Allender, J., Crago, M., & Leehey, K. (1992). Comparing obligatory and nonobligatory runners. **Psychosomatics, 33**, 180-189. (Running)

Personal Attributes Questionnaire (PAQ)

743. Andre, T., & Holland, A. (1995). Relationship of sport participation to sex role orientation and attitudes toward women among high school males and females. **Journal of Sport Behavior, 18**, 241-253. (Various Sports)

744. Campbell, T., Gillaspy, J. A., & Thompson, B. (1997). The factor structure of the Bem Sex Role Inventory (BSRI): Confirmatory analysis of long and short forms. **Educational and Psychological Measurement, 57**, 118-124. (Psychometric)

745. Colker, R., & Widom, C. S. (1980). Correlates of female athletic participation: Masculinity, femininity, self-esteem and attitudes toward women. **Sex Roles, 6**, 47-58. (Basketball, Rowing, Swimming, Squash)

746. Del Rey, P., & Sheppard, S. (1981). Relationships of psychological androgyny in female sports to self-esteem. **International Journal of Sport Psychology, 12**, 165-175. (Various Sports)

747. Helmreich, R. L., Spence, J. T., & Wilhem, J. A. (1981). A psychometric analysis of the Personal Attributes Questionnaire. **Sex Roles, 7**, 1097-1108. (Psychometric)

748. Hill, S. A., Fekken, G. C., & Bond, S. L. (2000). Factor structure of the Personal Attributes Questionnaire: An English-French comparison. **Canadian Journal of Behavioural Science, 32**, 234-242. (Psychometric)

749. Hochstetler, S., Rejeski, W. J., & Best, D. L. (1985). The influence of sex-role orientation on ratings of perceived exertion. **Sex Roles, 12,** 825-835. (Exercise)

750. Rejeski, W. J., & Sanford, B. (1984). Feminine-typed females: The role of affective schema in the perception of exercise intensity. **Journal of Sport Psychology, 6,** 197-207. (Exercise)

751. Rejeski, W. J., Best, D. L., Griffith, P., & Kenney, E. (1987). Sex-role orientation and the responses of men to exercise stress. **Research Quarterly, 58,** 260-264. (Exercise)

752. Rich, E. L., & Shaffer, D. R. (2000). "If you let me play sports": How might sport participation influence the self-esteem of adolescent females? **Psychology of Women Quarterly, 24,** 189-199. (Review Article)

753. Shifren, K., & Bauserman, R. (1996). The relationship between instrumental and expressive traits, health behaviors and perceived physical health. **Sex Roles, 34,** 841-864. (Health Behavior)

754. Spence, J. T., & Buckner, C. E. (2000). Instrumental and expressive traits, trait stereotypes, and sexist attitudes. **Psychology of Women Quarterly, 24,** 44-62. (Psychometric)

755. Spence, J. T. & Hall, S. (1996). Children's gender-related self-perceptions, activity preferences, and occupational stereotypes: A test of three models of gender constructs. **Sex Roles, 35,** 659-691. (Psychometric)

756. Spence, J. T., & Helmreich, R. L. (1978). **Masculinity and femininity: Their psychological dimensions, correlates, and antecedents**. Austin: University of Texas Press. (Test Manual)

SECTION TWO

MEASURES OF TEMPORARY STATES

As opposed to the measurement of enduring traits, other psychometric instruments have been created to measure more transitory or temporary aspects of personality. Among these temporary states are such constructs as anxiety, depression, and other aspects of mood or affect. With regard to mood or affect, it is important to note that not all of these states are negative, though the measurement of positive mood states lags behind the assessment of negative states.

CHAPTER ELEVEN

ANXIETY/DEPRESSION/MOOD

AUTHORS:

GEORGE CUNNINGHAM, PAUL KEIPER & MICHAEL SAGAS

Activation Deactivation Adjective Checklist (AD-ACL)

757.   Kubitz, K. A., & Pothakos, K. (1997). Does aerobic exercise decrease brain activation? **Journal of Sport & Exercise Psychology, 19**, 291-301. (Exercise)

758.   Rejeski, W. J., Hardy, C. J., & Shaw, J. (1991). Psychometric confounds of assessing state anxiety in conjunction with acute bouts of vigorous exercise. **Journal of Sport & Exercise Psychology, 13**, 65-74. (Cycling)

759.   Saklogske, D. H., Bloome, G. C., Kelly, I. W. (1992). The effects of exercise and relaxation on energetic and tense arousal. **Personality and Individual Differences, 13**, 623-625. (Exercise)

760.   Thayer, R. E. (1987). Problem perception, optimism, and related states as a function of time of day (diurnal rhythm) and moderate exercise: Two arousal systems in interaction. **Motivation and Emotion, 11**, 19-36. (Exercise)

761.   Thayer, R. E. (1987). Energy, tiredness, and tension effects of a sugar snack versus moderate exercise. **Journal of Personality and Social Psychology, 52**, 119-125. (Exercise)

762.   Thayer, R. E., Peters, D. P., Takahashi, P. J., Birkhead-Flight, A. M. (1993). Mood and behaviour (smoking and sugar snacking) following moderate exercise: A partial test of self-regulation theory. **Personality and Individual Differences, 14**, 97-104. (Exercise)

763. Van Landuyt, L. M., Ekkekakis, P., Hall, E. E., & Petruzello, S. J. (2000). Throwing the mountains into the lakes: On the perils of nomothetic conceptions of the exercise-affect relationship. **Journal of Sport & Exercise Psychology, 22**, 208-234. (Exercise)

764. Walker, M. B., & Hailey, B. J. (1987). Physical fitness levels and psychological states versus traits. **Perceptual and Motor Skills, 64**, 12-25. (Exercise)

Beck Depression Inventory (BDI)

765. Andersson, G. (1996). The benefits of optimism: A meta-analytic review of the life orientation test. **Personality and Individual Differences, 21**, 719-725. (Psychometric)

766. Babyak, M. A., Blumenthal, J. A., Herman, S., Khatri, P, Doraiswamy, M., Moore, K. A., Craighead, W. E., Baldewicz, T. T., & Krishnan, K. R. (2000). Exercise treatment for major depression: Maintenance of therapeutic benefits at 10 months. **Psychosomatic Medicine, 62**, 633-638. (Exercise)

767. Beck, A. T., Steer, R. A., & Garbin, M. G. (1988). Psychometric properties of the Beck Depression Inventory: 25 years of evaluation. **Clinical Psychology Review, 8**, 77-100. (Psychometric, Review Article)

768. Blumenthal, J. A., Babyak, M. A., Moore, K. A., Craighead, W. E., Herman, S., Khatri, P., Waugh, R., Napolitano, M. A., Forman, L. M., Appelbaum, M. C., Doraiswamy, P. M., & Krishnan, K. R. (1999). Effects of exercise training on older patients with major depression. **Archives of Internal Medicine, 159**, 2349-2356. (Exercise)

769. Cogan, K. D., Highlen, P. S., Petrie, T. A., Sherman, W. M., & Simonsen, J. (1991). Psychological and physiological effects of controlled intensive training and diet on collegiate rowers. **International Journal of Sport Psychology, 22**, 165-180. (Rowing)

770.   Dahlstrom, W. G., Brooks, J. D., & Peterson, C. D. (1990). The Beck Depression Inventory: Item order and the impact of response sets. **Journal of Personality Assessment, 55**, 224-233. (Psychometric)

771.   DiLorenzo, T. M., Bargman, E. P., Stucky-Ropp, R., Brassington, G. S., Frensch, P. A., & LaFontaine, T. (1999). Long-term effects of aerobic exercise on psychological outcomes. **Preventive Medicine, 28**, 78-85. (Exercise)

772.   Dozois, D. J. A., Dobson, K. S., & Ahnberg, J. L. (1998). A psychometric evaluation of the Beck Depression Inventory-II. **Psychological Assessment, 10**, 83-89. (Psychometric)

773.   Eensoo, D., Harro, J., Harro, M., Rimm, H., & Viru, A. M. (2000). Depressiveness, anxiety, perceived stress and self-efficacy in middle-aged men with different engagement in physical activity. **Medicina Della Sport, 53**, 69-74. (Exercise)

774.   Hassmen, P., Koivula, N., & Uutela, A. (2000). Physical exercise and psychological well-being: A population study in Finland. **Preventive Medicine, 30**, 17-25. (Exercise)

775.   Hayward, L. M., Sullivan, A. C., & Libonati, J. R. (2000). Group exercise reduces depression in obese women without weight loss. **Perceptual and Motor Skills, 90**, 204-208. (Exercise)

776.   Herrera, E., & Gomezamor, J. (1995). Differences in personality and menstrual variables between physically active and sedentary women. **Personality and Individual Differences, 19**, 389-392. (Exercise)

777.   Jacobs, K. W., & Boze, M. M. (1993). Correlations among scales of the Beck Depression Inventory and the Profile of Mood States. **Psychological Reports, 73**, 432-434. (Psychometric)

778.   Kendall, P. C., Hollon, S. D., Beck, A. T., Hammen, C. L., & Ingram, R. E. (1987). Issues and recommendations regarding use of the Beck Depression Inventory. **Cognitive Therapy and Research, 11**, 289-299. (Review Article)

779. Killgore, W. D. S. (1999). Empirically derived factor indices for the Beck Depression Inventory. **Psychological Reports, 84**, 1005-1013. (Psychometric)

780. Klock, S. C., & DeSouza, M. J. (1995). Eating disorder characteristics and psychiatric symptomatology of eumenorrheic and amenorrheic runners. **International Journal of Eating Disorders, 17**, 161-166. (Running)

781. Louks, J., Hayne, C., & Smith, J. (1989). Replicated factor structure of the Beck Depression Inventory. **Journal of Nervous and Mental Disease, 177**, 473-479. (Psychometric)

782. Mertens, D. J., Rhind, S., Berkhoff, F., Dugmore, D., Shek, P. N., & Shephard, R. J. (1996). Nutritional, immunologic, and psychological responses to a 7250 meter run. **Journal of Sports Medicine and Physical Fitness, 36**, 132-138. (Ultramarathon/Ultrarunning)

783. Moore, K. A., Babyak, M. A., Wood, C. E., Napolitano, M. A., Khatri, P., Craighead, W. E., Herman, S., Krishnan, K. R., & Blumenthal, J. A. (1999). The association between physical activity and depression in older depressed adults. **Journal of Aging and Physical Activity, 7**, 55-61. (Exercise)

784. Nudelman, S., Rosen, J. C., & Leitenberg, H. (1988). Dissimilarities in eating attitudes, body image distortion, depression, and self-esteem between high-intensity male runners and women with bulimia nervosa. **International Journal of Eating Disorders, 7**, 625-633. (Running)

785. Osman, A., Downs, W. R., Barrios, F. X., Kopper, B. A., Gutierrez, P. M., & Chiros, C. E. (1997). Factor structure and psychometric characteristics of the Beck Depression Inventory. **Journal of Psychopathology and Behavioral Assessment, 19**, 359-376. (Psychometric)

786. Prussin, R. (1991). Depression, dietary restraint, and binge eating in female runners. **Addictive Behaviors, 16**, 295-301. (Running)

787. Richter, P., Werner, J., Heerlein, A., Kraus, A., & Sauer, H. (1998). On the validity of the Beck Depression Inventory: A review. **Psychopathology, 31**, 160-168. (Review Article)

788.   Robinson, B. E., & Kelley, L. (1996). Concurrent validity of the Beck Depression Inventory as a measure of depression. **Psychological Reports, 79**, 929-930. (Psychometric)

789.   Sanz, J., & Vazquez, C. (2000). Reliability, validity, and normative data of the Beck Depression Inventory. **Psicothema, 10**, 303-318. (Psychometric)

790.   Schmitt, M., & Maes, J. (2000). Simplification of the Beck Depression Inventory (BDI). **Diagnostica, 46**, 38-46. (Psychometric)

791.   Sharpe, J. P., & Gilbert, D. G. (1998). Effects of repeated administration of the Beck Depression Inventory and other measures of negative mood states. **Personality and Individual Differences, 24**, 457-463. (Psychometric)

792.   Stein, P. N., & Motta, R. W. (1992). Effects of aerobic and nonaerobic exercise on depression and self-concept. **Perceptual and Motor Skills, 74**, 79-89. (Swimming, Weight Training)

793.   Whisman, M. A., Perez, J. E., & Ramel, W. (2000). Factor structure of the Beck Depression Inventory Second Edition (BDI-II) in a student sample. **Journal of Clinical Psychology, 56**, 545-551. (Psychometric)

794.   Yates, A., Shisslak, C. M., Allender, J., Crago, M., & Leehey, K. (1992). Comparing obligatory and nonobligatory runners. **Psychosomatics, 33**, 180-189. (Running)

795.   Yin, P., & Fan, X. T. (2000). Assessing the reliability of the Beck Depression Inventory scores: Reliability generalization across studies. **Educational and Psychological Measurement, 60**, 210-223. (Psychometric)

Cognitive – Somatic Anxiety Questionnaire (CSAQ)

796.   Berger, B. G., & Owen, D. R. (1987). Anxiety reduction with swimming: Relationships between exercise and state, trait, and somatic anxiety. **International Journal of Sport Psychology, 18**, 286-302. (Swimming)

797.   Crits-Christoph, P. (1986). The factor structure of the Cognitive-Somatic Anxiety Questionnaire. **Journal of Psychosomatic Research, 30**, 685-690. (Psychometric)

798.   DeGood, D. E., & Trait, R. C. (1987). The Cognitive-Somatic Anxiety Questionnaire: Psychometric and validity data. **Journal of Psychopathology and Behavioral Assessment, 9**, 75-87. (Psychometric)

799.   Delmonte, M. M., & Ryan, G. M. (1983). The Cognitive-Somatic Anxiety Questionnaire (CSAQ): A factor analysis. **British Journal of Clinical Psychology, 22**, 209-212. (Psychometric)

800.   Edwards, P. W., Zeichner, A., & Greene, P. (1984). Gender differences on the Cognitive-Somatic Anxiety Questionnaire. **Psychological Reports, 55**, 123-124. (Psychometric)

801.   Freedland, K. E., & Carney, R. M. (1988). Factor analysis of the Cognitive-Somatic Anxiety Questionnaire. **Journal of Psychopathological and Behavioral Assessment, 10**, 367-375. (Psychometric)

802.   Hardy, L., & Whitehead, R. (1984). Specific modes of anxiety and arousal. **Current Psychological Research and Reviews, 3** (3), 14-24. (Physical Education Class(es), Rock Climbing)

803.   Heimberg, R. G., Gansler, D., Dodge, C. S., & Becker, R. E. (1987). Convergent and discriminant validity of the Cognitive-Somatic Anxiety Questionnaire in a social phobic population. **Behavioral Assessment, 9**, 379-388. (Psychometric)

804.   Sandin, B., Chorot, P., & McNally, R. J. (1996). Validation of the Spanish version of the Anxiety Sensitivity Index in a clinical sample. **Behaviour Research and Therapy, 34**, 283-290. (Psychometric)

805.   Sargunaraj, D., & Kumaraiah, V. (1991). The reliability of translations of STAI, CSAQ, EPI, and I-E Scale. **Journal of Personality and Clinical Studies, 7**, 99-101. (Psychometric)

806.   Schwartz, G. E., Davidson, R. J., & Goleman, D. J. (1978). Patterning of cognitive and somatic processes in the self-regulation of anxiety: Effects of mediation versus exercise. **Psychosomatic Medicine, 40**, 321-328. (Exercise)

807.   Senkfor, A. J., & Williams, J. M. (1995). The moderating effects of aerobic fitness and mental training on stress reactivity. **Journal of Sport Behavior, 18**, 130-156. (Exercise)

808.   Steptoe, A., & Kearsley, N. (1990). Cognitive and somatic anxiety. **Behaviour Research and Therapy, 28**, 75-81. (Various Sports)

809.   Tamaren, A. J., Carney, R. M. & Allen, T. W. (1985). Assessment of cognitive and somatic anxiety: A preliminary study. **Behavioral Assessment, 7**, 197-202. (Psychometric)

810.   Tamaren, A. J., Carney, R. M. & Allen, T. W. (1985). Predictive validity of the cognitive vs. somatic anxiety distinction. **Pavlovian Journal of Biological Science, 20**, 177-180. (Psychometric)

Depression Adjective Check List (DACL)

811.   Chakravorty, D., Trunnell, E. P., & Ellis, G. D. (1995). Ropes course participation and post-activity processing on transient depressed mood of hospitalized adult psychiatric patients. **Therapeutic Recreation Journal, 29**, 104-113. (Leisure Activity)

812.   Joesting, J. (1981). Running and depression. **Perceptual and Motor Skills, 52**, 442. (Running)

813.   Morgan, W. P., & Pollock. M. L. (1977). Psychologic characterization of the elite distance runner. **Annals of the New York Academy of Sciences, 301**, 382-403. (Running)

814.   Stein, P. N. & Motta, R. W. (1992). Effects of aerobic and nonaerobic exercise of depression and self-concept. **Perceptual and Motor Skills, 74**, 79-89. (Swimming, Weight Training)

Endler Multidimensional Anxiety Scales (EMAS)

815.   Bagby, R. M., & Cox, B. J. (1991). Multidimensionality of state and trait anxiety: Factor structure of the Endler Multidimensional Anxiety Scales. **Journal of Personality and Social Psychology, 60**, 919-926. (Psychometric)

816.   Endler, N. S., Denisoff, E., & Rutherford, A. (1998). Anxiety and depression: Evidence for the differentiation of commonly co-occuring constructs. **Journal of Psychopathology and Behavioral Assessment, 20**, 149-171. (Psychometric)

817.   Endler, N. S., Parker, J. D. A., Bagby, R. M., & Cox, B. J.(1991). Multidimensionality of state and trait anxiety: Factor structure of the Endler Multidimensional Anxiety Scales. **Journal of Personality and Social Psychology, 60**, 919-926. (Psychometric)

818.   Jackson, D. J., & King, P. R. (1993). Interactional anxiety in an athletic competition situation: An empirical test of a composite predictor for state anxiety. **Personality and Individual Differences, 14**, 507-511. (Football)

Mood Adjective Checklist

819.   Lichtman, S., & Poser, E. G. (1983). The effects of exercise on mood and cognitive functioning. **Journal of Psychosomatic Research, 27**, 43-52. (Exercise)

820.   More, T. A., & Payne, B. R. (1978). Affective responses to natural areas near cities. **Journal of Leisure Research, 10**, 7-12. (Leisure Activity)

821.   Naruse, K., & Hirai, T. (2000). Effects of slow tempo exercise on respiration, heart rate, and mood state. **Perceptual and Motor Skills, 91**, 729-740. (Exercise)

822.   Nowlis, D. P., & Greenberg, N. (1979). Empirical description of effects of exercise on mood. **Perceptual and Motor Skills, 49**, 1001-1002. (Running)

Multiple Affect Adjective Checklist (MAACL)

823. Anderson, C. A., & Ford, C. M. (1986). Affect of game player: Short-term effects of highly and mildly aggressive video games. **Personality and Social Psychology Bulletin, 14,** 390-402. (Leisure Activity)

824. Celozzi, M. J., Kazelskis, R., & Gutsch, K. U. (1981). The relationship between viewing televised violence in ice hockey and subsequent levels of personal aggression. **Journal of Sport Behavior, 4,** 157-162. (Ice Hockey)

825. Doan, B. T. T., Plante, T. G., DiGregorio, M. P., & Manuel, G. M. (1995). Influence of aerobic exercise activity and relaxation training on coping with test-taking anxiety. **Anxiety, Stress and Coping, 8,** 101-111. (Exercise)

826. Flory, J. D., & Holmes, D. S. (1991). Effects of an acute bout of aerobic exercise on cardiovascular and subjective responses during subsequent cognitive work. **Journal of Psychosomatic Research, 35,** 225-230. (Exercise)

827. Folkins, C. H. (1976). Effects of physical training on mood. **Journal of Clinical Psychology, 32,** 385-388. (Exercise)

828. Francis, K. T., & Carter, R. (1982). Psychological characteristic of joggers. **Journal of Sports Medicine, 22,** 386-391. (Running)

829. Gough, H. G., & Heilbrun, A. B. (1965). **Adjective Checklist Manual.** Palo Alto, CA: Consulting Psychologists Press. (Test Manual)

830. Hardy, C. J., & Rejeski, W. J. (1989). Not what, but how one feels: The measurement of affect during exercise. **Journal of Sport & Exercise Psychology, 11,** 304-317. (Exercise)

831. Hatfield, B. D., Goldfarb, A. H., Sforzo, G. A., & Flynn, M. G. (1987). Serum beta-endorphin and affective responses to graded exercise in young and elderly men. **Journal of Gerontology, 42,** 429-431. (Exercise)

832. Plante, T. G., Chizmar, L., & Owen, D. (1999). The contribution of perceived fitness to physiological and self-reported responses to laboratory stress. **International Journal of Stress Management, 6,** 5-19. (Exercise)

833. Plante, T. G., Marcotte, D. Manuel, G. M., & Willemsen, E. (1996). The influence of brief episodes of aerobic exercise activity, soothing music-nature scenes condition, and suggestion on coping with test-taking anxiety. **International Journal of Stress Management, 3**, 155-166. (Exercise)

834. Reeves, D. L., Levinson, D. M., Justesen, D. R., & Lubin, B. (1985). Endogenous hyperthermia in normal human subjects: Experimental study of emotional states. **International Journal of Psychosomatics, 32**, 18-23. (Exercise)

835. Rejeski, W. J., Thompson, A., Brubaker, P. H., & Miller, H. S. (1992). Acute exercise: Buffering psychosocial stress responses in women. **Health Psychology, 11**, 355-362. (Cycling)

836. Tuson, K. M., Sinyor, D., & Pelletier, L. G. (1995). Acute exercise and positive affect: An investigation of psychological processes leading to affective change. **International Journal of Sport Psychology, 26**, 138-159. (Exercise)

837. York, R., Brown, L. P., Persily, C. A., & Jacobsen, B. S. (1996). Affect in diabetic women during pregnancy and postpartum. **Nursing Research, 45**, 54-56. (Exercise)

838. Zuckerman, M., & Lubin, B. (1965). **Manual for the Multiple Affect Adjective Check List.** San Diego, CA: Educational and Industrial Testing Service. (Test Manual)

Positive and Negative Affect Schedule (PANAS-X)

839. Bagozzi, R. P. (1993). An examination of the psychometric properties of measures of negative affect in the PANAS-X scales. **Journal of Personality and Social Psychology, 65**, 836-51. (Psychometric)

840. Bartholomew, J. B. (1999). The effect of resistance on manipulated preexercise mood states for male exercisers. **Journal of Sport & Exercise Psychology, 21**, 39-51. (Exercise)

841. Boutcher, S. H., McAuley, E., & Courneya, K. S. (1997). Positive and negative affective response of trained and untrained subjects during and after aerobic exercise. **Australian Journal of Psychology, 49,** 28-32. (Exercise)

842. Crocker, P. R. E. (1997). A confirmatory factor analysis of the positive affect negative affect schedule (PANAS) with youth sport sample. **Journal of Sport & Exercise Psychology, 19,** 91-97. (Psychometric)

843. Fry, S. K., & Heubeck, B. G. (1998). The effects of personality and situational variables on mood states during outward bound wilderness courses: An exploration. **Personality and Individual Differences, 24,** 649-659. (Leisure Activity)

844. Killgore, W. D. S. (2000). Evidence for a third factor on the positive and negative affect schedule in a college student sample. **Perceptual and Motor Skills, 90,** 147-152. (Psychometric)

845. Laurent, J., Catanzaro, S. J., Joiner, T. E., Rudolph, K. D., Potter, K. I., Lambert, S. M., Osborne, L., & Gathright, T. (1999). A measure of positive and negative affect for children: Scale development and preliminary validation. **Psychological Assessment, 11,** 326-338. (Psychometric)

846. Mackinnon, A., Jorm, A. F., Christensen, H., Korten, A. E., Jacomb, P. A., & Rodgers, B. (1999). A short form of the Positive and Negative Affect Schedule: Evaluation of factorial validity and invariance across demographic variables in a community sample. **Personality and Individual Differences, 27,** 405-416. (Psychometric)

847. Ntoumanis, N., & Biddle, S. J. H. (1998). The relationship of coping and its perceived effectiveness to positive and negative affect in sport. **Personality and Individual Differences, 24,** 773-788. (Various Sports)

848. Russell, J. A., & Carroll, J. M. (1999). On the bipolarity of positive and negative affect. **Psychological Bulletin, 125,** 3-30. (Psychometric)

849.   Russell, W. D. & Cox, R. H. (2000). A laboratory investigation of positive and negative affect within individual zones of optimal functioning theory. **Journal of Sport Behavior, 23**, 164. (Basketball, Football)

850.   Sandin, B., Chorot, P., Lostao, L., Joiner, T. E., Santed, M. A., & Valiente, R. M. (1999). The PANAS scales of positive and negative affect: Factor analytic validation and cross-cultural convergence. **Psicothema, 11**, 37-51. (Psychometric)

851.   Treasure, D. C., Monson, J., & Lox, C. L. (1996). Relationship between self-efficacy, wrestling performance, and affect prior to competition. **The Sport Psychologist, 10**, 73-83. (Wrestling)

852.   Vlachopolous, S. P., Karageorghis, C. I., & Terry, P. C. (2000). Motivation profiles in sport: A self-determination theory perspective. **Research Quarterly for Exercise and Sport, 71**, 387-397. (Various Sports)

853.   Watson, D., & Clark, W. A. (1994). **The PANAS-X: Manual for the Positive and Negative Affect Schedule: Expanded Form.** Iowa City, IA: The University of Iowa. (Test Manual)

854.   Yeung, R. R., & Hemsley, D. R. (1997). Exercise behavior in an aerobics class: The impact of personality traits and efficacy cognitions. **Personality and Individual Differences, 23**, 425-431. (Exercise)

Profile of Mood States (POMS)

855.   Albrecht, R. R., & Ewing, S. (1989). Standardizing the administration of the Profile of Mood States (POMS): Development of alternative word lists. **Journal of Personality Assessment, 53**, 31-39. (Psychometric)

856.   Allen, M., & Coen, D. (1987). Naloxone blocking and running-induced mood changes. **Annals of Sports Medicine, 3**, 190-195. (Running)

857.   Annesi, J. J. (2000). Effects of minimal exercise and cognitive behavior modification on adherence, emotion change, self-image, and physical change in obese women. **Perceptual and Motor Skills, 91**, 322-336. (Exercise)

858. Anshel, M. H. (1995). Examining social loafing among elite female rowers as a function of task and duration and mood. **Journal of Sport Behavior, 18**, 39-49. (Rowing)

859. Bahrke, M. S., Wright, J. E., Strauss, R. H., & Catlin, D. H. (1992). Psychological moods and subjectively perceived behavioral and somatic changes accompanying anabolic-androgenic steroid use. **American Journal of Sports Medicine, 20**, 717-724. (Steroids/Drugs)

860. Bahrke, M. S., Thompson, C., & Thomas, T. R. (1986). Mood alterations following aerobic exercise withdrawal. **Indiana Alliance for Health, Physical Education, Recreation and Dance Journal, 15**, 8-10. (Exercise)

861. Bahrke, M. S., Wright, J. E., O'Connor, P. J., Strauss, R. H., & Catlin, D. H. (1990). Selected psychological characteristics of anabolic-androgenic steroid users. **New England Journal of Medicine, 323**, 834-835. (Steroids/Drugs)

862. Barabasz, M. (1991). Effects of aerobic exercise on transient mood state. **Perceptual and Motor Skills, 73**, 657-658. (Exercise)

863. Beebe, D., Finer, E., & Holmbeck, G. (1996). Low-end specificity of four depression measures: Findings and suggestions for the research use of depression tests. **Journal of Personality Assessment, 67**, 272-284. (Psychometric)

864. Beedie, C. J., Lane, A. M., & Terry, P. C. (2001). Distinguishing emotion from mood in psychological measurement: A pilot study examining anxiety. **Journal of Sports Sciences, 19**, 69-70. (Psychometric)

865. Beedie, C. J., Terry, P. C., & Lane, A. M. (2000). The Profile of Mood States and athletic performance: Two meta-analyses. **Journal of Applied Sport Psychology, 12**, 49-68. (Psychometric)

866. Berger, B. G. (1986). Use of exercise for stress reduction: The state-of-the-art. In L.E. Unestahl (Ed.), **Sport psychology**. Orebro, Sweden: Veje Publishing Inc. (Exercise)

867.   Berger, B. G. (1987). Stress levels in swimmers. In W. P. Morgan and S. E. Goldston (Eds.), **Exercise and mental health**. (pp. 139-143). Washington, D. C.: Hemisphere Publishing Corporation. (Steroids/Drugs)

868.   Berger, B. G., & Owen, D. R. (1983). Mood alteration with swimming: Swimmers really do "feel better." **Psychosomatic Medicine, 45**, 425-433. (Steroids/Drugs, Swimming)

869.   Berger, B. G., & Owen, D. R. (1986). Mood alteration with swimming: A reexamination. In L. Vander Velden & J.H. Humphrey (Eds.), **Psychology and sociology of sport**. New York: AMS Press. (Steroids/Drugs, Swimming)

870.   Berger, B. G., & Owen, D. R. (1988). Stress reduction and mood enhancement in four exercise modes: Swimming, body conditioning, hatha yoga, and fencing. **Research Quarterly for Exercise and Sport, 59**, 148-159. (Fencing, Swimming, Yoga)

871.   Berger, B. G., & Owen, D. R. (1992). Mood alteration with yoga and swimming: Aerobic exercise may not be necessary. **Perceptual and Motor Skills, 75**, 1331-1343. (Steroids/Drugs, Swimming, Yoga)

872.   Berger, B. G., & Owen, D. R. (1992). Preliminary analysis of a causal relationship between swimming and stress reduction: Intense exercise may negate the effects. **International Journal of Sport Psychology, 23**, 70-85. (Steroids/Drugs, Swimming)

873.   Berger, B. G., & Owen, D. R. (1998). Relation of low and moderate intensity exercise with acute mood change in college joggers. **Perceptual and Motor Skills, 87**, 611-621. (Exercise)

874.   Berger, B. G., Friedman, E., & Eaton, M. (1988). Comparison of jogging, the relaxation response, and group interaction for stress reduction. **Journal of Sport & Exercise Psychology, 10**, 431-447. (Exercise, Running)

875.   Berger, B. G., Owen, D. R., & Man, R. (1993). A brief review of literature and examination of acute mood benefits of exercise in Czechoslovakian and United States swimmers. **International Journal of Sport Psychology, 24**, 130-150. (Exercise, Steroids/Drugs)

876.   Berger, B. G., Grove, J. R., Prapavessis, H., & Butki, B. D. (1997). Relationship of swimming distance, expectancy, and performance to mood states of competitive athletes. **Perceptual and Motor Skills, 84**, 1199-1210. (Swimming)

877.   Berger, B. G., Owen, D. R., Motl, R. W., & Parks, L. (1998). Relationship between expectancy of psychological benefits and mood alteration in joggers. **International Journal of Sport Psychology, 29**, 1-16. (Exercise)

878.   Berger, B. G., & Motl, R. W. (2000). Exercise and mood: A selective review and synthesis of research employing the profile of mood states. **Journal of Applied Sport Psychology, 12**, 69-92. (Review Article)

879.   Berger, B. G., Motl, R. W., Butki, B. D., Martin, D. T., Wilkinson, J. G., & Owen, D. R. (1999). Mood and cycling performance in response to three weeks of high-intensity, short-duration overtraining, and a two-week taper. **The Sport Psychologist, 13**, 444-457. (Cycling)

880.   Berglund, B., & Safstrom, H. (1994). Psychological monitoring and modulation of training load of world-class canoeists. **Medicine and Science in Sports and Exercise, 26**, 1036-1040. (Rowing)

881.   Biasiotto, J., Ritter, E., & Ferrando, E. (1987). POMS and powerlifters. **Powerlifting USA, 11**, 31. (Weightlifting)

882.   Blumenthal, J. A., Schocken, D., Needels, T., & Hindle, P. (1982). Psychological and physiological effects of physical conditioning for the elderly. **Journal of Psychosomatic Research, 26**, 505-510. (Exercise)

883.   Blumenthal, J. A., Williams, R., Needels, T., & Wallace, A. G. (1982). Psychological changes accompany aerobic exercise in healthy middle-aged adults. **Psychosomatic Medicine, 44**, 529-536. (Exercise)

884. Bourgeois. A. E., LeUnes, A., Burkett, S., Driggars-Bourgeois, T., Friend, J., & Meyers, M. C. (1995). Factors influencing intramural sport participation. **Journal of the National Intramural and Recreational Sports Association, 19**, 44-48. (Intramural Sports)

885. Boutcher, S. H., & Landers, D. M. (1988). The effects of vigorous exercise in anxiety, heart rate, and alpha activity of runners and nonrunners. **Psychophysiology, 25**, 696-702. (Running)

886. Boyle, G. J. (1987). A cross-validation of the factor structure of the Profile of Mood States: Were the factors correctly identified in the 1st instance? **Psychological Reports, 60**, 343-354. (Psychometric)

887. Boyle, G. J. (1987). Quantitative and qualitative intersections between the Eight State Questionnaire and the Profile of Mood States. **Educational and Psychological Measurement, 47**, 437-443. (Psychometric)

888. Boyle, G. J, (1988). Central clinical states: An examination of the Profile of Mood States and the Eight State Questionnaire. **Journal of Psychopathology and Behavioral Assessment, 10**, 205-215. (Psychometric)

889. Brand, N., Verspui, L., & Oving, A. (1997). Induced mood and selective attention. **Perceptual and Motor Skills, 84**, 455-463. (Psychometric)

890. Brewer, B. W. (1999). Causal attribution and adjustment to sport injury. **Journal of Personal and Interpersonal Loss, 4**, 215-224. (Injury)

891. Brignall, R., Karageorghis, C. I., & Terry, P. C. (1999). Discriminant effectiveness of psychological state measures in predicting selection during schoolboy rugby trials. **Journal of Sports Sciences, 17**, 49-50. (Rugby)

892. Brown, D. R., Wang, Y. D., Ward, A., Ebbeling, C. B., Fortlage, L., Puleo, E., Benson, H., & Rippe, J. M. (1995). Chronic psychological effects of exercise and exercise plus cognitive strategies. **Medicine and Science in Sports and Exercise, 27**, 765-775. (Exercise)

893. Brown, S. W., Welsh, M. C., Labbe, E. E., Vitulli, W. F., & Kulkarni, P. (1992). Aerobic exercise in the psychological treatment of adolescents. **Perceptual and Motor Skills, 74**, 555-560. (Exercise)

894. Buffenstein, R., Karklin, A., & Driver, H. S. (2000). Beneficial physiological and performance responses to a month of restricted energy intake in healthy overweight women. **Physiology and Behavior, 68**(4), 439-444. (Motor Task)

895. Burnett, K., & Kleiman, M. (1994). Psychological characteristics of adolescent steroid users. **Adolescence, 29**, 81-89. (Steroids/Drugs)

896. Byrne, A., & Byrne, D. (1993). The effect of exercise on depression, anxiety and other mood states: A review. **Journal of Psychosomatic Research, 37**, 565-574. (Review Article)

897. Cai, S. (2000). Physical exercise and mental health: A content integrated approach in coping with college students' anxiety and depression. **Physical Educator, 57**, 69-76. (Martial Arts)

898. Campbell, E. (1995). Psychological well-being of participants in wheelchair sports: Comparisons of individuals with congenital and acquired disabilities. **Perceptual and Motor Skills, 81**, 563-568. (Disabled Athletes)

899. Campbell, E., & Jones, J. G. (1994). Psychological well-being in wheelchair sport participants and nonparticipants. **Adapted Physical Education Quarterly, 11**, 404-415. (Disabled Athletes)

900. Canabal, M. Y., Sherrill, C., & Rainbolt, W. (1987). Psychological mood profiles of elite palsied athletes. In M. E. Berridge & G. R. Ward (Eds.), **International perspectives on adapted physical activity** (pp. 157-163). Champaign, IL: Human Kinetics. (Disabled Athletes)

901. Chan, C., & Grossman, H. (1988). Psychological effects of running loss on consistent runners. **Perceptual and Motor Skills, 66**, 875-883. (Running)

902.   Cheung, S. Y. (1999, Winter). A Chinese version of the Profile of Mood States. **Journal of the International Council for Health, Physical Education, Recreation, Sport, and Dance**, 24-27. (Psychometric)

903.   Choi, P., Parrott, A. C., & Cowan, D. (1990). High-dose anabolic steroids in strength athletes: Effects upon hostility and aggression. **Human Psychopharmacology, 5**, 349-356. (Steroids/Drugs)

904.   Clements, K., & Turpin, G. (2000). Life event exposure, physiological reactivity, and psychological strain. **Journal of Behavioral Medicine, 23**, 73-94. (Exercise)

905.   Cockerill, I. M., Nevill, A. M., & Byrne, N. (1992). Mood, mileage and the menstrual cycle. **British Journal of Sports Medicine, 26**, 145-150. (Running)

906.   Cockerill, I. M., Nevill, A. M., & Lyons, N. (1991). Modelling mood states in athletic performance. **Journal of Sports Sciences, 9**, 205-212. (Running)

907.   Cockerill, I. M., Wormington, J., & Nevill, A. M. (1994). Menstrual-cycle effects on mood and perceptual-motor performance. **Journal of Psychosomatic Research, 38**, 763-77 (Psychometric)

908.   Cogan, H., & Parfitt, C. G. (1994). The relationship between intensity of running and psychological mood state in female runners. **Journal of Sports Sciences, 12**, 188. (Running)

909.   Cogan, K. D., Highlen, P. S., Petrie, T. A., Sherman, W. M., & Simonsen, J. (1991). Psychological and physiological effects of controlled intensive training and diet of collegiate rowers. **International Journal of Sport Psychology, 22**, 165-180. (Rowing)

910.   Coker, C.A., & Mickle, A. (2000). Stability of the iceberg profile as a function of perceived difficulty in defeating an opponent. **Perceptual and Motor Skills, 90**, 1135-1138. (Softball)

911.   Conboy, J. (1994). The effects of exercise withdrawal on mood states in runners. **Journal of Sport Behavior, 17**, 188-203. (Running)

912. Craighead, D., Privette, G., Vallianos, F., & Byrkit, D. (1986). Personality characteristics of basketball players, starters and non-starters. **International Journal of Sport Psychology, 17**, 110-119. (Basketball)

913. Cramer, S. R., Nieman, D. C., & Lee, J. W. (1991). The effects of moderate exercise training on psychological well-being and mood state in women. **Journal of Psychosomatic Research, 35**, 437-449. (Exercise)

914. Curran, S. L., Andrykowski, M. A., & Studts, J. L. (1995). Short form of the Profile of Mood States (POMS-SF): Psychometric information. **Psychological Assessment, 7**, 80-83. (Psychometric)

915. Curry, L. A., Snyder, C. R., Cook, D. L., Ruby, B. C., & Rehm, M. (1997). Role of hope in academic and sport achievement. **Journal of Personality and Social Psychology, 73**, 1257-1267. (Review Article)

916. Daiss, S., LeUnes, A., & Nation, J. R. (1986). Mood and locus of control of college and professional football players. **Perceptual and Motor Skills, 63**, 733-734. (Football)

917. Daniel, M., Martin, A., & Carter, J. (1992). Opiate receptor blockade by naltrexone and mood state after physical activity. **British Journal of Sports Medicine, 26**, 111-115. (Exercise)

918. Daus, A. T., Wilson, J., & Freeman, W. M. (1986). Psychological testing as an auxiliary means of selecting successful college and professional football players. **Journal of Sports Medicine and Physical Fitness, 26**, 274-278. (Football)

919. DeGeus, E., Van Doomen, L., & Orlebeke, J. (1993). Regular exercise and aerobic fitness in relation to psychological make-up and physiological stress reactivity. **Psychosomatic Medicine, 55**, 347-363. (Exercise)

920. DeMers, G. (1983, May-July). Emotional states of high caliber divers. **Swimming Technique**, 33-35. (Steroids/Drugs)

921.   DeVaney, S., Hughey, A., & Osborne, W. (1994). Comparative effects of exercise reduction and relaxation training on mood states and type A scores in habitual aerobic exercisers. **Perceptual and Motor Skills, 79**, 1635-1644. (Exercise)

922.   DiLorenzo, T. M., Bargman, E. P., Stucky-Ropp. R., Brassington, G. S., & LaFontaine, T. (1999). Long-term effects of aerobic exercise on psychological outcomes. **Preventive Medicine, 28**, 75-85. (Exercise)

923.   Dimeo, F. C., Stieglitz, R. D., Novelli-Fischer, U., Fetscher, S., & Keul, J. (1999). Effects of physical activity on the fatigue and psychologic status of cancer patients during chemotherapy. **Cancer, 85**, 2273-2277. (Exercise)

924.   Doyle, J., & Parfitt, C. G. (1999). The effect of induced mood states on performance profile areas of perceived need. **Journal of Sports Sciences, 17**, 115-127. (Psychometric)

925.   Durtschi, S., & Weiss, M. R. (1986). Psychological characteristics of elite and nonelite marathon runners. In D. Landers (Ed.), **Sport and elite performers**. Champaign, IL: Human Kinetics. (Marathon)

926.   Dyer, J., & Crouch, J. (1987). Effects of running on moods: A time series study. **Perceptual and Motor Skills, 64**, 783-789. (Running)

927.   Dyer, J., & Crouch, J. (1988). Effects of running and other activities on mood. **Perceptual and Motor Skills, 67**, 43-50. (Running, Weightlifting)

928.   Edwards, S., & Huston, S. (1984). The clinical aspects of sport psychology. **Physical Educator, 41**, 142-148. (Gymnastics)

929.   Eichman, W. (1978). Review of Profile of Mood States. In O. K. Buros (Ed.), **The eighth mental measurements yearbook** (pp. 1016-1018). Highland Park, NJ.: The Gryphon Press. (Psychometric)

930.   Emery, C., & Blumenthal, J. A., (1988). Effects of exercise training on psychological functioning in healthy type-A men. **Psychology and Health, 2**, 367-379. (Exercise)

931. Evans, M., Weinberg, R. S., & Jackson, A. (1992). Psychological factors related to drug use in college athletes. **The Sport Psychologist, 6**, 24-41. (Steroids/Drugs)

932. Ewing, J., Scott, D., Mendez, A., & McBride, T. (1984). Effects of aerobic exercise upon affect and cognition. **Perceptual and Motor Skills, 59**, 407-414. (Exercise)

933. Fahey, T. D. (1997). Biological markers of overtraining. **Biology of Sport, 14**, 3-19. (Overtraining)

934. Farrell, P., Gustafson, A. B., Morgan, W. P., & Pert, C. (1987). Enkephalins, catecholamines, and psychological mood alterations: Effects of prolonged exercise. **Medicine and Science in Sports and Exercise, 19**, 347-353. (Exercise)

935. Farrell, P., Gates, W., Maksud, M., & Morgan, W. P. (1982). Increases in plasma B-endorphin/B-lipotropin immuno-reactivity after treadmill running in humans. **Journal of Applied Psychology, 52**, 1245-1249 (Running)

936. Feher, P., Meyers, M. C., & Skelly, W. A. (1998). Psychological profile of rock climbers. **Journal of Sport Behavior, 21**, 167-180. (Rock Climbing)

937. Fillingim, R., Roth, D., & Haley, W. (1989). The effects of distraction on the perception of exercise-induced symptoms. **Journal of Psychosomatic Research, 33**, 241-248. (Exercise)

938. Fillion, L., & Gagnon, P. (1999). French adaptation of the shortened version of the Profile of Mood States. **Psychological Reports, 84**, 188-190. (Psychometric)

939. Flory, J. D., & Holmes, D. S. (1991). Effects of an acute bout of aerobic exercise on cardiovascular and subjective responses during subsequent cognitive work. **Journal of Psychosomatic Research, 35**, 225-230. (Exercise)

940. Flynn, M. G., Pizza, F., Boone, J., Andres, F. F., Michaud, T. J., & Rodriguez-Zayas, J. (1994). Indices of training stress during competitive running and swimming seasons. **International Journal of Sports Medicine, 15**, 21-26. (Running, Steroids/Drugs, Swimming)

941. Focht, B. C., & Koltyn, K. F. (1999). Influence of resistance exercise of different intensities on state anxiety and blood pressure. **Medicine and Science in Sports and Exercise, 31**, 456-463. (Exercise)

942. Frazier, E. (1988). Mood states profiles of chronic exercisers with differing abilities. **International Journal of Sport Psychology, 19**, 65-71. (Exercise)

943. Freedson, P., Mihevic, P., Loucks, A., & Girandola, R. (1983). Physique, body composition, and psychological characteristics of competitive female body builders. **Physician and Sportsmedicine, 11**(5), 85-93. (Bodybuilding)

944. Fremont, J., & Craighead, L. (1987). Aerobic exercise and cognitive therapy in the treatment of dysphoric moods. **Cognitive Therapy and Research, 11**, 241-251. (Exercise)

945. Friedman, E., & Berger, B. G. (1991). Influence of gender, masculinity and femininity on the effectiveness of three stress reduction techniques: Jogging, relaxation response, and group interaction. **Journal of Applied Sport Psychology, 3**, 61-86. (Running)

946. Friend, J., & LeUnes, A. (1990). Predicting baseball player performance. **Journal of Sport Behavior, 13**, 73-86. (Baseball)

947. Fry, R., Grove, J. R., Morton, A., Zeroni, P., Gaudieri, S., & Keast, D. (1994). Psychological and immunological correlates of acute overtraining. **British Journal of Sports Medicine, 28**, 241-246. (Overtraining)

948. Fuchs, C., & Zaichkowsky, L. D. (1983). Psychological characteristics of male and female body builders: The iceberg profile. **Journal of Sport Behavior, 6**, 136-145. (Bodybuilding)

949. Fung, L., & Fu, F. H. (1995). Psychological determinants between wheelchair sport finalists and non-finalists. **International Journal of Sport Psychology, 26**, 568-579. (Disabled Athletes)

950. Gal-or, Y., & Tenenbaum, G. (1986). Psychological determinants of performance under threat. **International Journal of Sport Psychology, 17**, 199-214. (Skydiving)

951. Gat, I., & McWhirter, B. T. (1998). Personality characteristics of competitive and recreational cyclists. **Journal of Sport Behavior, 21**, 408-420. (Cycling)

952. Glazer, A., & O'Connor, P. J. (1992). Mood improvements following exercise and quiet rest in bulimic women. **Scandinavian Journal of Medicine and Science in Sports, 3**, 73-79. (Exercise)

953. Gondola, J. C., & Tuckman, B. (1982). Psychological mood states in "average" marathon runners. **Perceptual and Motor Skills, 55**, 1295-1300. (Marathon)

954. Gondola, J. C., & Tuckman, B. (1983). Extent of training and mood enhancement in women runners. **Perceptual and Motor Skills, 57**, 333-334. (Running)

955. Goode, K., & Roth, D. (1993). Factor analysis of cognitions during running: Association with mood change. **Journal of Sport & Exercise Psychology, 15**, 375-389. (Running)

956. Gordin, R. G., & Henschen, K. P. (1989). Preparing the USA women's artistic gymnastics team for the 1988 Olympics: A multimodal approach. **The Sport Psychologist, 3**, 366-373. (Gymnastics)

957. Goss, J. D. (1994). Hardiness and mood disturbances in swimmers while overtraining. **Journal of Sport and Exercise Psychology, 16**, 135-149. (Overtraining, Steroids/Drugs, Swimming)

958.   Green, E., Burke, K. L., Nix, C., Lambrecht, K., & Mason, D. (1995). Psychological factors associated with alcohol use by high school athletes. **Journal of Sport Behavior, 18,** 195-208. (Steroids/Drugs)

959.   Greenwood, C., Dzewaltowski, D. A., & French, R. (1990). Self-efficacy and psychological well being of wheelchair tennis participants and wheelchair nontennis participants. **Adapted Physical Activity Quarterly, 7,** 12-21. (Disabled Athletes, Tennis)

960.   Grove, J. R., & Prapavessis, H. (1992). Preliminary evidence for the reliability and validity of an abbreviated Profile of Mood States. **International Journal of Sport Psychology, 23,** 93-109. (Psychometric)

961.   Guadagnoli, E., & Mor, V. (1989). Measuring cancer patients' affect: Revision and psychometric properties of the Profile of Mood States (POMS). **Psychological Assessment, 1,** (Psychometric)

962.   Gutmann, M., Pollock, M. L., Foster, C. D., & Schmidt, D. (1984). Training stress in Olympic speed skaters: A psychological perspective. **Physician and Sportsmedicine, 12**(12), 45-57. (Figure Skating/Ice Skating)

963.   Hagberg, J. M, Mullin, J. P., Bahrke, M. S., & Limburg, J. (1979). Physiological profiles and selected psychological characteristics of national class American cyclists. **Journal of Sports Medicine, 19,** 341 346. (Cycling)

964.   Hall, A., & Terry, P. C. (1995). Trends in mood profiles in the preparation phase and racing phase of the 1993 world rowing championships, Roundnice, the Czech Republic. **Journal of Sports Sciences, 13,** 56-57. (Rowing)

965.   Hall, E. G., Church, G. E., & Stone, M., (1980). Relationship of birth order to selected personality characteristics of nationally ranked Olympic weight-lifters. **Perceptual and Motor Skills, 51,** 971-976. (Weightlifting)

966.   Hall, S., Munoz, R., Reus, V., Sees, K., Duncan, C., Humfleet, G., & Hartz, D. (1996). Mood management and nicotine gum in smoking treatment: A therapeutic contact and placebo-controlled study. **Journal of Consulting and Clinical Psychology, 64,** 1003-1009. (Psychometric)

967. Hanson, C. J., Stevens, L. C., & Coast, J. R. (2001). Exercise duration and mood state: How much is enough to feel better? **Health Psychology, 20,** 267-275. (Exercise)

968. Harris, S., & Dawson-Hughes, B. (1993). Seasonal mood changes in 250 normal women. **Psychiatry Research, 49,** 77-87. (Psychometric)

969. Harte, J., & Eifert, G. (1993). The effects of running, environment, and attentional focus on athletes' catecholamine and cortisol levels and mood. **Psychophysiology, 32,** 49-54. (Running)

970. Hassmen, P., & Blomstrand, E. (1991). Mood change and marathon running: A pilot study using a Swedish version of the POMS test. **Scandinavian Journal of Psychology, 32,** 225-232. (Marathon)

971. Hassmen, P., & Blomstrand, E. (1995). Mood state relationships and soccer team performance. **The Sport Psychologist, 9,** 297-308. (Soccer)

972. Hassmen, P., Koivula, N., & Hansson, T. (1998). Precompetitive mood states and performance of elite male golfers: Do trait characteristics make a difference? **Perceptual and Motor Skills, 86,** 1443-1457. (Golf)

973. Heitman, R. J., Pugh, S. F., Erdman, J. W., & Kovaleski, J. E. (2000). Measurement of upper and lower body strength and its relationship to underhand pitching speed. **Perceptual and Motor Skills, 90,** 1139-1144. (Softball)

974. Henderson, J., Bourgeois, A. E., LeUnes, A., & Meyers, M. C. (1998). Group cohesiveness, mood disturbance, and stress in female basketball players. **Small Group Research, 29,** 212-225. (Basketball)

975. Henschen, K. P., Horvat, M., & French, R. (1984). A visual comparison of psychological profiles between able-bodied and wheelchair athletes. **Adapted Physical Activity Quarterly, 1,** 118-124. (Disabled Athletes)

976. Henschen, K. P., Horvat, M., & Roswal, G. (1992). Psychological profiles of the United States wheelchair basketball team. **International Journal of Sport Psychology, 23,** 128-137. (Basketball, Disabled Athletes)

120

977. Hill, C., & Hill, D. W. (1991). Influence of time of day on responses to the Profile of Mood States. **Perceptual and Motor Skills, 72,** 434. (Psychometric)

978. Hill, D. W., & Smith, J. (1991). Effect of time of day on the relationship between mood state, anaerobic power, and capacity. **Perceptual and Motor Skills, 72,** 83-87. (Exercise)

979. Hilyer, J., Wilson, D., Dillon, C., Caro, L., Jenkins, C., Spencer, W., Meadows, M., & Booker, W. (1982). Physical fitness training and counseling as treatment for youthful offenders. **Journal of Counseling Psychology, 29,** 292-303. (Exercise)

980. Hoffman, J. R., Bar-Eli, M., & Tenenbaum, G. (1999). An examination of mood changes and performance in a professional basketball team. **Journal of Sports Medicine and Physical Fitness, 39,** 74-79. (Basketball)

981. Hooper, S. L., & Mackinnon, L. T. (1995). Monitoring overtraining in athletes. **Sports Medicine, 20,** 321-327. (Overtraining)

982. Hooper, S. L., Mackinnon, L. T., & Ginn, E. M. (1998). Effects of three tapering techniques on the performance, forces and psychometric measures of competitive swimmers. **European Journal of Applied Physiology and Occupational Physiology, 78,** 258-263. (Swimming)

983. Hooper, S., Mackinnon, L. T., & Hanrahan, S. J. (1997). Mood states as an indication of staleness and recovery. **International Journal of Sport Psychology, 28,** 1-12. (Overtraining, Steroids/Drugs, Swimming)

984. Hooper, S. L., Mackinnon, L. T., & Howard, A. (1999). Physiological and psychometric variables for monitoring recovery during tapering from major competition. **Medicine and Science in Sports and Exercise, 31,** 1205-1210. (Overtraining)

985. Horswill, C., Hickner, R., Scott, J., Costill, D. L., & Gould, D. (1990). Weight loss, dietary carbohydrate modifications, and high intensity physical performance. **Medicine and Science in Sports and Exercise, 22,** 470-476. (Exercise)

986.   Horvat, M., French, R., & Henschen, K. P. (1986). A comparison of the psychological characteristics of male and female able-bodied and wheelchair athletes. **Paraplegia, 24**, 115-122. (Disabled Athletes)

987.   Horvat, M., Roswal, G., & Henschen, K. P. (1991). Psychological profiles of disabled male athletes before and after competition. **Clinical Kinesiology, 45**, 14-18. (Disabled Athletes)

988.   Houmard, J. (1991). Impact of reduced training on performance in endurance athletes. **Sports Medicine, 12**, 380-393. (Exercise)

989.   Houmard, J., Costill, D. L., Mitchell, J., Park, S., Fink, W., & Burns, J. (1990). Testosterone, cortisol, and creatine kinase levels in male distance runners during reduced training. **International Journal of Sports Medicine, 11**, 41-45. (Running)

990.   Houmard, J., Costill, D. L., Mitchell, J., Park, S., Hickner, R., & Roemmich, J. (1990). Reduced training maintains performance in distance runners. **International Journal of Sports Medicine, 11**, 46-52. (Running)

991.   Howe, B. L., & Bell, G. (1986). Mood states and motivations of triathletes. In J. Watkins, T. Reilly, & L. Burwitz (Eds.), **Sports science**. New York: E. & FN. Spon LTD. (Triathlon)

992.   Hughes, J., Casal, D., & Leon, A. (1986). Psychological effects of exercise: A randomized cross-over trial. **Journal of Psychosomatic Research, 30**, 355-360. (Exercise)

993.   Jackson, A., & Lane, A. M. (2001).Self-regulatory mechanisms to explain mood changes following exercise. **Journal of Sports Sciences, 19**, 75-76. (Exercise)

994.   Jacobs, D., Roswal, G., Horvat, M., & Gorman, D. (1990). A comparison between the psychological profiles of wheelchair athletes, wheelchair nonathletes, and able-bodied athletes. In G. Tepper, C. Dahms, B. Doll, & H. von Selzam (Eds.), **Adapted physical activity** (pp. 75-79). Berlin: Springer-Verlag. (Disabled Athletes)

995.   Jacobs, K. W., & Blandino, S. E. (1992). Effects of color of paper on which the Profile of Mood States is printed on the psychological states it measures. **Perceptual and Motor Skills, 75**, 267-271. (Psychometric)

996.   Jacobs, K. W., & Boze, M. M. (1993). Correlations among scales of the Beck Depression Inventory and the Profile of Mood States. **Psychological Reports, 73**, 431-434. (Psychometric)

997.   Jean-Louis, G., von Gizycki, H., Zizi, F., & Nunes, J. (1998). Mood states and sleepiness in college students: Influences of age, sex, habitual sleep, and substance abuse. **Perceptual and Motor Skills, 87**, 507-512. (Psychometric)

998.   Jin, P. (1992). Efficacy of Tai Chi, brisk walking, meditation, and reading in reducing mental and emotional stress. **Journal of Psychosomatic Research, 36**, 361-370. (Martial Arts, Psychometrics)

999.   Joesting, J. (1981). Comparison of personalities of athletes who sail with those who run. **Perceptual and Motor Skills, 52**, 514. (Running, Sailing)

1000.   Johnson, A., Collins, P., Higgins, I., Harrington, D., Connolly, J., Dolphin, C., McCreery, M., Brady, L., & O'Brien, M. (1986). Psychological, nutritional and physical status of Olympic road cyclists. **Journal of Sports Medicine and Physical Fitness, 19**, 11-14. (Cycling)

1001.   Johnson, R. F., Branch, L., & McMenemy, D. (1989). Influence of attitude and expectation on moods and symptoms during cold weather military training. **Aviation, Space, and Environmental Medicine, 60**, 1157-1162. (Psychometric)

1002.   Kanters, M. A. (2000). Recreational sport participation as a moderator of college stress. **Journal of the National Intramural and Recreational Sport Association, 24**(2), 10-23. (Intramural Sports)

1003.   Karageorghis, C. I., & Terry, P. C. (2000). Affective and psychophysical responses to asynchronous music during submaximal treadmill running. **Journal of Sports Sciences, 18**, 555-556. (Exercise)

1004. Karageorghis, C. I., Dimitriou, L. A., & Terry, P. C. (1999). Effects of circadian rhythms on mood among athletes. **Journal of Sports Sciences, 17**, 56-57. (Review Article)

1005. Kaye, M., Lawton, M., Gitlin, L., Kleban, M., Windsor, L., & Kaye, D. (1988). Older people's performance on the Profile of Mood States (POMS). **Clinical Gerontologist, 7**, 35-56. (Psychometric)

1006. Keith, R., O'Keefe, K., Blessing, D. L., & Wilson, G. (1991). Alterations in dietary carbohydrate, protein and fat intake and mood state in trained female cyclists. **Medicine and Science in Sports and Exercise, 23**, 212-216. (Cycling)

1007. Kellmann, M., Altenburg, D., Lormes, W., & Steinacker, J. M. (2001). Assessing stress and recovery during preparation for the world championship in rowing. **The Sport Psychologist, 15**, 151-167. (Rowing)

1008. Kennedy, M. M., & Newton, M. L. (1997). Effects of exercise intensity on mood in step aerobics. **Journal of Sports Medicine and Physical Fitness, 37**, 200-204. (Exercise)

1009. King, A., Taylor, C., & Haskell, W. (1993). Effects of differing intensities and formats of 12 months of exercise training on psychological outcomes in older adults. **Health Psychology, 12**, 292-300. (Exercise)

1010. King, A., Taylor, C., Haskell, W., & DeBusk, R. (1989). Influence of regular aerobic exercise on psychological health: A randomized, controlled trial of healthy middle-aged adults. **Health Psychology, 8**, 305-324. (Exercise)

1011. Kirkby, R. J. (1996). Ultraendurance running: A case study. **International Journal of Sport Psychology, 27**,109-116. (Ultrarunning/Ultramarathon)

1012. Kolt, G., & Kirkby, R. J. (1994). Injury, anxiety, and mood in competitive gymnasts. **Perceptual and Motor Skills, 78**, 955-962. (Gymnastics, Injury)

1013. Koltyn, K. F., & Schultes S. S. (1997). Psychological effects of an aerobic exercise session and a rest session following pregnancy. **Journal of Sports Medicine and Physical Fitness, 37**, 287-291. (Exercise)

1014. Koltyn, K. F., Lynch, N. A., & Hill, D. W. (1998). Psychological responses to brief exhaustive cycling exercise in the morning and evening. **International Journal of Sport Psychology, 29,** 145-156. (Exercise)

1015. Kowal, D. M., Patton, J. F., & Vogel, J. A. (1978). Psychological states and aerobic fitness of male and female recruits before and after basic training. **Aviation, Space, and Environmental Medicine, 49,** 603-606. (Exercise)

1016. Kraemer, R., Dzewaltowski, D. A., Blair, M., Rinehardt, F., & Castracane, V. (1990). Mood alteration from treadmill running and its relationship to beta-endorphin, corticotropin, and growth hormone. **Journal of Sports Medicine and Physical Fitness, 30,** 241-246. (Running)

1017. Kreider, R. B., Hill, D., Horton, G., Downes, M., Smith, S., & Anders, B. (1995). Effects of carbohydrate supplementation during intense training on dietary patterns, psychological status, and performance. **International Journal of Sport Nutrition, 5,** 125-135. (Exercise)

1018. Lane, A. M. (2000). Relationships between performance satisfaction and post-competitive mood among runners. **Journal of Sports Sciences, 18,** 53. (Running)

1019. Lane, A. M. (2000). Mood and emotion in sport: A response to Jones, Mace, and Williams (2000). **Perceptual and Motor Skills, 91,** 649-652. (Review Article)

1020. Lane, A. M. (2001). Relationships between attitudes toward eating disorders and mood among student athletes. **Journal of Sports Sciences, 18,** 52-53. (Psychometric)

1021. Lane, A. M. (2001). Relationships between perceptions of performance expectations and mood among distance runners: The moderating effect of depressed mood. **Journal of Science in Medicine and Sport, 4,** 235-249. (Running)

1022. Lane, A. M., Crone-Grant, D., and Lane, H. J. (2001). Mood changes following exercise. **Perceptual and Motor Skills,** in press. (Exercise)

1023. Lane, A. M., & Lane, H. J. (2001). Predictive effectiveness of mood measures. **Perceptual and Motor Skills**, in press. (Exercise)

1024. Lane, A. M., & Lovejoy, D. J. (2001). The effects of exercise on mood changes: The moderating effect of depressed mood. **Journal of Sports Medicine and Physical Fitness**. in press. (Exercise)

1025. Lane, A. M., & Terry, P. C. (1998). Development of normative data for Profile of Mood States-C among adult and young athletes. **Journal of Sports Sciences, 16**, 93-94. (Psychometric)

1026. Lane, A. M., & Terry, P. C. (1998). Mood states as predictors of performance: A conceptual model. **The Psychologist**, (August), 109. (Psychometric)

1027. Lane, A. M., & Terry, P. C. (1998). Mood states as predictors of performance: Test of a conceptual model. In A. J. Sargeant & H. Siddons (Eds.), **From community health to elite sport: Proceedings of the 3rd Annual Congress of the European College of Sport Science Congress** (p. 145). Liverpool, U. K.: Health Care Development. (Psychometric)

1028. Lane, A. M., & Terry, P. C. (1998, August). Prediction of athletic performance from mood: Test of a conceptual model. **The Psychologist**, 109. (Psychometric)

1029. Lane, A. M., & Terry, P. C. (1998). Mood states as predictors of performance: A conceptual model. **Journal of Sports Sciences, 16**, 93-94. (Psychometric)

1030. Lane, A.M., & Terry, P. C. (1998). Development of normative data for Profile of Mood States-C among adult and young athletes. **Journal of Sports Sciences, 16**, 95-96. (Psychometric)

1031. Lane, A. M., & Terry, P. C. (1998). Predictive effectiveness of mood on cycling time trial performance. **Journal of Sports Sciences, 16**, 95. (Cycling, Psychometric)

1032. Lane, A. M., & Terry, P. C. (1999). The conceptual independence of tension and depression. **Journal of Sports Sciences, 17,** 605-606. (Psychometric)

1033. Lane, A. M., & Terry, P. C. (1999). Mood states as predictors of performance: Test of a conceptual model. **Journal of Sports Sciences, 17,** 606. (Psychometric)

1034. Lane, A. M., & Terry, P. C. (2000). The nature of mood: Development of a conceptual model with a focus on depression. **Journal of Applied Sport Psychology, 12,** 16-33. (Psychometric)

1035. Lane, A. M., Lane, H. J., & Firth, S. (2000). Relationships between performance satisfaction and post-competition mood among runners. **Journal of Sports Sciences, 18,** 53. (Running)

1036. Lane, A. M., Mills, M., & Terry, P. C. (1998). Mood regulation among corporate workers: Effects of exercise on mood. **Journal of Sports Sciences, 16,** 92-93. (Exercise)

1037. Lane, A. M., Terry, P. C., & Lane, H. J. (1996). The antecedents of mood in distance runners. **Journal of Sports Sciences, 14,** 94. (Running)

1038. Lane, A. M., Beedie, C. J., Lane, H. J., & Firth, S. (2000). Relationships between performance satisfaction and post-competition mood among runners. **Journal of Sports Sciences, 18,** 53. (Running)

1039. Lane, A. M., Terry, P. C., Karageorghis, C. I., & Lawson, J. (1999). Mood state as predictors of kickboxing performance: A test of a conceptual model. **Journal of Sports Sciences, 17,** 61-62. (Martial Arts)

1040. Lavalee, L., & Flint, F. (1996). The relationship of stress, competitive anxiety, mood state, and social support to athletic injury. **Journal of Athletic Training, 31,** 296-299. (Football, Injury, Rugby)

1041. Lee, C. (1990). Psyching up for a muscular endurance task: Effects of image content on performance and mood state. **Journal of Sport and Exercise Psychology, 12,** 66-73. (Exercise)

1042. Lee, K. A., Hicks, G., & Ninomurcia, G. (1991). Validity and reliability of a scale to assess fatigue. **Psychiatry Research, 36**, 291-298. (Psychometric)

1043. Leiderbach, M., Gleim, G. W., & Nicholas, J. A. (1992). Monitoring training status in professional ballet dancers. **Journal of Sports Medicine and Physical Fitness, 32**, 187-195. (Dance, Overtraining)

1044. Leith, L. (1990). Psychological aspects of exercise: A decade literature review. **Journal of Sport Behavior, 13**, 219-239. (Exercise, Review Article)

1045. Leon, G., McNally, C., & Ben-Porath, Y. (1989). Personality characteristics, mood, and coping patterns in a successful North Pole expedition team. **Journal of Research in Personality, 23**, 162-179. (Psychometric)

1046. LeUnes, A. (2000). Updated bibliography on the profile of mood states in sport and exercise psychology research. **Journal of Applied Sport Psychology, 12**, 110-113. (Review Article)

1047. LeUnes, A., & Burger, J. (2000). Profile of mood states research in sport and exercise psychology: Past, present, and future. **Journal of Applied Sport Psychology, 12**, 5-15. (Review Article)

1048. LeUnes, A., & Nation, J. R. (1982). Saturday's heroes: A psychological portrait of college football players. **Journal of Sport Behavior, 5**, 139-149. (Football)

1049. LeUnes, A., Daiss, S., and Nation, J. R. (1986). Some psychological predictors of continuation in a collegiate football program. **Journal of Applied Research in Coaching and Athletics, 1**, 1-8 (Football)

1050. Lichtman, S., & Poser, E, (1983). The effects of exercise on mood and cognitive functioning. **Journal of Psychosomatic Research, 27**, 43-52. (Exercise)

1051. Liederbach, M., Gleim, G. W., & Nicholas, J. A. (1992). Monitoring training status in professional ballet dancers. **Journal of Sports Medicine and Physical Fitness, 32**, 187-195. (Dance, Overtraining)

1052. Lloyd, A., Gandevia, S., Brockman, A., Hales, J., & Wakefield, D. (1994). Cytokine production and fatigue in patients with chronic fatigue syndrome and healthy control subjects in response to exercise. **Clinical Infectious Diseases, 18,** S142-S146. (Exercise)

1053. Lovejoy, D., & Lane, A. M. (2000). The effects of exercise on mood changes: The moderating effect of depressed mood. **Journal of Sports Sciences, 18,** 53-54. (Exercise)

1054. Lowther, J., & Lane, A. M. (2001). Relationships between mood, cohesion and performance among soccer players. **Journal of Sports Sciences,** 19. (Soccer)

1055. Mahoney, C. A., & Smith, L. M. (1997). An exercise effect on mood during the menstrual cycle: A preliminary investigation. **Irish Journal of Psychology, 18,** 397-403. (Exercise)

1056. Mahoney, M. J. (1989). Psychological predictors of elite and non-elite performance in Olympic weight-lifting. **International Journal of Sport Psychology, 20,** 1-12. (Weightlifting)

1057. Markoff, R., Ryan, P., & Young, T (1982). Endorphins and mood changes in long-distance running. **Medicine and Science in Sports and Exercise, 14,** 11-15. (Running)

1058. Maroulakis, E., & Zervas, Y. (1993). Effects of aerobic exercise on mood of adult women. **Perceptual and Motor Skills, 76,** 795-801. (Exercise)

1059. Martin, D. T., Andersen, M. B., and Gates, W. (2000). Using Profile of Mood States (POMS) to monitor high-intensity training in cyclists: Group versus case studies. **The Sport Psychologist, 14,** 138-156. (Cycling)

1060. Martin, D. T., Andersen, M. B., & Gates, W. (2000). Using the Profile of Mood States (POMS) to monitor high-intensity training in cyclists: Group versus case studies. **The Sport Psychologist, 14,** 138-156. (Cycling)

1061. Mastro, J. V., Canabal, M. Y., & French, R. (1988). Psychological mood profiles of sighted and unsighted beep baseball players. **Research Quarterly for Exercise and Sport, 59,** 262-264. (Baseball, Disabled Athletes)

1062. Mastro, J. V., French, R., & Hall, M. (1987). Test-retest reliability of the Profile of Mood States using visually impaired athletes. **Perceptual and Motor Skills, 65,** 593-594. (Disabled Athletes)

1063. Mastro, J. V., French, R., Henschen, K. P., & Horvat, M. (1986). Selected psychological characteristics of blind golfers and their coaches. **American Corrective Therapy Journal, 40,** 111-114. (Coaching, Disabled Athletes, Golf)

1064. Mastro, J. V., Sherrill, C., Gench, B., & French, R. (1987). Psychological characteristics of-elite visually impaired athletes: The iceberg profile. **Journal of Sport Behavior, 10,** 39-46. (Disabled Athletes)

1065. Matsubara, F., Shimomitsu, T., Okamura, K., Odagiri, Y., & Katsumura, T. (1999). Implications of the amino acid metabolism regarding changes in the mood profile following ultra-endurance. **Japanese Journal of Physical Fitness and Sports Medicine, 48,** 201-210. (Exercise)

1066. McDonald, S., & Hardy, C. J. (1990). Affective response patterns of the injured athlete: An exploratory analysis. **The Sport Psychologist, 4,** 261-274. (Injury)

1067. McGill, J. C., Hall, J. R., Ratliff, W. R., & Moss, R. F. (1986). Personality characteristics of professional rodeo cowboys. **Journal of Sport Behavior, 9,** 143-151. (Rodeo)

1068. McGowan, R. W., & Jordan, C. (1988). Mood states and physical activity. **Louisiana Alliance for Health, Physical Education, Recreation and Dance Journal, 15,** 12-13, 17, 32. (Martial Arts)

1069. McGowan, R. W., & Shultz, B. B. (1989). Task complexity and affect in collegiate football. **Perceptual and Motor Skills, 69,** 671-674. (Football)

1070. McGowan, R.W., Miller, M., & Henschen, K. P. (1990). Differences in mood states between belt ranks in karate tournament competitors. **Perceptual and Motor Skills, 71,** 147-150. (Martial Arts)

1071. McGowan, R. W., Pierce, E. F., & Jordan, D. (1991). Mood alterations with a single bout of physical activity. **Perceptual and Motor Skills, 72,** 1203-1209. (Exercise)

1072. McGowan, R. W., Pierce, E. F., & Jordan, R. (1992). Differences in precompetitive mood states between black-belt ranks. **Perceptual and Motor Skills, 75,** 123-128. (Martial Arts)

1073. McGowan, R. W., Talton, B., & Thompson, M. (1996). Changes in scores of the Profile of Mood States following a single bout of physical activity: Heart rate and changes in affect. **Perceptual and Motor Skills, 83,** 859-866. (Exercise)

1074. McGowan, R. W., Pierce, E. F., Williams, M., & Eastman, N. (1994). Athletic injury and self diminution. **Journal of Sports Medicine and Physical Fitness, 34,** 299-304. (Injury)

1075. McGowan, R. W., Pierce, E. F., Eastman, N., Tripathi, H. L., Dewey, T., & Olson, K. (1993). Beta-endorphins and mood states during resistance exercise. **Perceptual and Motor Skills, 76,** 376-378. (Exercise)

1076. McInman, A. D., & Berger, B. G. (1993). Self-concept and mood changes associated with aerobic dancing. **Australian Journal of Psychology, 45,** 134-140. (Dance, Exercise)

1077. McNair, D., Lorr, M., & Droppleman, L. (1971). **Manual for the Profile of Mood States.** San Diego, CA.: Educational and Industrial Testing Service. (Test Manual)

1078. Meney, I., Waterhouse, J., Atkinson, G., Reilly, T., & Davenne, D. (1998). The effect of one night's sleep deprivation on temperature, mood, and physical performance in subjects with different amounts of habitual physical activity. **Chronobiology International, 15,** 349-363. (Exercise)

1079. Meyers, M. C., Sterling, J. C., & LeUnes, A. (1988). Psychological characterization of the collegiate rodeo athlete. **Journal of Sport Behavior, 11,** 59-65. (Rodeo)

1080. Meyers, M. C., Bourgeois, A. E., LeUnes, A., & Murray, N. G. (1999). Mood and psychological skills of elite and sub-elite equestrian athletes. **Journal of Sport Behavior, 22,** 399-409. (Equestrian)

1081. Meyers, M. C., Sterling, J. C., Bourgeois, A. E., Treadwell, S., & LeUnes, A. (1994). Mood and psychological skills of world-ranked female tennis players. **Journal of Sport Behavior, 17,** 156-165. (Tennis)

1082. Meyers, M. C., Sterling, J. C., LeUnes, A., & Elledge, J. (1990). Precompetitive mood state changes in collegiate rodeo athletes. **Journal of Sport Behavior, 13,** 114-12 1. (Rodeo)

1083. Meyers, M. C., LeUnes, A., Elledge, J., Tolson, H., & Sterling, J. C. (1992). Injury incidence and psychological mood state patterns in collegiate rodeo athletes. **Journal of Sport Behavior, 15,** 297-306. (Rodeo)

1084. Miller, B. P., & Edgington, G. (1984). Psychological mood state distortion in a sporting context. **Journal of Sport Behavior, 7,** 92-94. (Psychometric)

1085. Miller, B. P., & Miller, A. J. (1985). Psychological correlates of success in elite sportswomen. **Journal of Sport Psychology, 16,** 289-295. (Netball)

1086. Momas, T, Zebas, C., Bahrke, M. S., Araujo, J., & Etheridge, G. (1980). Physiological and psychological correlates of success in track and field athletes. **British Journal of Sports Medicine, 17,** 102-109. (Track and Field)

1087. Moore, K., Stanley, R., & Burrows, G. (1990). Profile of Mood States: Australian normative data. **Psychological Reports, 66,** 509-510. (Psychometric)

1088. Morgan, W. P. (1978, April). The mind of the marathoner. **Psychology Today,** 38-49. (Marathon)

1089. Morgan, W. P. (1980). The trait psychology controversy. **Research Quarterly for Exercise and Sport, 51,** 50-76. (Review Article)

1090. Morgan, W. P. (1980, July). Test of champions. **Psychology Today,** 92-99. (Review Article)

1091. Morgan, W. P. (1995). Anxiety and panic in recreational scuba divers. **Sports Medicine, 20,** 398-421. (Scuba)

1092. Morgan, W. P., & Horstman, D. (1978). Psychometric correlates of pain perception. **Perceptual and Motor Skills, 47**, 27-39. (Injury)

1093. Morgan, W. P., & Johnson, R. W. (1978). Personality characteristics of successful and unsuccessful oarsmen. **International Journal of Sport Psychology, 9**, 119-133. (Rowing)

1094. Morgan, W. P., & Pollock, M. L. (1977). Psychologic characterization of the elite distance runner. **Annals of the New York Academy of Sciences, 301**, 382-403. (Running)

1095. Morgan, W. P., Brown, D. R., Raglin, J. S., O'Connor, P. J., & Ellickson, K. A. (1987). Psychological monitoring of overtraining and staleness. **British Journal of Sports Medicine, 21**, 107-114. (Overtraining, Steroids/Drugs, Swimming)

1096. Morgan, W. P., Costill, D. L., Flynn, M. G., Raglin, J. S., & O'Connor, P. J. (1988). Mood disturbance following increased training in swimmers. **Medicine and Science in Sports and Exercise, 20**, 408-414. (Steroids/Drugs, Swimming)

1097. Morgan, W. P., O'Connor, P. J., Ellickson, K. A., & Bradley, P. W. (1992). Elite male distance runners: Personality structure, mood states and performance. **Track & Field Quarterly, 92**, 59-62. (Running)

1098. Morgan, W. P., O'Connor, P. J., Sparling, P. B., & Pate, R. R. (1987). Psychological characterization of the elite female distance runner. **International Journal of Sports Medicine, 8**, 124-131. (Running)

1099. Morgan, W. P., Sparling, P. B., O'Connor, P. J., & Pate, R. R. (1992). The elite female distance runner: Psychological characterization. **Track & Field Quarterly, 92**, 63-67. (Running)

1100. Morrey, M. A., Stuart, M. J., Smith, A. M., & Wiese-Bjornstal, D. M. (1999). A longitudinal examination of athletes' emotional and cognitive responses to anterior cruciate ligament injury. **Clinical Journal of Sport Medicine, 9**, 63-69. (Injury, Overtraining)

1101. Morris, M., & Salmon, P. (1994). Qualitative and quantitative effects of running on mood. **Journal of Sports Medicine and Physical Fitness, 34,** 284-291. (Running)

1102. Moses, J., Steptoe, A., Mathews, A., & Edwards, S. (1989). The effects of exercise training on mental well-being in the normal population: A controlled trial. **Journal of Psychosomatic Research, 33,** 47-61. (Exercise)

1103. Moss, H., Panzak, G., & Tarter, R. (1992). Personality, mood, and psychiatric symptoms among anabolic steroid users. **American Journal on Addictions, 1,** 315-324. (Bodybuilding, Steroids/Drugs)

1104. Motl, R. W., Berger, B. G., & Leuschen, P. S. (2000). The role of enjoyment in the exercise-mood relationship. **International Journal of Sport Psychology, 31,** 347-363. (Rock Climbing)

1105. Muraki, S., Tsunawake, N., Hiramatsu, S., & Yamasaki, M. (2000). The effect of frequency and mode of sports activity on the psychological status in tetraplegics and paraplegics. **Spinal Cord, 38,** 309-314. (Exercise)

1106. Murphy, S. M., Fleck, S. J., Dudley, G., & Callister, R. (1990). Psychological and performance concomitants of increased volume training in elite athletes. **Journal of Applied Sport Psychology, 2,** 34-50. (Martial Arts)

1107. Naessens, G., Chandler, T. J., Kibler, W. B., & Driessens, M. (2000). Clinical usefulness of nocturnal urinary noradrenaline excretion patterns in the follow-up of training processes in high-level soccer players. **Journal of Strength and Conditioning Research, 14,** 125-131. (Soccer)

1108. Nagle, F. J., Morgan, W. P., Hellickson, R. O., Serfass, R. C., & Alexander, J. F. (1975). Spotting success traits in Olympic contenders. **Physician and Sportsmedicine, 3**(12), 31-43, 84. (Wrestling)

1109. Nagy, S., & Frazier, S. E. (1988). The impact of exercise on locus of control, self-esteem and mood states. **Journal of Social Behavior and Personality, 3,** 263-268. (Exercise)

1110. Nation, J. R., & LeUnes, A. (1981, September). Semi-tough and supernormal. **Psychology Today**, 66-67. (Football)

1111. Nation, J. R., & LeUnes, A. (1983). A personality profile of the black athlete in college football. **Psychology, 20**, 1-3. (Football)

1112. Nation, J. R., & LeUnes, A. (1983). Personality characteristics of intercollegiate players as determined by position, classification, and redshirt status. **Journal of Sport Behavior, 6**, 92-102. (Football)

1113. Newby, R. W., & Simpson, S .(1994). Basketball performance as a function of scores on Profile of Mood States. **Perceptual and Motor Skills, 78**, 1142. (Basketball)

1114. Newby, R. W., & Simpson, S. (1991). Personality profile of nonscholarship college football players. **Perceptual and Motor Skills, 73**, 1083-1089. (Football)

1115. Newby, R. W., & Simpson, S. (1996). Correlations between mood state scores and volleyball performance. **Perceptual and Motor Skills, 83**, 1153-1154. (Volleyball)

1116. Newcombe, P. A., & Boyle, G. J. (1995). High school students' sport personalities: Variations across participation level, gender, type of sport, and success. **International Journal of Sport Psychology, 26**, 277-294. (Various Sports)

1117. Nieman, D. C., Custer, W. F., Butterworth, D. E., Utter, A. C., & Henson, D. A. (2000). Psychological response to exercise training and/or energy restriction in obese women. **Journal of Psychosomatic Research, 48**, 23-29. (Exercise)

1118. Norcross, J. C., Guadagnoli, E., & Prochaska, J. (1984). Factor structure of the Profile of Mood States (POMS): Two partial replications. **Journal of Clinical Psychology, 40**, 1270-1277. (Psychometric)

1119. O'Brien, P. M., & O'Connor, P. J. (2000). Effect of bright light on cycling performance. **Medicine and Science in Sports and Exercise, 32**, 439-447. (Cycling)

1120. O'Connor, P. J., & Morgan, W. P. (1990). Athletic performance following rapid traversal of multiple time zones. **Sports Medicine, 10**, 20-30. (Exercise)

1121. O'Connor, P. J., Morgan, W. P., & Raglin, J. S. (1991). Psychobiologic effects of 3 d of increased training in female and male swimmers. **Medicine and Science in Sports and Exercise, 23**, 1055-1061. (Steroids/Drugs)

1122. O'Connor, P. J., Raglin, J. S., & Morgan, W. P. (1996). Psychometric correlates of perception during arm ergometry in males and females. **International Journal of Sports Medicine, 17**, 462-466. (Exercise)

1123. O'Connor, P. J., Morgan, W. P., Raglin, J. S., Barksdale, C., & Kalin, N. (1989). Mood state and salivary cortisol levels following overtraining in female swimmers. **Psychoneuroendocrinology, 14**, 303-310. (Overtraining, Steroids/Drugs, Swimming)

1124. O'Connor, P. J., Morgan, W. P., Koltyn, K. F., Raglin, J. S., Turner, J., & Kalin, N. (1991). Air travel across four time zones in college swimmers. **Journal of Applied Physiology, 70**, 756-763. (Steroids/Drugs)

1125. Oda, S., Matsumoto, T., Nakagawa, K., & Moriya, K. (1999). Relaxation effects in humans of underwater exercise of moderate intensity. **European Journal of Applied Physiology and Occupational Physiology, 80**, 253-259. (Exercise)

1126. Ogden, J., Veale, D., & Summers, Z. (1997). The development and validation of the exercise dependence questionnaire. **Addiction Research, 5**, 343-355. (Exercise)

1127. Oldridge, N., Streiner, D., Hoffmann, R., & Guyatt, G. (1995). Profile of Mood States and cardiac rehabilitation after acute myocardial infarction. **Medicine and Science in Sports and Exercise, 27**, 900-905. (Exercise)

1128. Owens, A. J. N., Lane, A. M., & Terry, P. C. (2000). Mood states as predictors of tennis performance: A test of a conceptual model. **Journal of Sports Sciences, 18**, 558. (Tennis)

1129. Palinkas, L., Suedfeld, P., & Steel, G. (1995). Psychological functioning among members of a small polar expedition. **Aviation, Space, and Environmental Medicine, 66**, 943-950. (Psychometric)

1130. Patten, C., Harris, W., & Leatherman, D. (1994). Psychological characteristics of elite wheelchair athletes: The iceberg profile. **Perceptual and Motor Skills, 79**, 1390. (Disabled Athletes)

1131. Paulsen, P., French, R., & Sherrill, C. (1990). Comparison of wheelchair athletes and nonathletes on selected mood states. **Perceptual and Motor Skills, 71**, 1160-1162. (Disabled Athletes)

1132. Paulsen, P., French, R., & Sherrill, C. (1991). Comparison of mood states of college able-bodied and wheelchair basketball players. **Perceptual and Motor Skills, 73**, 396-398. (Basketball, Disabled Athletes)

1133. Perczek, R., Carver, C. S., Price, A. A., & Pozo-Kaderman, C. (2000). Coping, mood, and aspects of personality in Spanish translation and evidence of convergence with English versions. **Journal of Personality Assessment, 74**, 63-87. (Exercise)

1134. Petajan, J. H., Gappmaier, E., White, A. T., Spencer, M. K., Mino, L., & Hicks, R. W. (1996). Impact of aerobic training on fitness and quality of life in multiple sclerosis. **Annals of Neurology, 39**, 432-441. (Exercise)

1135. Pierce, E. F., & Pate, D. (1994). Mood alterations in older adults following acute exercise. **Perceptual and Motor Skills, 79**, 191-194. (Exercise)

1136. Pinhas, L., Toner, B. B., Ali, A., Garfinkel, P. E., & Stuckless, N. (1999). The effects of the ideal of female beauty on mood and body satisfaction. **International Journal of Eating Disorders, 25**, 223-226. (Psychometric)

1137. Pistacchio, T., Weinberg, R. S., & Jackson, A. (1989). The development of a psychobiologic profile of individuals who experience and those who do not experience exercise related mood enhancement. **Journal of Sport Behavior, 12**, 151-166. (Exercise)

1138. Poole, R., & Henschen, K. P. (1984). Brigham Young's psychological program for women's cross-country and track. **Scholastic Coach, 53,** 52-53, 73-74, 77. (Running)

1139. Porter, K. (1985). Psychological characteristics of the average female runner. **Physician and Sportsmedicine, 13**(5), 171-175. (Running)

1140. Power, S. L. (1986). Psychological assessment procedures of a track and field national event squad training weekend. In J. Watkins, T Reilly, and L. Burwitz (Eds.), **Sports science.** New York: E. & FN. Spon. (Track and Field)

1141. Prapavessis, H. (2000). The POMS and sports performance: A review. **Journal of Applied Sport Psychology, 12,** 34-48. (Review Article)

1142. Prapavessis, H., & Grove, J. R. (1991). Precompetitive emotions and shooting performance: The mental health and zone of optimal function models. **The Sport Psychologist, 5,** 223-234. (Running, Shooting)

1143. Prapavessis, H., & Grove, J. R. (1994). Personality variables as antecedents of precompetitive mood states. **International Journal of Sport Psychology, 25,** 81-99. (Shooting)

1144. Prapavessis, H., & Grove, J. R. (1994). Personality variables as antecedents of precompetitive mood state temporal planning. **International Journal of Sport Psychology, 25,** (Shooting)

1145. Prapavessis, H., Berger, B., G., & Grove, J. R. (1992). 'The relationship of training and pre-competition mood states to swimming performance: An exploratory investigation. **Australian Journal of Science and Medicine in Sport, 24,** 12-17. (Steroids/Drugs, Swimming)

1146. Pronk, N., Crouse, S., & Rohack, J. (1994). Maximal exercise and acute mood response in women. **Physiology and Behavior, 57,** 1-4. (Exercise)

1147. Pronk, N., Jawad, A., Crouse, S., & Rohack, J. (1994). Acute effects of walking on mood profiles in women: Preliminary findings in postmenopausal women. **Medicine, Exercise, Nutrition, and Health, 3,** 148-155. (Exercise)

1148. Prusaczyk, W., Dishman, R. K., & Cureton, K. J. (1992). No effects of glycogen depleting exercise and altered diet composition on mood states. **Medicine and Science in Sports and Exercise, 24**, 708713. (Exercise)

1149. Quinn, A. M., & Fallon, B. J. (1999). The changes in psychological characteristics and reactions of elite athletes from injury onset until full recovery. **Journal of Applied Sport Psychology, 11**, 210-229. (Injury)

1150. Raglin, J.S. (1990). Exercise and mental health-beneficial and detrimental effects. **Sports Medicine, 9**, 323-329. (Exercise)

1151. Raglin, J.S. (2001). Psychological factors in sport performance: The mental health model revisited. **Journal of Sports Medicine, 31**, 879-890. (Review Article)

1152. Raglin, J. S., & Morgan, W. P. (1994). Development of a scale for use in monitoring training-induced distress in athletes. **International Journal of Sports Medicine, 15**, 84-88. (Exercise, Overtraining, Psychometrics, Steroids/Drugs, Swimming)

1153. Raglin, J. S., Eksten, F., & Garl, T. (1995). Mood state responses to a pre-season conditioning program in male collegiate basketball players. **International Journal of Sport Psychology, 26**, 214-225. (Basketball)

1154. Raglin, J. S., Morgan, W. P., & Luchsinger, A. (1990). Mood and self-motivation in successful and unsuccessful female rowers. **Medicine and Science in Sports and Exercise, 22**, 849-853. (Rowing)

1155. Raglin, J. S., Morgan, W. P., & O'Connor, P. J. (1991). Changes in mood states during training in female and male college swimmers. **International Journal of Sports Medicine, 12**, 585-589. (Steroids/Drugs, Swimming)

1156. Raglin, J. S., Koceja, D., Stager, J., & Harms, C. (1996). Mood, neuromuscular function, and performance during training in female swimmers. **Medicine and Science in Sports and Exercise, 28**, 372-377. (Steroids/Drugs, Swimming)

1157. Raglin, J. S., O'Connor, P. J., Carlson, N., & Morgan, W. P. (1996). Responses to underwater exercise in scuba divers differing in trait anxiety. **Undersea and Hyperbaric Medicine, 23,** 77-82. (Running, Scuba)

1158. Rainey, D. W., Amunategui, F., Agocs, H., & Larick, J. (1992). Sensation seeking and competitive trait anxiety among college rodeo athletes. **Journal of Sport Behavior, 15,** 307-317. (Rodeo)

1159. Rasmussen, P. R., & Jeffrey, A. C. (1995). Assessment of mood states: Biases in single administration instruments. **Journal of Psychopathology and Behavioral Assessment, 17,** 177-184. (Psychometric)

1160. Rasmussen, P. R., Jeffrey, A. C., Willingham, J. K., & Glover, T. L. (1994). Implications of the true score model in assessment of mood state. **Journal of Social Behavior and Assessment, 9,** 107-118. (Psychometric)

1161. Reddon, J., Marceau, R., & Holder, R. (1985). A confirmatory evaluation of the Profile of Mood States: Convergent and discriminant item validity. **Journal of Psychopathology and Behavior Assessment, 7,** 243-259. (Psychometric)

1162. Rehor, P. R., Dunnagan, T., Stewart, C., & Cooley, D. (2001). Alteration of mood state after a single bout of noncompetitive and competitive exercise programs. **Perceptual and Motor Skills, 93,** 249-256. (Exercise)

1163. Reilly, T., & Piercy, M. (1994). The effect of partial sleep deprivation on weight-lifting performance. **Ergonomics, 37,** 107-115. (Weightlifting)

1164. Rejeski, W. J., Gregg, E., Thompson, A., & Berry, M. (1991). The effects of varying doses of acute aerobic exercise on psychophysiological stress responses in highly trained cyclists. **Journal of Sport & Exercise Psychology, 13,** 188-199. (Cycling)

1165. Renger, R. (1993). A review of the Profile of Mood States (POMS) in the prediction of athletic success. **Journal of Applied Sport Psychology, 5,** 78-84. (Review Article)

1166. Riddick, C. C. (1984). Comparative psychological profiles of three groups of female collegians: Competitive swimmers, recreational swimmers and inactive swimmers. **Journal of Sport Behavior, 7**, 160-174. (Steroids/Drugs, Swimming)

1167. Robinson, D. W., & Howe, B. L. (1987). Causal attribution and mood state relationships of soccer players in a sport achievement setting. **Journal of Sport Behavior, 10**, 137-146. (Soccer)

1168. Roth, D. (1989). Acute emotional and psychophysiological effects of aerobic exercise. **Psychophysiology, 26**, 593-602. (Exercise)

1169. Roth, D., Bachtler, S., & Fillingim, R. (1990). Acute emotional and cardiovascular effects of stressful mental work during aerobic exercise. **Psychophysiology, 27**, 694-701. (Exercise)

1170. Rowley, A., Landers, D. M., Kyllo, L., & Etnier, J. (1995). Does the iceberg profile discriminate between successful and less successful athletes? A meta-analysis. **Journal of Sport & Exercise Psychology, 17**, 185-199. (Psychometric)

1171. Segebartt, K., Nieman, D. C., Pover, N., Arabatzis, K., & Johnson, M. (1988). Psychological well-being in physically active and inactive healthy young old to very old women. **Annals of Sports Medicine, 4**, 130-136. (Exercise)

1172. Segerstrom, S. C., Taylor, S. E., Kemeny, M. E., & Fahey J. L. (1998). Optimism is associated with mood, coping, and immune change in response to stress. **Journal of Personality and Social Psychology, 74**, 1646-1655. (Psychometric)

1173. Shacham, S. (1983). A shortened version of the Profile of Mood States. **Journal of Personality Assessment, 47**,305-306. (Psychometric)

1174. Sharpe, J. P., & Gilbert, D. G. (1998). Effects of repeated administration of the Beck Depression Inventory and other measures of negative mood states. **Personality and Individual Differences, 24**, 457-463. (Psychometric)

1175. Shin, Y. H. (1999). The effects of a walking exercise program on physical function and emotional state of elderly Korean women. **Public Health Nursing, 16**, 146-154. (Exercise)

1176. Shukitt-Hale, B., Rauch, T, & Foutch, R. (1990). Altitude symptomatology and mood states during a climb to 3,630 meters. **Aviation, Space, and Environmental Medicine, 61**, 225-228. (Rock Climbing)

1177. Silva, J. M., Schultz, B., Haslam, R. W., & Murray, D. F. (1981). A psychophysiological assessment of elite wrestlers. **Research Quarterly for Exercise and Sport, 52**, 348-358. (Wrestling)

1178. Silva, J. M., Shultz, B. B., Haslam, R.W., Martin, T. P., & Murray, D. F. (1985). Discriminating characteristics of contestants at the United States Olympic wrestling trials. **International Journal of Sports Psychology, 16**, 79-102. (Wrestling)

1179. Simons, C. W., & Birkimer, J. C. (1988). An exploration of factors predicting the effects of aerobic conditioning on mood state. **Journal of Psychosomatic Research, 32**, 63-75. (Exercise)

1180. Simpson, S., & Newby, R. W. (1994). Scores on Profile of Mood States of college football players from nonscholarship and scholarship programs. **Perceptual and Motor Skills, 78**, 635-640. (Football)

1181. Skirka, N. (2000). The relationship of hardiness, sense of coherence, sports participation, and gender to perceived stress and psychological symptoms among college students. **Journal of Sports Medicine and Physical Fitness, 40**, 63-70. (Various Sports)

1182. Slaven, L., & Lee, C. (1994). Psychological effects of exercise among adult women: The impact of menopausal status. **Psychology and Health, 9**, 297-303. (Exercise)

1183. Slaven, L., & Lee, C. (1997). Mood and symptom reporting among middle-aged women: The relationship between menopausal status, hormone replacement therapy, and exercise participation. **Health Psychology, 16,** 203-208. (Exercise)

1184. Smith, A. M., Stuart, M. J., Wiese-Bjornstal, D. M., & Gunnon, C. (1997). Predictors of injury in ice hockey players: A multivariate, multidisciplinary approach. **American Journal of Sports Medicine, 25,** 500-507. (Ice Hockey, Injury)

1185. Smith, A. M., Scott, S., & Wiese, D. M. (1990). The psychological effects of sports injuries-coping. **Sports Medicine, 9,** 352-369. (Injury)

1186. Smith, A. M., Scott, S., O'Fallon, W., & Young, M. (1990). Emotional responses of athletes to injury. **Mayo Clinic Proceedings, 65,** 38-50. (Injury)

1187. Smith, A. M., Stuart, M. J., Wiese-Bjornstal, D. M., Milliner, E., O'Fallon, W., & Crowson, C. (1993). Competitive athletes: Preinjury and postinjury mood state and self-esteem. **Mayo Clinic Proceedings, 68,** 939-947. (Injury)

1188. Sothmann, M., Horn, T. S., Hart, B. A., & Gustafson, A. B. (1987). Comparison of discrete cardiovascular fitness groups on plasma catecholamine and selected behavioral responses to psychological stress. **Psychophysiology, 24,** 47-54. (Exercise)

1189. Stanton, J., & Arroll, B. (1996). The effect of moderate exercise on mood in mildly hypertensive volunteers: A randomized control study. **Journal of Psychosomatic Research, 40,** 637-642. (Exercise)

1190. Steptoe, A., & Bolton, J. (1988). The short-term influence of high and low intensity physical exercise on mood. **Psychology and Health, 2,** 91-106. (Exercise)

1191. Steptoe, A., & Cox, S. (1988). Acute effects of aerobic exercise on mood. **Journal of Health Psychology, 1,** 329-340. (Exercise)

1192. Steptoe, A., Kearsley, N., & Walters, N. (1993). Acute mood response to maximal and submaximal exercise in active and inactive men. **Psychology and Health, 8**, 89-99. (Exercise)

1193. Steptoe, A., Kearsley, N., & Walters, N. (1993). Cardiovascular activity during mental stress following vigorous exercise in sportsmen and inactive men. **Psychophysiology, 30**, 245-252. (Exercise)

1194. Steptoe, A., Edwards, S., Moses, J., & Mathews, A. (1989). The effects of exercise training on mood and perceived coping ability in anxious adults from the general population. **Journal of Psychosomatic Research, 33**, 537-547. (Exercise)

1195. Stevens, M., & Lane, A. M. (2000). Mood-regulating strategies used by athletes. **Journal of Sports Sciences, 18**, 58-59. (Exercise)

1196. Stevens, M., Lane, A. M., & Terry, P. C. (2001). The impact of response set on measures of mood. **Journal of Sports Sciences, 19**, 82. (Psychometric)

1197. Straub, W.F., Spino, M. P., Alattar, M. M., Pfleger, B., Downes, J. W., Belizaire, M. A., Heinonen O. J., & Vasankari, T. (2001) The effect of chiropractic care on jet lag of Finnish junior elite athletes. **Journal of Manipulative and Physiological Therapeutics, 24**, 191-198. (Various Sports)

1198. Svrakic, D. M., Przybeck, T. R., & Cloninger, C. R. (1992). Mood states and personality traits. **Journal of Affective Disorders, 24**, 217-226. (Psychometric)

1199. Szabo, A., Pdronnet, E, Boudreau, G., Cote, L., Gauvin, L., & Seraganian, P. (1993). Psychophysiological profiles in response to various challenges during recovery from acute aerobic exercise. **International Journal of Psychophysiology, 14**, 285 -292. (Exercise)

1200. Takahashi, A., Suzuki, S., Takahashi, H., & Sato, T. (2000). Effects of amino acid supplementation on endocrine responses and profile of mood states during intermittent exercise for 24 hours. **Japanese Journal of Physical Fitness and Sports Medicine, 49**, 561-569. (Exercise)

1201. Tanaka, H., Dake, G. A., & Bassett, D. R. (1999). Influence of regular swimming on profile of mood states in college students: Transient experiences and quantitative EEG responses. **Japanese Journal of Physical Fitness and Sport, 48**, 447-452. (Swimming)

1202. Terry, P. C. (1994). Pre-performance mood profiles of the England cricket team during the 1993 'ashes' series. **Proceedings of the Commonwealth Scientific Congress.** (Victoria, British Columbia), 11, 213-240. (Cricket)

1203. Terry, P. C. (1994). Mood state profiles as indicators among Olympic and World Championship athletes. In S. Serpa, J. Alves, V. Ferreira, and A. Paulo-Brito (Eds.), **Proceedings of the V111th ISSP World Congress of Sport Psychology** (pp. 963-967). Lisbon, Portugal: ISSP. (Bobsledding, Rowing)

1204. Terry, P. C. (1994). Mood state profiles as indicators of performance among Olympic and World Championship athletes. **Journal of Sports Sciences, 12**, 214. (Bobsledding, Rowing)

1205. Terry, P. C. (1995). The efficacy of mood state profiling with elite performers: A review and synthesis. **The Sport Psychologist, 9**, 309-324. (Review Article)

1206. Terry, P. C. (1995). Discriminant capability of pre-performance mood state profiles during the 1993-1994 World Cup bobsleigh. **Journal of Sports Sciences, 13**, 77-78. (Bobsledding, Rowing)

1207. Terry, P. C. (1996). Discriminant capability of psychological state measures in predicting performance outcome in karate competition. **Journal of Sports Sciences, 14**, 48. (Martial Arts)

1208. Terry, P. C. (2000). Introduction to perspectives on mood in sport and exercise. **Journal of Applied Sport Psychology, 12**, 1-5. (Review Article)

1209. Terry, P. C. (2000). An overview of the relationship between mood and performance in sport. **Australian Journal of Psychology, 52**, S115. (Review Article)

1210. Terry, P. C., & Hall, A. (1996). Development of normative data for the Profile of Mood States for use with athletic samples. **Journal of Sports Sciences, 14,** 47-48. (Exercise, Psychometric)

1211. Terry, P. C., & Lane, A. M. (2000). Development of normative data for the profile of mood states for use with athletic samples. **Journal of Applied Sport Psychology, 12,** 69-85. (Basketball, Swimming)

1212. Terry, P. C., & Slade, A. (1995). Discriminant effectiveness of psychological state measures in predicting performance outcome in karate competition. **Perceptual and Motor Skills, 81,** 275-286. (Martial Arts)

1213. Terry, P. C., & Youngs, E. L. (1996). Discriminant effectiveness of psychological state measures in predicting selection during field hockey trials. **Perceptual and Motor Skills, 82,** 371-377. (Field Hockey)

1214. Terry, P. C., Keohane, L., & Lane, H. J. (1996). Development and validation of a shortened version of the Profile of Mood States suitable for use with young athletes. **Journal of Sports Sciences, 14,** 49. (Psychometric)

1215. Terry, P. C., Lane, A. M., & Warren. L. (1999). Eating attitudes, body shape perceptions and mood of elite rowers. **Journal of Science and Medicine in Sport, 2,** 67-77. (Rowing)

1216. Terry, P. C., Walrond, N., & Carron, A. V. (1998). The influence of game location on athletes' psychological states. **Journal of Medicine and Science in Sport, 1,** 27-39. (Rugby)

1217. Terry, P. C., Lane, A. M., Lane, H. J., & Keohane, L. (1999). Development and validation of a mood measure for adolescents: POMS-A. **Journal of Sports Sciences, 17,** 861-872. (Psychometric)

1218. Terry, P. C., Carron, A. V., Pink, M. J., Lane, A. M., Jones, G. J. W., & Hall, M. P. (2000). Team cohesion and mood in sport. **Group Dynamics: Theory, Research, and Practice, 4,** 244-253. (Netball, Rowing, Rugby)

1219. Tharion, W., McMenemy, D., Terry, A., & Rauch, T. (1990). Recovery of mood changes experienced when running an ultramarathon. **Perceptual and Motor Skills, 71,** 1311-1316. (Ultramarathon/Ultrarunning)

1220. Tharion, W., Strowman, S., & Rauch, T. (1988). Profile of changes in moods of ultramarathoners. **Journal of Sport and Exercise Psychology, 10,** 229-235. (Ultramarathon/Ultrarunning)

1221. Thaxton, L. (1982). Physiological and psychological effects of short-term exercise addiction on habitual runners. **Journal of Sport Psychology, 4,** 73-80. (Running)

1222. Thirlaway, K., & Benton, D. (1992). Participation in physical activity and cardiovascular fitness has different effects on mental health and mood. **Journal of Psychosomatic Research, 36,** 657-665. (Exercise)

1223. Thomas, T. R., Londeree, B., Lawson, D., Ziogas, G., & Cox, R. (1994). Physiological and psychological responses to eccentric exercise. **Canadian Journal of Applied Physiology, 19,** 91-100. (Exercise)

1224. Thomas, T. R., Zebas, C., Bahrke, M. S., Araujo, J., & Etheridge, G. (1980). Physiological and psychological correlates of success in track and field athletes. **British Journal of Sports Medicine, 17,** 102-109. (Track and Field)

1225. Trafton, T. A., Meyers, M. C., & Skelly, W. A. (1997). Psychological characteristics of the telemark skier. **Journal of Sport Behavior, 20,** 465-476. (Skiing)

1226. Toskovic, N. N. (2001). Alterations in selected measures of mood with a single bout of dynamic Taekwando exercise in college-age students. **Perceptual and Motor Skills, 92,** 1031-1038. (Martial Arts)

1227. Usala, P. D., & Hertzog, C. (1989). Measurement of affective states in adults: Evaluation of an adjective rating scale instrument. **Research on Aging, 11,** 403-426. (Psychometric)

1228. Ussher, J. M., & Swann, C. (2000). A double blind placebo controlled trial examining the relationship between health-related quality of life and dietary supplements. **British Journal of Health Psychology, 5,** 173-187. (Psychometric)

1229. Veale, D. (1991). Psychological aspects of staleness and dependence on exercise. **International Journal of Sports Medicine, 12,** S 19-S22. (Exercise)

1230. Verde, T., Thomas, S., & Shephard, R. J. (1992). Potential markers of heavy training in highly trained distance runners. **British Journal of Sports Medicine, 26,** 167-175. (Running)

1231. Vleck, V., Garbutt, G., & Terry, P. C. (1998). Development of triathlon-specific normative data for the Profile of Mood States-C. **Journal of Sports Sciences, 16,** 399. (Triathlon)

1232. Wald, F. D., & Mellenbergh, G. J. (1990). The shortened version of the Dutch translation of the Profile of Mood States. **Nederlands Tijdschrift voor de Psychologie en Haar Grensgebieden, 45,** 86-90. (Psychometric)

1233. Wann, D. L., Inman, S., Ensor, C. L., Gates, R. D., & Caldwell, D. S. (1999). Assessing the psychological well-being of sports fans using the Profile of Mood States: The importance of team identification. **International Sports Journal, 3,** 81-89. (Basketball, Sports Fans)

1234. Watanabe, E., Takeshima, N., Okada, A., & Inomata, K. (2001). Effects of increasing expenditure of energy during exercise on psychological well-being in older adults. **Perceptual and Motor Skills, 92,** 288-298. (Exercise)

1235. Watson, D., & Clark, L. A. (1997). Measurement and mismeasurement of mood: Recurrent and emergent issues. **Journal of Personality Assessment, 68,** 267-296. (Psychometric)

1236. Weckowicz, T. (1978). Review of Profile of Mood States. In O.K. Buros (Ed.), **The eighth mental measurements yearbook, 1,** 1018-1019. (Review Article)

1237. Weinberg, R. S., Jackson, A., & Kolodny, K. (1988). The relationship of massage and exercise to mood enhancement. **The Sport Psychologist, 2**, 202-211. (Exercise)

1238. Wilfley, D., & Kunce, J. (1986). Differential physical and psychological effects of exercise. **Journal of Counseling Psychology, 33**, 337-342. (Exercise)

1239. Williams, J. M., & Getty, D. (1986). Effect of levels of exercise on psychological mood states, physical fitness, and plasma beta-endorphin. **Perceptual and Motor Skills, 63**, 1099-1105. (Exercise)

1240. Williams, T. J., & Krahenbuhl, G. S. (1997). Menstrual cycle phase and running economy. **Medicine and Science in Sports and Exercise, 29**, 1609-1618. (Running)

1241. Williams, T. J., Krahenbuhl, G. S., & Morgan, D. W. (1991). Mood state and running economy in moderately trained male runners. **Medicine and Science in Sports and Exercise, 23**, 727-731. (Running)

1242. Willis, J. D., & Layne, B. H. (1988). A validation study of sport-related motive scales. **Journal of Applied Research in Coaching and Athletics, 3**, 297-307. (Football)

1243. Wilson, V. E., Ainsworth, M., & Bird, E. I. (1985). Assessment of attentional abilities in male volleyball athletes. **International Journal of Sport Psychology, 16**, 296-306. (Volleyball)

1244. Wilson, V. E., Morley, N., & Bird, E. I. (1980). Mood profiles of marathon runners, joggers and non-exercisers. **Perceptual and Motor Skills, 50**, 117-118. (Marathon, Running)

1245. Wilson-Fearon, C., & Parrott, A. C. (1999). Multiple drug use and dietary restraint in a Mr. Universe competitor: Psychobiological effects. **Perceptual and Motor Skills, 88**, 579-580. (Bodybuilding, Steroids/Drugs)

1246. Wittig, A. F., Houmard, J., & Costill, D. L. (1989). Psychological effects during reduced training in distance runners. **International Journal of Sports Medicine, 10**, 97-100. (Marathon, Running)

1247. Wittig, A. F., McConnell, G. K., Costill, D. L., & Schurr, K. T. (1992). Psychological effects during reduced training volume and intensity in distance runners. **International Journal of Sports Medicine, 13,** 497-499. (Running)

1248. Wormington, J., Cockerill, I. M., & Nevill, A. M. (1992). Mood alterations with running: The effects of mileage, gender, age and ability. **Journal of Human Movement Studies, 22,** 1-12. (Running)

1249. Wughalter, E., & Gondola, J. C. (1991). Mood states of professional female tennis players. **Perceptual and Motor Skills, 73,** 187-190. (Tennis)

1250. Yates, A., Shisslak, C. M., Allender, J., Crago, M., & Leehey, K. (1992). Comparing obligatory and nonobligatory runners. **Psychosomatics, 33,** 180-189. (Running)

1251. Yeung, R. R. (1996). The acute effects of exercise on mood state. **Journal of Psychosomatic Research, 40,** 123-141. (Exercise)

S-R Inventory of General Trait Anxiousness

1252. Fisher, A. C., & Zwart, E. F. (1982). Psychological analysis of athletes' anxiety responses. **Journal of Sport Psychology, 4,** 139-158. (Basketball)

1253. Fisher, A. C., Horsfall, J. S., Morris, H. H. (1977). Sport personality assessment: A methodological re-examination. **International Journal of Sport Psychology, 8,** 92-102. (Basketball)

1254. Flood, M., & Endler, N. S. (1980). Interaction model of anxiety: An empirical test in an athletic competition. **Journal of Research in Personality, 14,** 329-339. (Track and Field)

1255. Griffiths, T. J., Steel, D. H., & Vaccaro, P. (1982). Anxiety of scuba divers: A multidimensional approach. **Perceptual and Motor Skills, 55,** 611-614. (Scuba)

1256. Vitelli, R., & Frisch, G. R. (1982). Relationship between trait anxiety and leisure time activities: A comparison of the unidimensional and multidimensional models of anxiety, **Perceptual and Motor Skills, 52,** 371-376. (Psychometric)

State Trait Anxiety Inventory (STAI)

1257. Abadie, B. R. (1988). Relating trait anxiety to perceived physical fitness. **Perceptual and Motor Skills, 67**, 539-543. (Exercise)

1258. Annesi, J. J. (1997). Three-dimensional state anxiety recall: Implications for individual zone of optimal functioning research and application. **The Sport Psychologist, 11**, 43-52. (Field Hockey, Gymnastics)

1259. Annesi, J. J. (2000). Effects of minimal exercise and cognitive behavior modification on adherence, emotion change, self-image, and physical change in obese women. **Perceptual and Motor Skills, 91**, 322-326. (Exercise)

1260. Anshel, M. H. (1985). The effect of arousal on warm-up decrement. **Research Quarterly, 5**, 1-9. (Cyling)

1261. Bahrke, M. S., & Thomas, T. R. (1986). Mood alterations following aerobic exercise withdrawal. **Indiana Alliance for Health, Physical Education, Recreation and Dance Journal, 15**(2), 8-10. (Exercise)

1262. Beer, J. (1989). Relations of moderate physical exercise to scores on hostility, aggression, and trait-anxiety. **Perceptual and Motor Skills, 68**, 1191-1194. (Running)

1263. Berger, B. G., & Owen, D. R. (1987). Anxiety reduction with swimming: Relationships between exercise and state, trait, and somatic anxiety. **International Journal of Sport Psychology, 81**, 286-302. (Swimming)

1264. Berger, B. G., & Owen, D. R. (1992). Preliminary analysis of a causal relationship between swimming and stress reduction: Intense exercise may negate the effects. **International Journal of Sport Psychology, 23**, 70-85. (Swimming)

1265. Blais, M. R., & Vallerand R. J. (1986). Multimodal effects of electromyographic biofeedback: Looking at children's ability to control precompetitive anxiety. **Journal of Sport Psychology, 8**, 283-303. (Biofeedback, Psychometric, Youth)

1266. Blumenthal, J. A., Williams, R. S., Needels, T. L., & Wallace, A. G. (1982). Psychological changes accompany aerobic exercise in healthy middle-aged adults. **Psychosomatic Medicine, 44,** 529-536. (Exercise)

1267. Brandon, J. E., & Loftin, J. M. (1991). Relationship of fitness to depression, state and trait anxiety, internal health locus of control, and self-control. **Perceptual and Motor Skills, 73,** 563-568. (Cycling)

1268. Breivik, G., Roth, W. T., & Jorgensen, P. E. (1998). Personality, psychological states and heart rate in non-expert parachutists. **Personality and Individual Differences, 25,** 365-380. (Skydiving)

1269. Brewer, B. W., & Petrie, T. A. (1995). A comparison between injured and uninjured football players on selected psychosocial variables. **The Academic Athletic Journal,** Spring, 11-18. (Football, Injury)

1270. Brown, D. R., Morgan, W. P., & Raglin, J. S. (1993). Effects of exercise and rest on state anxiety and blood pressure of physically challenged college students. **Journal of Sports Medicine and Physical Fitness, 33,** 300-305. (Exercise)

1271. Brunelle, J. P., Janelle, C. M., & Tennant, L. K. (1999). Controlling competitive anger among male soccer players. **Journal of Applied Sport Psychology, 11,** 283-297. (Soccer)

1272. Bull, S. J. (1989). The role of the sport psychology consultant: A case study of ultra distance running. **The Sport Psychologist, 3,** 254-264. (Ultramarathon/Ultrarunning)

1273. Burke, S. T., & Jin, P. (1996). Predicting performance from a triathlon event. **Journal of Sport Behavior, 19,** 272-287. (Triathlon)

1274. Burton, E. C. (1971). State and trait anxiety, achievement motivation and skill attainment in college women. **Research Quarterly, 42,** 139-144. (Bowling)

1275. Carter, J. E. & Kelley, A. E. (1997). Using traditional and paradoxical imagery interventions with reactant intramural athletes. **The Sport Psychologist, 11,** 175-189. (Basketball, Intramural Sports)

1276. Cheung, S. Y., & Lo, C. (1996). Psychological profiles and stress management training for Hong Kong national gymnasts. **Journal of the International Council for Health, Physical Education, Recreation, Sport, and Dance, 32**(4), 61-64. (Gymnastics)

1277. Clingman, J. M., & Hilliard, D. V. (1994). Anxiety reduction in competitive running as a function of success. **Journal of Sport Behavior, 17**, 120-129. (Running)

1278. Colley, A., Roberts, N., & Chipps, A. (1985). Sex-role identity, personality and participation in team and individual sports by males and females. **International Journal of Sport Psychology, 16**, 103-112. (Various Sports)

1279. Cooley, E. J. (1987). Situational and trait determinants of competitive state anxiety. **Perceptual and Motor Skills, 64**, 767-773. (Tennis)

1280. Corbin, C. B. (1980). Effects of success-failure and opponents perceived ability on predictions of performance by males in cross-sex competition. **Perceptual and Motor Skills, 50**, 247-254. (Table Tennis)

1281. Corbin, C. B., Barnett, M. A., & Matthews, K. A. (1979). The effects of direct and indirect competition on children's state anxiety. **Journal of Leisure Research, 11**, 271-277. (Table Tennis)

1282. Corr, P. J., & Gray, J. A. (1996). Structure and validity of the attributional style questionnaire: A cross-sample comparison. **Journal of Psychology, 130**, 645-657. (Psychometric)

1283. Delignieres, D., Marcellini, A., & Brisswalter, J. (1994). Self-perception of fitness and personality traits. **Perceptual and Motor Skills, 78**, 843-851. (Physical Education Class(Es)

1284. DeMoja, C. A., & Reitano, M., & DeMarco, P. (1987). Anxiety, perceptual and motor skills in an underwater environment. **Perceptual and Motor Skills, 65**, 359-365. (Scuba)

1285. DeMoja, C. A., & DeMoja, G. (1986). Analysis of anxiety trend before a sport competition. **Perceptual and Motor Skills, 62**, 406. (Motorcross)

1286. DeMoja, C. A., & DeMoja, G. (1986). State-trait anxiety and motorcross performance. **Perceptual and Motor Skills, 62,** 107-110. (Motorcross)

1287. DiLorenzo, T. M., Bargman, E. P., Stucky-Ropp, R., Brassington, G. S., Frensch, P. A., & LaFontaine, T. (1999). Long-term effects of aerobic exercise on psychological outcomes. **Preventive Medicine, 28,** 75-85. (Exercise)

1288. Dishman, R. K., Farquhar, R. P., & Cureton, K. J. (1994). Responses to preferred intensities of exertion in men differing in activity levels. **Medicine and Science in Sports and Exercise, 26,** 783-790. (Exercise)

1289. Dudley, G., & Callister, R. (1990). Psychological and performance concomitants of increased volume training in elite athletes. **Journal of Applied Sport Psychology, 2,** 34-50. (Martial Arts)

1290. Eensoo, D., Harro, J., Harro, M., Rimm, H., & Viru, A. M. (2000). Depressiveness, anxiety, perceived stress and self-efficacy in middle-aged men with different engagement in physical activity. **Medicine Della Sport, 53,** 69-74. (Exercise)

1291. Ekkekakis, P., Hall, E. E., & Petruzzello, S. J. (1999). Measuring state anxiety in the context of acute exercise using the State Anxiety Inventory: An attempt to resolve the brouhaha. **Journal of Sport & Exercise Psychology, 21,** 205-229. (Exercise)

1292. Ewert, A. (1988). Reduction of trait anxiety through participation in outward bound. **Leisure Sciences, 10,** 107-117. (Leisure Activity)

1293. Ferreira, R. & Murray, J. (1983). Spielberger's state-trait anxiety inventory: Measuring anxiety with and without an audience during performance on a stabilometer. **Perceptual and Motor Skills, 57,** 15-18. (Motor Task)

1294. Filaire, E., LeScanff, C., Duche, P., & Lac, G. (1999). The relationship between salivary adrenocortical hormones changes during handball and volleyball competition. **Research Quarterly for Exercise and Sport, 70,** 297-301. (Handball, Volleyball)

1295. Filaire, E., Sagnol, M., Ferrand, C., Maso, G., & Lac, G. (2001). Psychophysiological stress in judo athletes during competitions. **Journal of Sports Medicine and Physical Fitness, 41**, 263-268. (Martial Arts)

1296. Focht, B. C., Koltyn, K. F., & Bouchard, L. J. (2000). State anxiety and blood pressure responses following different resistance exercise sessions. **International Journal of Sport Psychology, 31**, 376-390. (Exercise)

1297. Foster, Y. A. (1997). Brief Aikido training versus karate and golf training and university students' scores on self-esteem, anxiety, and expression of anger. **Perceptual and Motor Skills, 84**, 609-610. (Golf, Martial Arts)

1298. Francis, K. T., & Carter, R. (1982). Psychological characteristic of joggers. **Journal of Sports Medicine, 22**, 386-391. (Running)

1299. Freedson, P., Mihevic, P., Loucks, A., & Girandola, R. (1983). Physique, body composition, and psychological characteristics of competitive body builders. **Physician and Sportsmedicine, 11**(5), 85-93. (Bodybuilding)

1300. Fung, L., & Fu, F. H. (1995). Psychological determinants between wheelchair sport finalists and non-finalists. **International Journal of Sport Psychology, 26**, 568-579. (Disabled Athletes, Swimming, Table Tennis, Track and Field)

1301. Gemar, J. A., & Bynum, R. F. (1990). The effect of weight training and jogging on trait anxiety. **Wellness Perspectives: Research Theory and Practice, 7**, 13-20. (Running, Weight Training)

1302. Gill, D. L. (1980). Comparison of three measures of pre-competition arousal. **Perceptual and Motor Skills, 51**, 765-766. (Volleyball)

1303. Gould, D., Weinberg, R. S., & Jackson, A. (1980). Mental preparation strategies, cognitions, and strength performance. **Journal of Sport Psychology, 2**, 329-339. (Motor Task)

1304. Griffiths, T. J., Steel, D. H., & Vaccaro, P. (1978). Anxiety levels of beginning SCUBA students. **Perceptual and Motor Skills, 47**, 312-314. (Scuba)

1305. Griffiths, T. J., Steel, D. H., & Vaccaro, P. (1979). Relationship between anxiety and performance in scuba diving. **Perceptual and Motor Skills, 48,** 1009-1010. (Scuba)

1306. Griffiths, T. J., Steel, D. H., & Vaccaro, P. (1982). Anxiety of scuba divers: A multidimensional approach. **Perceptual and Motor Skills, 55,** 611-614. (Scuba)

1307. Griffiths, T. J., Steel, D. H., Vaccaro, P., & Karpman, M. B. (1981). The effects of relaxation techniques on anxiety and underwater performance. **International Journal of Sport Psychology, 12,** 176-182. (Scuba)

1308. Griffiths, T. J., Steel, D. H., Vaccaro, P., & Ostrove, S. M. (1987). Psychological implications for underwater archaeologists. **International Journal of Sport Psychology, 18,** 1-8. (Scuba)

1309. Griffiths, T. J., Steel, D. H., Vaccaro, P., Allen, R., & Karpman, M. (1985). The effects of relaxation and cognitive rehearsal on the anxiety levels and performance of scuba students. **International Journal of Sport Psychology, 16,** 113-119. (Scuba)

1310. Hall, E. G. (1980). Comparison of postperformance state anxiety of internals and externals following failure or success on a simple motor task. **Research Quarterly for Exercise and Sport, 51,** 306-314. (Motor Task)

1311. Hall, E. G., Church, G. E., & Stone, M. (1980). Relationship of birth order to selected personality characteristics of nationally ranked Olympic weight lifters. **Perceptual and Motor Skills, 51,** 971-976. (Weightlifting)

1312. Halvari, H., & Gjesme, T. (1995). Trait and state anxiety before and after competitive performance. **Perceptual and Motor Skills, 81,** 1059-1074. (Motor Task)

1313. Harger, G. J., & Raglin, J. S. (1994). Correspondence between actual and recalled precompetition anxiety in collegiate track and field athletes. **Journal of Sport & Exercise Psychology, 16,** 206-211. (Track and Field)

1314. Head, A., Kendall, M. J., Ferner, R., & Eagles, C. (1996). Acute effects of β blockade and exercise on mood and anxiety. **British Journal of Sport Medicine, 30**, 238-242. (Exercise)

1315. Heiby, E. M., Onorato, V. A. & Sato, R. (1987). Cross-validation of the Self- Motivation Inventory. **Journal of Sport Psychology, 9**, 394-399. (Running)

1316. Henschen, K. P., Horvat, M., & French, R. (1984). A visual comparison of psychological profiles between able-bodied and wheelchair athletes. **Adapted Physical Education Quarterly, 1**, 118-124. (Disabled Athletes)

1317. Henschen, K. P., Horvat, M., & Roswal, G. (1992). Psychological profiles of the United States wheelchair basketball team. **International Journal of Sport Psychology, 23**, 128-137. (Basketball, Disabled Athletes)

1318. Hinkle, J. S., Lyons, B., & Burke, K. L. (1989). Manifestation of type a behavior pattern among aerobic runners. **Journal of Sport Behavior, 12**, 131-138. (Running)

1319. Imlay, G. J., Carda, R. D., Stanbrough, M. E., Dreiling, A. M., & O'Connor, P. J. (1995). Anxiety and athletic performance: A test of zone of optimal function theory. **International Journal of Sport Psychology, 26**, 295-306. (Track and Field)

1320. Jones, J. G. (1995). More than just a game: Research developments and issues in competitive anxiety in sport. **British Journal of Psychology, 86**, 449-478. (Review Article)

1321. Jones, J. G., & Hardy, L. (1988). The effects of anxiety upon psychomotor performance. **Journal of Sport Sciences, 6**, 59-67. (Motor Task)

1322. Kerr, G. A. & Goss, J. D. (1997). Personal control in elite gymnasts: The relationships between locus of control, self-esteem, and trait anxiety. **Journal of Sport Behavior, 20**, 69-82. (Gymnastics)

1323. Kerr, G. A., & Minden, H. A. (1988). Psychological factors related to the occurrence of athletic injuries. **Journal of Sport and Exercise Psychology, 10**, 167-173. (Gymnastics)

1324. Kleine, D. (1990). Anxiety and sport performance: A meta-analysis. **Anxiety Research, 2,** 113-131. (Psychometrics, Review Article)

1325. Koltyn, K. F., Lynch, N. A., & Hill, D. W. (1998). Psychological responses to brief exhaustive cycling exercise in the morning and evening. **International Journal of Sport Psychology, 29,** 145-156. (Exercise)

1326. Koltyn, K. F., Raglin, J. S., O'Connor, P. J., & Morgan, W. P. (1995). Influence of weight training on state anxiety, body awareness and blood pressure. **International Journal of Sports Medicine, 16,** 266-269. (Weight Training)

1327. Koltyn, K. F., & Schultes, S. S. (1997). Psychological effects of an aerobic exercise session and a rest session following pregnancy. **Journal of Sports Medicine and Physical Fitness, 37,** 287-291. (Exercise)

1328. Kowal, D. M., Patton, J. F., & Vogel, J. A. (1978). Psychological states and aerobic fitness of male and female recruits before and after basic training. **Aviation, Space, and Environmental Medicine,** April, 603-606. (Exercise)

1329. Kroll, W. (1979). The stress of high performance athletics. In P. Klavora & J. Daniel (Eds.), **Coach, athlete and the sport psychologist** (pp. 211-219). Champaign, IL: Human Kinetics. (Review Article)

1330. Krotee, M. L. (1980). Effects of various physical activity situational settings on the anxiety level of children. **Journal of Sport Behavior, 3,** 158-164. (Running)

1331. Labbe, E. E., Welsh, M. C., & Delaney, D. (1988). Effects of consistent aerobic exercise on the psychological functioning of women. **Perceptual and Motor Skills, 67,** 919-925. (Exercise)

1332. LaGuardia, R., & Labbe, E. E. (1993). Self-efficacy and anxiety and their relationship to training and race performance. **Perceptual and Motor Skills, 77,** 27-34. (Running)

1333. Landers, D. M., Boutcher, S. H., & Wang, M. Q. (1986). A psychobiological study of archery performance. **Research Quarterly, 57,** 236-244. (Archery)

1334. Layton, C. (1986). Test-retest characteristics of state-trait anxiety inventory, A-state scale. **Perceptual and Motor Skills, 62,** 586. (Psychometric)

1335. Layton, C. (1990). Anxiety in black-belt and nonblack-belt traditional karateka. **Perceptual and Motor Skills, 71,** 905-906. (Martial Arts)

1336. Layton, C. (2000). Scores on trait and state anxiety of female karateka before the commencement of shotokan karate training. **Perceptual and Motor Skills, 91,** 1020. (Martial Arts)

1337. Leddy, M. H., Lambert, M. J., & Ogles, B. M. (1994). Psychological consequences of athletic injury among high-level competitors. **Research Quarterly for Exercise and Sport, 65,** (Injury, Various Sports)

1338. Legros, P. (1994). Self-perception of fitness and personality traits. **Perceptual and Motor Skills, 78,** 843-851. (Exercise)

1339. Levine, H. G., & Langness, L. L. (1983). Context, ability, and performance: Comparison of competitive athletics among mildly mentally retarded and nonretarded adults. **American Journal of Mental Deficiency, 87,** 528-538. (Disabled Athletes)

1340. Long, B. C. (1984). Aerobic conditioning and stress inoculation: A comparison of stress-management interventions. **Cognitive Therapy and Research, 8,** 517-542. (Exercise)

1341. Long, B. C. (1985). Stress-management interventions: A 15-month follow-up of aerobic conditioning and stress inoculation training. **Cognitive Therapy and Research, 9,** 471-478. (Exercise)

1342. Long, B. C., & Stavel, R. V. (1995). Effects of exercise training on anxiety: A meta-analysis. **Journal of Applied Sport Psychology, 7,** 167-189. (Psychometric, Review article)

1343. Mace, R. D., & Carroll, D. (1985). The control of anxiety in sport: Stress inoculation training prior to abseiling. **International Journal of Sport Psychology, 16,** 165- 175. (Abseiling)

159

1344. Mahler, D. A. (1994). Psychological components of effort sense. **Medicine and Science in Sports and Exercise, 26**, 1071-1077. (Exercise)

1345. Man, F., Stuchlikova, I., & Kindlmann, P. (1995). Trait-state anxiety, worry, emotionality, and self-confidence in top-level soccer players. **The Sport Psychologist, 9**, 212-224. (Soccer)

1346. Martens, R., Gill, D. L., & Scanlan, T. K. (1976). Competitive trait anxiety, success-failure and sex as determinants of motor performance. **Perceptual and Motor Skills, 43**, 1199-1208. (Exercise)

1347. Martin, J. D., Blair, G. E. & Hatzel, D. J. (1987). Rorschach correlates of state and trait anxiety in college students. **Perceptual and Motor Skills, 64**, 539-543. (Psychometric)

1348. Mastro, J. V., & French, R. (1984). Sport anxiety and elite blind athletes. In C. Sherrill (Ed.), **Sport and disabled athletes: The 1984 Olympic scientific congress proceedings**, (Vol. 9), Champaign, IL: Human Kinetics. (Disabled Athletes)

1349. Mastro, J. V., French, R., Henschen, K. P., & Horvat, M. (1985). Use of the state-trait anxiety inventory for visually impaired athletes. **Perceptual and Motor Skills, 61**, 775- 778. (Various Sports)

1350. Mears, J. D., & Cleary, P. J. (1980). Anxiety as a factor in underwater performance. **Ergonomics, 23**, 549-557. (Scuba)

1351. Miller, B. P., & Miller, A. J. (1985). Psychological correlates of success in elite sportswomen. **International Journal of Sport Psychology, 16**, 289-295. (Netball)

1352. Missoum, G., Rosnet, E., & Richalet, J. P. (1992). Control anxiety and acute mountain sickness in Himalayan mountaineers. **International Journal of Sports Medicine, 13**, S37-S39. (Mountain Climbing)

1353. Mondin, G. W., Morgan, W. P., Piering, P. N., Stegner, A. J., Stotesbery, C. L., Trine, M. R., & Wu, M. (1996). Psychological consequences of exercise deprivation in habitual exercisers. **Medicine and Science in Sports and Exercise, 28**, 1199-1203. (Exercise)

1354. Morgan, W. P., (1995). Anxiety and panic in recreational scuba divers. **Sports Medicine, 20**, 398-421. (Scuba)

1355. Morgan, W. P., & Johnson, R. W. (1978). Personality characteristics of successful and unsuccessful oarsmen. **International Journal of Sport Psychology, 9**, 119-133. (Rowing)

1356. Morgan, W. P., & Pollock, M. L. (1977). Psychologic characterization of the elite distance runner. **Annals of the New York Academy of Sciences, 301**, 382-403. (Running)

1357. Morgan, W. P., O'Connor, P. J., Ellickson, K. A. & Bradley, P. W. (1988). Personality structure, mood states, and performance in elite male distance runners. **International Journal of Sport Psychology, 19**, 247-263. (Running)

1358. Morgan, W. P., O'Connor, P. J., Sparling, P. B., & Pate, R. R. (1987). Psychological characterization of the elite female distance runner. **International Journal of Sports Medicine, 8**, 124-131. (Running)

1359. Muraki, S., Tsunawake, N., Hiramatsu, S., & Yamasaki, M. (2000). The effect of frequency and mode of sports activity on the psychological status in tetraplegics and paraplegics. **Spinal Cord, 38**, 309-314. (Exercise)

1360. Myung Woo, H. (1996). Psychological profiles of Korean elite judoists. **American Journal of Sports Medicine, 24**, S67-S71. (Martial Arts)

1361. Naruse, K., & Hirai, T. (2000). Effects of slow tempo exercise on respiration, heart rate, and mood state. **Perceptual and Motor Skills, 91**, 729-740. (Exercise)

1362. Newcombe, P. A., & Boyle, G. J. (1995). High school students' sports personalities: Variations across participation level, gender, type of sport, and success. **International Journal of Sport Psychology, 26,** 277-294. (Various Sports)

1363. Nowlis, D. P., & Greenberg, N. (1979). Empirical description of effects of exercise on mood. **Perceptual and Motor Skills, 49,** 1001-1002. (Running)

1364. O'Connor, P. J., Raglin, J. S., & Morgan, W. P. (1996). Psychometric correlates of perception during arm ergometry in males and females. **International Journal of Sports Medicine, 17,** 462-466. (Exercise)

1365. O'Connor, P. J., Bryant, C. X., Veltri, J. P., & Gebhardt. S. M. (1993). State anxiety and ambulatory blood pressure following resistance exercise in females. **Medicine and Science in Sports and Exercise, 25,** 516-521. (Exercise)

1366. O'Connor, P. J., Petruzzello, S. J., Kubitz, K. A., & Robinson, T. L. (1995). Anxiety responses to maximal exercise testing. **British Journal of Sport Medicine, 29,** 97-102. (Exercise)

1367. Owen, H., & Lanning, W. (1982). The effects of three treatment methods upon anxiety and inappropriate attentional style among high school athletes. **International Journal of Sport Psychology, 13,** 154-162. (Various Sports)

1368. Palleschi, L., DeGennaro, E., Sottosanti, G., Vetta, F., Ronzoni, S., Lato, P. F. A., & Marigliano, V. (1998). The role of exercise training in aged subjects with anxiety-depression syndrome. **Archives of Gerontology and Geriatrics, 6,** 381-384. (Exercise)

1369. Pemberton, C. L., & Cox, R. H. (1981). Consolidation theory and the effects of stress and anxiety on motor behavior. **International Journal of Sport Psychology, 12,** 131-139. (Motor Task)

1370. Peters, M. L., Turner, S. M., & Blanchard, E. B. (1996). The effects of aerobic exercise on chronic tension-type headache. **Headache Quarterly-Current Treatment and Research, 7,** 330-334. (Exercise)

1371. Petruzzello, S. J., & Landers, D. M. (1994). State anxiety reduction and exercise: Does hemispheric activation reflect such changes? **Medicine and Science in Sports and Exercise, 26**, 1028-1035. (Exercise)

1372. Piedmont, R. L. (1988). The relationship between achievement, motivation, anxiety, and situational characteristics on performance in a cognitive task. **Journal of Research in Personality, 22**, 177-187. (Exercise)

1373. Porat, Y., Lufi, D., & Tenenbaum, G. (1989). Psychological components contribute to select young female gymnasts. **International Journal of Sport Psychology, 20**, 279-286. (Gymnastics)

1374. Porretta, D. L., Moore, W., & Sappenfield. C. (1992). Situational anxiety in special Olympic athletes. **Palaestra, 8**, 46-50. (Disabled Athletes)

1375. Poteet, D., & Weinberg, R. S. (1980). Competition trait anxiety, state anxiety, and performance. **Perceptual and Motor Skills, 50**, 651-654. (Weight Training)

1376. Powell, F. M., & Verner, J. P. (1982). Anxiety and performance relationships in first time parachutists. **Journal of Sport Psychology, 4**, 184-188. (Skydiving)

1377. Power, S. L. (1986). Psychological assessment procedures of a track and field national event squad weekend. In J. Watkins, T. Reilly, & L. Burwitz (Eds.), **Sports science**. New York: E & FN Spon. (Track and Field)

1378. Raglin, J. S., & Morgan, W. P. (1987). Influence of exercise and quiet rest on state anxiety and blood pressure. **Medicine and Science in Sports and Exercise, 19**, 456-463. (Exercise)

1379. Raglin, J. S., & Morgan, W. P. (1988). Predicted and actual pre-competition anxiety in college swimmers. **Journal of Swimming Research, 4**(2), 5-7. (Swimming)

1380. Raglin, J. S., & Morris, J. (1994). Precompetition anxiety in women volleyball players: A test of ZOF theory in a team sport. **British Journal of Sports Medicine, 28**, 47-51. (Volleyball)

1381. Raglin, J. S., & Turner, P. E. (1993). Anxiety and performance in track and field athletes: A comparison of the inverted-U hypothesis with the zone of optimal function theory. **Personality and Individual Differences, 14,** 163-171. (Track and Field)

1382. Raglin, J. S., & Wilson, M. (1996). State anxiety following 20 minutes of bicycle ergometry exercise at selected intensities. **International Journal of Sports Medicine, 17,** 467-471. (Exercise)

1383. Reilly, T., & Walsh, T. J. (1981). Physiological, psychological and performance measures during an endurance record for a 5-A-Side soccer play. **British Journal of Sports Medicine, 15,** 122-128. (Soccer)

1384. Rejeski, W. J., Hardy, C. J., & Shaw, J. (1991). Psychometric confounds of assessing state anxiety in conjunction with acute bouts of vigorous exercise. **Journal of Sport & Exercise Psychology, 13,** 65-74. (Exercise)

1385. Robertson, K., & Mellor, S., & Hughes, M., & Sanderson, F. H., & Reilly, T. (1988). Psychological health and squash play. **Ergonomics, 31,** 1567-1572. (Squash)

1386. Rodrigo, G., Lusiardo, M., & Pereira, G. (1990). Relationship between anxiety and performance in soccer players. **International Journal of Sport Psychology, 21,** 112-120. (Soccer)

1387. Ryska, T. A. (1993). The relationship between trait and precompetitive state anxiety among high school athletes. **Perceptual and Motor Skills, 76,** 431-414. (Tennis)

1388. Sanderson, F. H., & Ashton, M. K. (1981). Analysis of anxiety levels before and after badminton competition. **International Journal of Sport Psychology, 12,** 23-28. (Badminton)

1389. Sargunaraj, D., & Kumaraiah, V. (1991). The reliability of translations of STAI, CSAQ, EPI, and I-E Scale. **Journal of Personality and Clinical Studies, 7,** 99-101. (Psychometric)

1390. Scanlan, T. K., & Passer, M. W. (1978). Factors related to competitive stress among male youth sport participants. **Medicine and Science in Sports, 10**, 103-108. (Soccer)

1391. Scanlan, T. K., & Passer, M. W. (1979). Sources of competitive stress in young female athletes. **Journal of Sport Psychology, 1**, 151-159. (Soccer)

1392. Schwartz, G. E., Davidson, R. J., & Goleman, D. J. (1978). Patterning of cognitive and somatic processes in the self-regulation of anxiety: Effects of meditation versus exercise. **Psychosomatic Medicine, 40**, 321-328. (Exercise)

1393. Senkfor, A. J., & Williams, J. M. (1995). The moderating effects of aerobic fitness and mental training on stress reactivity. **Journal of Sport Behavior, 18**, 130-156. (Exercise)

1394. Silva, J. M., Shultz, B. B., Haslam, R.W., & Murray, D. F. (1981). A psychological assessment of elite wrestlers. **Research Quarterly, 52**, 348-358. (Wrestling)

1395. Silva, J. M., Shultz, B. B., Haslam, R.W., Martin, T. P., & Murray, D. F. (1985). Discriminating characteristics of contestants at the United States Olympic wrestling trials. **International Journal of Sport Psychology, 16**, 79-102. (Wrestling)

1396. Sonstroem, R. J., & Bernardo, P. (1982). Intraindividual pregame state anxiety and basketball performance: A re-examination of the inverted-U curve. **Journal of Sport Psychology, 4**, 235-245. (Basketball)

1397. Sothmann, M. S., Horn, T. S., Hart, B. A., & Gustafson, A. B. (1987). Comparison of discrete cardiovascular fitness groups on plasma catecholamine and selected behavioral responses to psychological stress. **Psychophysiology, 24**, 47-54. (Exercise)

1398. Spano, L. (2001). The relationship between exercise and anxiety, obsessive-compulsiveness, and narcissism. **Personality and Individual Differences, 30**, 87-93. (Exercise)

1399. Spielberger, C. D. (1973). **State-trait anxiety inventory for children: Preliminary manual.** Palo Alto, Calif.: Consulting Psychologists Press.

1400. Spielberger, C. D., Gorsuch, R. L., & Lushene, R. E. (1970). **Manual for the State-Trait Anxiety Inventory.** Palo Alto, Calif.: Consulting Psychologists Press. (Test Manual)

1401. Starek, J., & McCullagh, P. (1999). The effect of self-modeling on the performance of beginning swimmers. **The Sport Psychologist, 13,** 269-287. (Swimming)

1402. Steptoe, A., Edwards, S., Moses, J., & Mathews, A. (1989). The effects of exercise training on mood and perceived coping ability in anxious adults from the general population. **Journal of Psychosomatic Research, 33,** 537-547. (Exercise)

1403. Subhan, S., & White, J. A., & Kane, J. (1987). The influence of exercise on stress states using psychophysiological indices. **Journal of Sports Medicine, 27,** 223-229. (Exercise)

1404. Sugiyama, Y., & Ichimura, S. (1994). Preference for practicing location in table tennis classes and students' personalities. **Perceptual and Motor Skills, 79,** 195-199. (Table Tennis)

1405. Sugiyama, Y., Shiraki, H., & Ichimura, S. (1994). Relation of preference for location with scores on anxiety and on visibility in golf practice. **Perceptual and Motor Skills, 79,** 812-814. (Golf)

1406. Takemura, Y., Kikuchi, S., & Inaba, Y. (1999). Does psychological stress improve physical performance? **Tohoku Journal of Experimental Medicine, 187,** 111-120. (Exercise)

1407. Turner, P. E., & Raglin, J. S. (1996). Variability in precompetition anxiety and performance in college track and field athletes. **Medicine and Science in Sports and Exercise, 28,** 378-385. (Track and Field)

1408. Vitelli, R., & Frisch, G. R. (1982). Relationship between trait anxiety and leisure time activities: A comparison of the unidimensional and multidimensional models of anxiety. **Perceptual and Motor Skills, 54**, 371-376. (Leisure Activity)

1409. Wagner, A. M., & Houlihan, D. D. (1994). Sensation seeking and trait anxiety in hang glider pilots and golfers. **Personality and Individual Differences, 16**, 975-977. (Golf, Hang Gliding)

1410. Weinberg, R. S., Seabourne, T. G., & Jackson, A. (1981). Effects of visuo-motor behavior rehearsal, relaxation, and imagery on karate performance. **Journal of Sport Psychology, 3**, 228-238. (Martial Arts)

1411. Wilfley, D., & Kunce, J. (1986). Differential physical and psychological effects of exercise. **Journal of Counseling Psychology, 33**, 337-342. (Exercise)

1412. Williams, J. M., Tonymon, P., & Andersen, M. B. (1991). The effects of stressors and coping resources on anxiety and peripheral narrowing. **Journal of Applied Sport Psychology, 3**, 126-141. (Physical Education Class(es)

1413. Wilson, G. S., Raglin, J. S., & Harger, G. J. (2000). A comparison of the STAI and CSAI-2 in five-day recalls of precompetition anxiety in collegiate track and field athletes. **Scandinavian Journal of Medicine and Science in Sports, 10**, 51-54. (Track and Field)

1414. Wilson, V. E., Berger, B. G., & Bird, E. I. (1981). Effects of running and of an exercise class on anxiety. **Perceptual and Motor Skills, 53**, 472-474. (Exercise)

SECTION THREE
SPORT-SPECIFIC MEASURES

Over the years, there has been an awareness that the standard psychometric inventories that had been used in sport and exercise research were often inadequate or inappropriate. As a result, there has been a substantial increase in the creation of instruments normed on and intended for use with athletes and exercise participants. These instruments are called sport-specific and they attempt to assess a broad range of sport-related constructs. Among the broad areas in which sport-specific assessment devices have been created are aggression, anxiety, attributions, group cohesion, sport leadership, mental skills, motivation, and self-concept. Also, the assessment of more specific aspects of sport and exercise participation has been undertaken, and include such areas as athletic identity, competitive orientation, flow, negative addiction, pain, and attentional style, just to name a few. Clearly, these instruments represent an exciting addition to the assessment repertoire of the sport and exercise psychologist.

CHAPTER TWELVE

AGGRESSION

Bredemeier Athletic Aggression Inventory (BAAGI)

1415. Mintah, J. D., Huddleston, S., & Doody, S. G. (1999). Justifications of aggressive behavior in contact and semi-contact sports. **Journal of Applied Social Psychology, 29,** 597-605. (Various Sports)

1416. Sachs, M. L. (1978). Analysis of aggression in female softball players. **Review of Sports and Leisure, 3,** 85-97. (Softball)

1417. Wall, B. R., & Gruber, J. J. (1985). Relationships between anxiety and aggression inventory scores in women's intercollegiate basketball. **Kansas Alliance for Health, Physical Education, Recreation and Dance Journal, 21,** 2-3. (Basketball)

1418. Wall, B. R., & Gruber, J. J. (1986). Relevancy of athletic aggression inventory for use in women's intercollegiate basketball: A pilot investigation. **International Journal of Sport Psychology, 17,** 23-33. (Basketball)

1419. Worrell, G. L., & Harris, D. V. (1986). The relationship of perceived and observed aggression of ice hockey players. **International Journal of Sport Psychology, 17,** 34-40. (Ice Hockey)

CHAPTER THIRTEEN
ANXIETY

AUTHORS:

Michael Sagas, Paul Keiper, George Cunningham, & Shannon Champion

Competitive State Anxiety Inventory (CSAI & CSAI-2)

1420. Albrecht, R. R., & Feltz D. L. (1987). Generality and specificity of attention related to competitive anxiety and sport performance. **Journal of Sport Psychology, 9**, 231-248. (Baseball, Softball)

1421. Alexander, V., & Krane, V. (1996). Relationships among performance expectations, anxiety, and performance in collegiate volleyball players. **Journal of Sport Behavior, 19**, 246-269. (Volleyball)

1422. Annesi, J. J. (1997). Three-dimensional state anxiety recall: Implications for individual zone of optimal functioning research and application. **The Sport Psychologist, 11**, 43-52. (Field Hockey, Gymnastics)

1423. Annesi, J. J. (1998). Applications of the individual zones of optimal functioning model for the multimodal treatment of precompetitive anxiety. **The Sport Psychologist, 12**, 300-316. (Tennis)

1424. Armstrong, M., & Dowthwaite, P. (1984). An investigation into the anxiety levels of soccer players. **International Journal of Sport Management, 15**, 149-159. (Soccer)

1425. Bakker, F. C., & Kayser, C. S. (1994). Effect of a self-help mental training programme. **International Journal of Sport Psychology, 25**, 158-175. (Field Hockey)

1426. Barber, H., Sukhi, H., & White, S. A. (1999). The influence of parent-coaches on participant motivation and competitive anxiety in youth sport participants. **Journal of Sport Behavior, 22**, 162-180. (Baseball, Basketball, Football, Soccer, Softball)

1427. Barnes, M. W., Sime, W., Dienstbier, R., & Plake, B. (1986). A test of construct validity of the CSAI-2 questionnaire on male elite college swimmers. **International Journal of Sport Psychology, 17**, 364-374. (Swimming)

1428. Bird, A. M., & Horn, M. A. (1990). Cognitive anxiety and mental errors in sport. **Journal of Sport & Exercise Psychology, 12**, 217-222. (Softball)

1429. Bunker, L. K., Cook, D. L., Gansneder, B., Malone C., & Owens, D. R. (1983). Relationship among competitive state anxiety, ability, and golf performance. **Journal of Sport Psychology, 5**, 460-465. (Golf)

1430. Burke, K. L., Joyner, A. B., Pim, A., & Czech, D. R. (2000). An exploratory investigation of the perceptions of anxiety among basketball officials before, during, and after the contest. **Journal of Sport Behavior, 23**, 11. (Basketball, Sports Officials)

1431. Burke, S. T., & Jin, P. (1996). Predicting performance from a triathlon event. **Journal of Sport Behavior, 19**, 272-287. (Triathlon)

1432. Burton, D. (1988). Do anxious swimmers swim slower? Reexamining the elusive anxiety-performance relationship. **Journal of Sport & Exercise Psychology, 10**, 45-61. (Swimming)

1433. Burton, D. (1989). Winning isn't everything: Examining the impact of performance goals on collegiate swimmers' cognitions and performance. **The Sport Psychologist, 3**, 105-132. (Swimming)

1434. Burton, D., & Naylor, S. (1997). Is anxiety really facilitative? Reaction to the myth that cognitive anxiety always impairs sport performance. **Journal of Applied Sport Psychology, 9**, (Review Article)

1435. Brustad, R. J., & Ritter-Taylor, M. (1997). Applying social psychology perspectives to the sport psychology consulting process. **The Sport Psychologist, 11**, 107-119. (Review Article)

1436. Campbell, E., & Jones, J. G. (1997). Precompetition anxiety and self-confidence in wheelchair sport participants. **Adapted Physical Activity Quarterly, 14**, 95-107. (Disabled Athletes)

1437. Carter, J. E., & Kelley, A. E. (1997). Using traditional and paradoxical imagery interventions with reactant intramural athletes. **The Sport Psychologist, 11**, 175-189. (Basketball, Intramural Sports)

1438. Caruso, C. M., Dzewaltowski, D. A., Gill, D. L., & McElroy, M. A. (1990). Psychological and physiological changes in competitive state anxiety during noncompetition and competitive success and failure. **Journal of Sport & Exercise Psychology, 12**, 6-20. (Cycling)

1439. Chapman, C. L., Lane, A. M., Brierley, J. H., & Terry, P.C. (1997). Anxiety, self-confidence and performance in Tae Kwon-Do. **Perceptual and Motor Skills, 85**, 1275-1278. (Martial Arts)

1440. Chartrand, J. M., Jowdy, D. P., & Danish, S. J. (1992). The psychological skills inventory for sports: Psychometric characteristics and applied implications. **Journal of Sport & Exercise Psychology, 14**, 405-413. (Psychometric, Various Sports)

1441. Cogan, K. D., & Petrie, T. A. (1995). Sport consultation: An evaluation of a season-long intervention with female collegiate gymnasts. **The Sport Psychologist, 9**, 282-296. (Gymnastics)

1442. Cox, R. H. (1986). Relationship between skill performance in women's volleyball and competitive state anxiety. **International Journal of Sport Psychology, 17**, 183-190. (Volleyball)

1443. Cox, R. H., Davis, J. E., & Robb, M. (1998). Test-retest reliability of the Anxiety Rating Scale (ARS*)*. **Research Quarterly for Exercise and Sport, 69**, A-111. (Volleyball)

1444. Cox, R. H., Reed, C., & Robb, M. (1997). Comparative validity of the MRF-L and ARS competitive state anxiety rating scales for intramural athletes competing in six individual sports. **Research Quarterly for Exercise and Sport, 68**, A-101. (Intramural Sports, Various Sports)

1445. Cox, R. H., Robb, M., & Russell, W. D. (1999). Order of scale administration and concurrent validity of the Anxiety Rating Scale. **Perceptual and Motor Skills, 88,** 297-303. (Basketball, Track and Field)

1446. Cox, R. H., Russell, W. D., & Robb, M. (1998). Development of a CSAI-2 short form for assessing competitive state anxiety during and immediately prior to competition. **Journal of Sport Behavior, 21,** 30-40. (Basketball, Volleyball)

1447. Cox, R. H., Russell, W. D., & Robb, M. (1999). Comparative concurrent validity of the MRF-L and ARS competitive state anxiety rating scales for volleyball and basketball. **Journal of Sport Behavior, 22,** 310-320. (Basketball, Volleyball)

1448. Crocker, P. R. E. (1989). A follow-up of cognitive-affective stress management training. **Journal of Sport & Exercise Psychology, 11,** 236-242. (Volleyball)

1449. Crocker, P. R. E. (1989). Evaluating stress management training under competition conditions. **International Journal of Sport Psychology, 20,** 191-204. (Volleyball)

1450. Crocker, P. R. E., Alderman, R. B., & Smith M. R. (1988). Cognitive-affective stress management training with high performance youth volleyball players: Effects on affect, cognition, and performance. **Journal of Sport & Exercise Psychology, 10,** 448-460. (Volleyball)

1451. Davids, K., & Gill, A. (1995). Multidimensional state anxiety prior to different levels of sport competition: Some problems with simulation tasks. **International Journal of Sport Psychology, 26,** 359-382. (Ice Hockey)

1452. Dudley, G., & Callister, R. (1990). Psychological and performance concomitants of increased volume training in elite athletes. **Journal of Applied Sport Psychology, 2,** 34-50. (Martial Arts)

1453. Durr, K. R., & Cox, R. H. (1997). Relationship between state anxiety performance in high school divers: A test of catastrophe theory. **Research Quarterly for Exercise and Sport, 68,** A-102. (Swimming)

1454. Ebbeck, V., & Weiss, M. R. (1988). The arousal-performance relationship: Task characteristics and performance measures in track and field athletics. **The Sport Psychologist, 2**, 13-27. (Track and Field)

1455. Edwards, T., & Hardy, L. (1996). The interactive effects of intensity and direction of cognitive and somatic anxiety and self-confidence upon performance. **Journal of Sport & Exercise Psychology, 18**, 296-312. (Netball)

1456. Eidson, T. A. (1997). Assessment of hearing-impaired athletes' anxiety and self-perceptions. **Perceptual and Motor Skills, 85**, 491-496. (Basketball)

1457. Elko, K. P., & Ostrow, A. C. (1991). Effects of a rational-emotive education program on heightened anxiety levels of female collegiate gymnasts. **The Sport Psychologist, 5**, 235-255. (Gymnastics)

1458. Elko, K. P., & Ostrow, A. C. (1992). The effects of three mental preparation strategies on strength performance of young and older adults. **Journal of Sport Behavior, 15**, 34-41. (Exercise)

1459. Eubank, M. R., & Collins, D. (2000). Coping with pre- and in-event fluctuations in competitive state anxiety: A longitudinal approach. **Journal of Sports Sciences, 18**, 121-131. (Psychometric)

1460. Eubank, M. R., Smith, N. C., & Smethurst, C. J. (1995). Intensity and direction of multidimensional competitive state anxiety: Relationships to performance in racket sports. **Journal of Sports Sciences, 13**, 52-53. (Badminton, Tennis)

1461. Filaire, E., Sagnol, M., Ferrand, C., Maso, G., & Lac, G. (2001). Psychophysiological stress in judo athletes during competitions. **Journal of Sports Medicine and Physical Fitness, 41**, 263-268. (Martial Arts)

1462. Finkenberg, M. E., DiNucci, J. M., McCune, E. D., & McCune, S. L. (1992). Cognitive and somatic state anxiety and self-confidence in cheerleading competition. **Perceptual and Motor Skills, 75**, 835-839. (Cheerleading)

1463. Ford, S. K., & Summers, J. J. (1992). The factorial validity of the TAIS attentional-style subscales. **Journal of Sport & Exercise Psychology, 14,** 283-297. (Psychometric)

1464. Garza, D. L. & Feltz, D. L. (1998). Effects of selected mental practice on performance, self-efficacy, and competition confidence of figure skaters. **The Sport Psychologist, 12,** 1-15. (Figure Skating/Ice Skating)

1465. George, T. R. (1994). Self-confidence and baseball performance: A causal examination of self-efficacy theory. **Journal of Sport & Exercise Psychology, 16,** 381-399. (Baseball)

1466. Gill, D. L., & Lan, L. (1984). The relationships among self-efficacy, stress responses, and a cognitive feedback manipulation. **Journal of Sport Psychology, 6,** 227-238. (College Students)

1467. Gould, D., Petlichkoff, L., & Weinberg, R. S. (1984). Antecedents of temporal changes in, and relationships between CSAI-2 subcomponents. **Journal of Sport Psychology, 6,** 289-304. (Volleyball, Wrestling)

1468. Gould, D., Weinberg, R. S., & Jackson, A. (1980). Mental preparation strategies, cognitions, and strength performance. **Journal of Sport Psychology, 2,** 329-339. (Weight Training)

1469. Gould, D., Petlichkoff, L., Simon, J. A., & Vevera, M. (1987). Relationship between Competitive State Anxiety Inventory-2 subscale scores and pistol shooting performance. **Journal of Sport Psychology, 9,** 33-42. (Shooting)

1470. Gould, D., Tuffey, S., Hardy, L., & Lochbaum, M. (1993). Multidimensional state anxiety and middle distance running performance: An exploratory examination of Hanin's (1980) zones of optimal functioning hypothesis. **Journal of Applied Sport Psychology, 5,** 85-95. (Running)

1471. Gould, D., Eklund, R. C., Petlichkoff, L., Peterson, K., & Bump, L. (1991). Psychological predictors of state anxiety and performance in age group wrestlers. **Pediatric Exercise Science, 3,** 198-208. (Wrestling)

1472. Gruber, J. J., & Beauchamp, D. (1979). Relevancy of the Competitive State Anxiety Inventory in a sport environment. **Research Quarterly, 50**, 207-214. (Basketball)

1473. Hackfort, D., & Spielberger, C. D. (1989). **Anxiety in sports: An international perspective**. New York: Hemisphere Publishing Company. (Book/Test Manual)

1474. Hale, B. D., & Whitehouse, A. (1998). The effects of imagery-manipulated appraisal on intensity and direction of competitive anxiety. **The Sport Psychologist, 12**, 40-51. (Soccer)

1475. Hall, H. K. & Kerr, A. W. (1997). Motivational antecedents of precompetitive anxiety in youth sport. **The Sport Psychologist, 11**, 24-42. (Fencing)

1476. Hall, H. K., & Kerr, A. W. (1998). Predicting achievement anxiety: A social-cognitive perspective. **Journal of Sport & Exercise Psychology, 20**, 98-111. (Fencing)

1477. Hall, H. K., Kerr, A. W., & Matthews, J. (1998). Precompetitive anxiety in sport: The contribution of achievement goals and perfectionism. **Journal of Sport & Exercise Psychology, 20**, 194-217. (Cross Country)

1478. Hammermeister, J., & Burton, D. (1995). Anxiety and the ironman: Investigating the antecedents and consequences of endurance athletes' state anxiety. **The Sport Psychologist, 9**, 29-40. (Cycling, Running, Triathlon)

1479. Hanson, T. W., & Gould, D. (1988). Factors affecting the ability of coaches to estimate their athletes' trait and state anxiety levels. **The Sport Psychologist, 2**, 298-313. (Cross Country)

1480. Hanton, S., & Jones, J. G. (1999). The acquisition and development of cognitive skills and strategies: Making the butterflies fly in formation. **The Sport Psychologist, 13**, 1-21. (Swimming)

178

1481. Hanton, S., & Jones, J. G. (1999). The effects of a multimodal intervention program on performers: II. Training the butterflies to fly in formation. **The Sport Psychologist, 13,** 22-41. (Swimming)

1482. Hanton, S., Jones, J. G., & Mullen, R. (2000). Intensity and direction of competitive state anxiety as interpreted by rugby players and rifle shooters. **Perceptual and Motor Skills, 90,** 513-521. (Rugby, Shooting)

1483. Huband, E. D. & McKelvie, J. S. (1986). Pre and post game state anxiety in team athletes high and low in competitive trait anxiety. **International Journal of Sport Psychology, 17,** 191-198. (Various Sports)

1484. Huddleston, S., & Gill, D. L. (1981). State anxiety as a function of skill level and proximity to competition. **Research Quarterly for Exercise and Sport, 52,** 31-34. (Track and Field)

1485. Jambor, E. A., Rudisill, M. E., Weekes, E. M., & Michaud, T. J. (1994). Association among fitness components, anxiety, and confidence following aerobic training in aquarunning. **Perceptual and Motor Skills, 78,** 595-602. (Exercise)

1486. Janelle, C. M., Singer, R. N., & Williams, A. M. (1999). External distraction and attentional narrowing: Visual search evidence. **Journal of Sport & Exercise Psychology, 21,** 70-91. (Automobile Racing)

1487. Jerome, G. J., & Williams, J. M. (2000). Intensity and interpretation of competitive state anxiety: Relationship to performance and repressive coping. **Journal of Applied Sport Psychology, 12,** 236-250. (Bowling)

1488. Jones, J. G. (1995). More than just a game: Research developments and issues in competitive anxiety in sport. **British Journal of Psychology, 86,** 449-478. (Review Article)

1489. Jones, J. G., & Cale, A. (1989). Precompetition temporal patterning of anxiety and self-confidence in males and females. **Journal of Sport Behavior, 12,** 183-195. (Field Hockey, Netball, Rugby, Soccer, Squash)

1490. Jones, J. G., & Hanton, S. (1995). Antecedents of multidimensional state anxiety in elite competitive swimmers. **International Journal of Sport Psychology, 26**, 512-523. (Swimming)

1491. Jones, J. G., & Hanton, S. (1996). Interpretation of competitive anxiety symptoms and goal attainment expectancies. **Journal of Sport & Psychology, 18**, 144-157. (Swimming)

1492. Jones, J. G. & Hanton, S. (2001). Pre-competitive feeling states and directional anxiety interpretations. **Journal of Sports Sciences, 19**, 385-395. (Swimming)

1493. Jones, J. G., & Swain, A. (1992). Intensity and direction as dimensions of competitive state anxiety and relations with competitiveness. **Perceptual and Motor Skills, 74**, 467-472. (Basketball, Field Hockey, Rugby, Soccer)

1494. Jones, J. G., & Swain, A. (1995). Predisposition to experience debilitative and facilitative anxiety in elite and nonelite performers. **The Sport Psychologist, 9**, 201-211. (Cricket)

1495. Jones, J. G., Hanton, S., & Swain, A. (1994). Intensity and interpretation of anxiety symptoms in elite and non-elite sports performers. **Personality and Individual Differences, 17**, 657-663. (Swimming)

1496. Jones, J. G., Swain, A., & Cale, A. (1990). Antecedents of multidimensional competitive state anxiety and self-confidence in elite intercollegiate middle-distance runners. **The Sport Psychologist, 4**, 107-118. (Running)

1497. Jones, J. G., Swain, A., & Cale, A. (1991). Gender differences in precompetition temporal patterning and antecedents of anxiety and self-confidence. **Journal of Sport & Exercise Psychology, 13**, 1-15. (Field Hockey, Netball, Rugby)

1498. Jones, J. G., Swain, A., & Hardy, L. (1993). Intensity and direction dimensions of competitive state anxiety and relationships with performance. **Journal of Sport Sciences, 11**, 525-532. (Gymnastics)

1499. Jones, J. G., & Hardy, L. (1990). **Stress and performance in sport.** Chichester, England: Wiley. (Book/Test Manual)

1500. Jones, J. G., Cale, A., & Kerwin, D. G. (1988). Multi-dimensional competitive state anxiety and psychomotor performance. **The Australian Journal of Science and Medicine in Sport**, **20**, 3-7. (Cricket)

1501. Karteroliotis, C., & Gill, D. L. (1987). Temporal changes in psychological and physiological components of state anxiety. **Journal of Sport Psychology, 9,** 261-274. (Physical Education Class(es)

1502. Kenow, L. J., & Williams, J. M. (1992). Relationship between anxiety, self-confidence, and evaluation of coaching behaviors. **The Sport Psychologist, 6,** 344-357. (Basketball, Coaching)

1503. Kenow, L. J., & Williams, J. M. (1999). Coach-athlete compatibility and athlete's perception of coaching behaviors. **Journal of Sport Behavior, 22,** 251-259. (Basketball, Coaching)

1504. Kingston, K. M. & Hardy, L. (1997). Effects of different types of goals on processes that support performance. **The Sport Psychologist, 11,** 277-293. (Golf)

1505. Kirkby, R. J., & Liu, J. (1999). Precompetition anxiety in Chinese athletes. **Perceptual and Motor Skills, 88,** 297-303. (Basketball, Track and Field)

1506. Kleine, D. (1990). Anxiety and sport performance: A meta-analysis. **Anxiety Research, 2,** 113-131. (Psychometric)

1507. Kolt, G., & Kirkby, R. J. (1994). Injury, anxiety, and mood in competitive gymnasts. **Perceptual and Motor Skills, 78,** 955-962. (Gymnastics, Injury)

1508. Krane, V. (1993). A practical application of the anxiety-athletic performance relationship: The zone of optimal functioning hypothesis. **The Sport Psychologist, 7,** 113-126. (Soccer)

1509. Krane, V. (1994). The mental readiness form as a measure of competitive state anxiety. **The Sport Psychologist, 8,** 189-202. (Rugby, Softball, Tennis, Track and Field)

1510. Krane, V., & Williams, J. M. (1987). Performance and somatic anxiety, cognitive anxiety, and confidence changes prior to competition. **Journal of Sport Behavior, 10,** 47-56. (Golf, Gymnastics)

1511. Krane, V., & Williams, J. M. (1994). Cognitive anxiety, somatic anxiety, and confidence in track and field athletes: The impact of gender, competitive level and task characteristics. **International Journal of Sport Psychology, 25,** 203-217. (Track and Field)

1512. Krane, V., Joyce, D., & Rafeld, J. (1994). Competitive anxiety, situation criticality, and softball performance. **The Sport Psychologist, 8,** 58-72. (Softball)

1513. Krane, V., Williams, J. M, & Feltz, D. L. (1992). Path analysis examining relationships among cognitive anxiety, somatic anxiety, state confidence, performance expectations, and golf performance. **Journal of Sport Behavior, 15,** 279-295. (Golf)

1514. Lane, A. M., Rodger, J. S. E., & Karageorghis, C. I. (1997). Antecedents of state anxiety in rugby. **Perceptual and Motor Skills, 84,** 427-433. (Rugby)

1515. Lane, A. M., Terry, P. C., & Karageorghis, C. I. (1995). Path analysis examining relationships among antecedents of anxiety, multidimensional state anxiety, and triathlon performance. **Perceptual and Motor Skills, 81,** 1255-1266. (Triathlon)

1516. Lane, A. M, Terry, P. C., & Karageorghis, C. I. (1995). Antecedents of multidimensional competitive state anxiety and self-confidence in duathletes. **Perceptual and Motor Skills, 80,** 911-919. (Duathlon)

1517. Lane, A. M., Sewell, D. F., Terry, P. C., Bartram, D., & Nesti, A. S. (1999). Confirmatory factor analysis of the Competitive State Anxiety Inventory-2. **Journal of Sports Sciences, 17,** 505-512. (Psychometric)

1518. Lewthwaite, R., & Scanlan, T. K. (1984). Social psychological aspects of competition for male youth sport participants: Predictors of competitive stress. **Journal of Sport Psychology, 6,** 208-226. (Wrestling)

1519. Mallet, C. J., & Hanrahan, S. J. (1997). Race modeling: An effective cognitive strategy for the 100 m Sprinter? **The Sport Psychologist, 11**, 72-85. (Track and Field)

1520. Man, F., Stuchlíková, I., & Kindlmann, P. (1995). Trait-state anxiety, worry, emotionality, and self-confidence in top-level soccer players. **The Sport Psychologist, 9**, 212-224. (Soccer)

1521. Marchant, D. B., Morris, T., & Andersen, M. B. (1998). Perceived importance of outcome as a contributing factor in competitive state anxiety. **Journal of Sport Behavior, 21**, 71-91. (Golf)

1522. Martens, R., Burton, D., Rivkin, F., & Simon, J. A. (1980). Reliability and validity of the Competitive State Anxiety Inventory (CSAI). In C. H. Nadeau, W. C. Halliwell, K. M. Newell, & G. C. Roberts (Eds.), **Psychology of motor behavior and sport-1979** (pp. 91-99). Champaign, IL: Human Kinetics. (Psychometric, Various Sports)

1523. Martin, J. J., & Gill, D. L. (1991). The relationships among competitive orientation, sport-confidence, self-efficacy, anxiety, and performance. **Journal of Sport & Exercise Psychology, 13**, 149-159. (Running)

1524. Martin, K. A. & Hall, C. R. (1998). Situational and intrapersonal moderators of sport competition state anxiety. **Journal of Sport Behavior, 20**, 435-446. (Figure Skating/Ice Skating)

1525. Maynard I. W. & Howe, B. L (1987). Interrelations of trait and state anxiety with game performance of rugby players. **Perceptual and Motor Skills, 64**, 599-602. (Rugby)

1526. Maynard, I. W., & Cotton, P. C. J. (1993). An investigation of two stress-management techniques in a field setting. **The Sport Psychologist, 7**, 375-387. (Field Hockey)

1527. Maynard, I. W., Hemmings, B., & Warwick-Evans, L. (1995). The effects of somatic intervention strategy on competitive state anxiety and performance in semiprofessional soccer players. **The Sport Psychologist, 9**, 51-64. (Soccer)

1528. Maynard, I. W., MacDonald, A., & Warwick-Evans, L. (1997). Anxiety in novice rock climbers: A further test of the matching hypothesis in a field setting. **International Journal of Sport Psychology, 28**, 67-78. (Rock Climbing)

1529. Maynard, I. W., Smith, M. J., & Warwick-Evans, L. (1995). The effects of a cognitive intervention strategy on competitive state anxiety and performance in semiprofessional soccer players. **Journal of Sport & Exercise Psychology, 17**, 428-446. (Soccer)

1530. McAuley, E. (1985) State anxiety: Antecedent or result of sport performance. **Journal of Sport Behavior, 8**, 71-77. (Golf)

1531. Murphy, S. M., Fleck, S. J., Dudley, G., & Callister, R. (1990). Psychological and performance concomitants of increased volume training in elite athletes. **Journal of Applied Sport Psychology, 2**, 34-50. (Martial Arts)

1532. Myung Woo, H. (1996). Psychological profiles of Korean elite judoists. **American Journal of Sports Medicine, 24**, S67-S71. (Martial Arts)

1533. Newton, M. L., & Duda, J. L. (1995). Relations of goal orientations and expectations on multidimensional state anxiety. **Perceptual and Motor Skills, 81**, 1107-1112. (Tennis)

1534. Nordell, K. A., & Sime, W. (1993). Competitive trait anxiety, state anxiety, and perceptions of anxiety: Interrelationships in practice and in competition. **Journal of Swimming Research, 9** (Fall), 19-24. (Swimming)

1535. Ntoumanis, N. & Jones, J. G. (1998). Interpretation of competitive trait anxiety symptoms as a function of locus of control beliefs. **International Journal of Sport Psychology, 29**, 99-114. (Cricket, Ice Hockey, Rugby, Swimming)

1536. Ntoumanis, N., & Biddle, S. J. H. (1998). The relationship between competitive anxiety, achievement goals, and motivational climates. **Research Quarterly for Exercise and Sport, 69**, (2), 176-187. (Basketball, Ice Hockey, Rugby, Soccer, Volleyball)

1537. Page, S. J., Sime, W., & Nordell, K. A. (1999). The effects of imagery on female college swimmer's perceptions of anxiety. **The Sport Psychologist, 13,** 458-469. (Swimming)

1538. Papaioannou, A., & Kouli, O. (1999). The effect of task structure, perceived motivational climate and goal orientations on students' task involvement and anxiety. **Journal of Applied Sport Psychology, 11,** 51-71. (Physical Education Class(es)

1539. Parfitt, C. G., & Pates, J. (1999). The effects of cognitive and somatic anxiety and self-confidence on components of performance during competition. **Journal of Sports Sciences, 17,** 351-356. (Basketball)

1540. Parfitt, C. G., Jones, J. G., & Hardy, L. (1990). Multidimensional anxiety and performance. In J. G. Jones & L. Hardy (Eds.), **Stress and performance in sport** (pp. 43-80). New York: Wiley. (Review Article)

1541. Parfitt, C. G., Hardy, L., & Pates, J. (1995). Somatic anxiety and physiological arousal: Their effects upon a high anaerobic, low memory demand task. **International Journal of Sport Psychology, 26,** 196-213. (Basketball)

1542. Perraullt, S., & Marisi, D. Q. (1997). A test of multidimensional anxiety theory with male wheelchair basketball players. **Adapted Physical Activity Quarterly, 14,** 108-118. (Basketball, Disabled Athletes)

1543. Perry, J. D., & Williams, J. M. (1998). Relationship of intensity and direction of competitive trait anxiety to skill level and gender in tennis. **The Sport Psychologist, 12,** 169-179. (Tennis)

1544. Prapavessis, H., & Carron, A.V. (1996). The effect of group cohesion on competitive state anxiety. **Journal of Sport & Exercise Psychology, 18,** 64-74. (Basketball, Ice Hockey, Rugby, Soccer)

1545. Prapavessis, H., Grove, J. R., McNair, P. J., & Cable, N. T. (1992). Self-regulation training, state anxiety, and sport performance: A psychophysiological case study. **The Sport Psychologist, 6,** 213-229. (Shooting)

1546. Prapavessis, H., Cox, R. H., & Brooks, L. (1996). A test of Martens, Vealey and Burton's theory of competitive anxiety. **The Australian Journal of Science and Medicine and Sport, 28,** 24-29. (Various Sports)

1547. Raedeke, T. D., & Stein, G. L. (1994). Felt arousal, thoughts/feelings, and ski performance. **The Sport Psychologist, 8,** 360-375. (Skiing)

1548. Raglin, J. S., & Turner, P. E. (1993). Anxiety and performance in track and field athletes: A comparison of the inverted-U hypothesis with the zone of optimal function theory. **Personality and Individual Differences, 14,** 163-171. (Track and Field)

1549. Randle S., & Weinberg, R. S. (1997). Multidimensional anxiety and performance: An exploratory examination of the zone of optimal functioning hypothesis. **The Sport Psychologist, 11,** 160-174. (Softball)

1550. Robazza, C. & Bortoli, L. (1998). Performance-related emotions in skilled athletes: Hedonic tone and functional impact. **Perceptual and Motor Skills, 87,** 547-564. (Figure Skating/Ice Skating, Track and Field)

1551. Rodrigo, G., Lusiardo, M., & Pereira, G. (1990). Relationship between anxiety and performance in soccer players. **International Journal of Sport Psychology, 21,** 112-120. (Soccer)

1552. Russell, W. D., Robb, M., & Cox, R. H. (1998). Sex, sport, situation, and competitive state anxiety. **Perceptual and Motor Skills, 86,** 816-818. (Basketball, Volleyball)

1553. Ryska, T.A. (1998). Cognitive-behavorial strategies and precompetitive anxiety among recreational athletes. **Psychological Record, 48,** 697-708. (Tennis)

1554. Ryska, T. A. (1993). The relationship between trait and precompetitive state anxiety among high school athletes. **Perceptual and Motor Skills, 76,** 413-414. (Tennis)

1555. Savoy, C. (1993). A yearly mental training program for a college basketball player. **The Sport Psychologist, 7,** 173-190. (Basketball)

1556. Savoy, C. (1997). Two individualized mental training programs for a team sport. **International Journal of Sport Psychology, 28**, 259-270. (Basketball)

1557. Savoy, C., & Beitel, P. (1997). The relative effect of a group and group/individualized program on state anxiety and state self-confidence. **Journal of Sport Behavior, 20**, 364-376. (Basketball)

1558. Scanlan, T. K., & Lewthwaite, R. (1984). Social psychological aspects of competition for male and female youth sport participants: I. Predictors of competitive stress. **Journal of Sport Psychology, 6**, 208-226. (Wrestling)

1559. Scanlan, T. K., & Passer, M. W. (1979). Sources of competitive stress in young female athletes. **Journal of Sport Psychology, 1**, 151-159. (Soccer)

1560. Sewell, D. F., & Edmondson, A. M. (1996). Relationships between field position and pre-match competitive state anxiety in soccer and field hockey. **International Journal of Sport Psychology, 27**, 159-172. (Field Hockey, Soccer)

1561. Simon, J. A., & Martens, R. (1979). Children's anxiety in sport and nonsport evaluative activities. **Journal of Sport Psychology, 1**, 160-169. (Various Sports)

1562. Smith, R. E. (1989). Conceptual and statistical issues in research involving multidimensional anxiety scales. **Journal of Sport & Exercise Psychology, 11**, 452-457. (Review Article)

1563. Summers, J. J., Miller, K., & Ford, S. K. (1991). Attentional style and basketball performance. **Journal of Sport & Exercise Psychology, 8**, 239-253. (Basketball)

1564. Swain, A., & Jones, J. G. (1991). Gender role endorsement and competitive anxiety. **International Journal of Sport Psychology, 22**, 50-65. (Track and Field)

1565. Swain, A., & Jones, J. G. (1992). Relationships between sport achievement orientation and competitive state anxiety. **The Sport Psychologist, 6**, 42-54. (Track and Field)

1566. Swain, A., & Jones, J. G. (1993). Intensity and frequency dimensions of competitive state anxiety. **Journal of Sport Sciences, 11**, 533-542. (Track and Field)

1567. Swain, A., & Jones, J. G. (1996). Explaining performance variance: The relative contribution of intensity and direction dimensions of competitive state anxiety. **Anxiety, Stress, and Coping, 9**, 1-18. (Basketball)

1568. Swain, A., Jones, J. G., & Cale, A. (1990). Interrelationships among multidimensional competitive state anxiety components as a function of the proximity of competition. **Perceptual and Motor Skills, 71,** 1111-1114. (Soccer, Field Hockey, Rugby)

1569. Taylor, J. (1987). Predicting athletic performance with self-confidence and somatic and cognitive anxiety as a function of motor and physiological requirements in six sports. **Journal of Personality, 55**, 141-152. (Basketball, Cross Country, Skiing, Tennis, Track and Field)

1570. Tenenbaum, G., Stewart, E., Singer, R. N., & Duda, J. L. (1997). Aggression and violence in sport: An ISSP position stand. **The Sport Psychologist, 11**, 1-7. (Review Article)

1571. Terry, P. C., & Mayer, J. L. (1998). Effectiveness of a mental training program for novice scuba divers. **Journal of Applied Sport Psychology, 10**, 251-267. (Scuba)

1572. Terry, P. C., & Slade, A. (1995). Discriminant effectiveness of psychological state measures in predicting performance outcome in karate competition. **Perceptual and Motor Skills, 81**, 275-286. (Martial Arts)

1573. Terry, P. C., & Youngs, E. L. (1996). Discriminant effectiveness of psychological state measures in predicting selection during field hockey trials. **Perceptual and Motor Skills, 82**, 371-377. (Field Hockey)

1574. Terry, P. C., Coakley, L., & Karageorghis, C. I. (1995). Effects of intervention upon precompetition state anxiety in elite junior tennis players: The relevance of the matching hypothesis. **Perceptual and Motor Skills, 81**, 287-296. (Tennis)

1575. Terry, P. C., Walrond, N., & Carron, A. V. (1998). The influence of game location on athletes' psychological states. **Journal of Science and Medicine in Sport, 1**, 29-37. (Rugby)

1576. Terry, P. C., Cox, J. A., Lane, A. M., & Karageorghis, C. I. (1996). Measures of anxiety among tennis players in singles and doubles matches. **Perceptual and Motor Skills, 83**, 595-603. (Tennis)

1577. Thelwell, R. C. & Maynard, I. W. (1998). Anxiety-performance relationships in cricketers: Testing the zone of optimal functioning hypothesis. **Perceptual and Motor Skills, 87**, 675-689. (Cricket)

1578. Thomas, P. R., & Fogarty, G. J. (1997). Psychological skills training in golf: The role of individual differences in cognitive preferences. **The Sport Psychologist, 11**, 86-106. (Golf)

1579. Thuot, S. M., & Kavouras, S. A. (1998). Effect of perceived ability, game location, and state anxiety on basketball performance. **Journal of Sport Behavior, 21**, 311-321. (Basketball)

1580. Treasure, D. C., Monson, J., & Lox, C. L. (1996). Relationship between self-efficacy, wrestling performance, and affect prior to competition. **The Sport Psychologist, 10**, 73-83. (Wrestling)

1581. Vadocz, E. A., Hall, C. R., & Moritz, S. E. (1997). The relationship between competitive anxiety and imagery use. **Journal of Applied Sport Psychology, 9**, 241-253. (Rollerskating)

1582. Vealey, R. S., & Campbell, J. L. (1988). Achievement goals of adolescent figure skaters: Impact on self-confidence, anxiety, and performance. **Journal of Adolescent Research, 3**, 227-243. (Figure Skating/Ice Skating)

1583. Wall, B. R., & Gruber, J. J. (1986). Relevance of athletic aggression inventory for use in women's intercollegiate basketball: A pilot investigation. **International Journal of Sport Psychology,** 17, 23-33. (Basketball)

1584. Wankel, L. M., & Sefton, J. M. (1989). A season-long investigation of fun in youth sports. **Journal of Sport & Exercise Psychology,** 11, 355-366. (Ice Hockey, Ringette)

1585. Wann, D. L., Schrader, M. P., & Adamson, D. R. (1998). The cognitive and somatic anxiety of sport spectators. **Journal of Sport Behavior, 21,** 322-337. (Sports Fans)

1586. Weekes, E. M., & Rudisill, M. E. (1994). Association among fitness components, anxiety, and confidence following aerobic training in aquarunning. **Perceptual and Motor Skills, 78,** 595-602. (Exercise)

1587. Weinberg, R. S., Seabourne, T. G., & Jackson, A. (1987). Arousal and relaxation instructions prior to the use of imagery. **International Journal of Sport Psychology, 18,** 205-214. (Martial Arts)

1588. Weiss, M. R., Wiese, D. M., & Klint, K. A. (1989). Head over heels with success: The relationship between self-efficacy and performance in competitive youth gymnastics. **Journal of Sport & Exercise Psychology,** 11, 444-451. (Gymnastics)

1589. Wiggins, M. S. (1998). Anxiety intensity and direction: Preperformance temporal patterns and expectations in athletes. **Journal of Applied Sport Psychology, 10,** 201-211. (Soccer, Swimming, Track and Field)

1590. Wiggins, M. S., & Brustad, R. J. (1996). Perception of anxiety and expectations of performance. **Perceptual and Motor Skills, 83,** 1071-1074. (Soccer, Swimming, Track and Field)

1591. Wiggins, M. S., & Freeman, P. (2000). Anxiety and flow: An examination of anxiety direction and the flow experience. **International Sports Journal, 4,** 78-87. (Volleyball)

1592. Wiggins, M. S., & Moode, F. M. (2000). Analysis of body esteem in female college athletes and nonathletes. **Perceptual and Motor Skills, 90**, 851-854. (Soccer)

1593. Williams, D. M., Frank, M. L., & Lester, D. (2000). Predicting anxiety in competitive sports. **Perceptual and Motor Skills, 90**, 847-850. (Various Sports)

1594. Williams, J. M., & Krane, V. (1989). Response distortion on self-report questionnaires with female collegiate golfers. **The Sport Psychologist, 3**, 212-218. (Golf)

1595. Williams, J. M., & Krane, V. (1992). Coping styles and self-reported measures of state anxiety and self-confidence. **Journal of Applied Sport Psychology, 4**, 134-143. (Golf)

1596. Williams, L. (1998). Contextual influences and goal perspectives among female youth sport participants. **Research Quarterly for Exercise and Sport, 69**, 47-57. (Softball)

1597. Wilson, G. S., Raglin, J. S., & Harger, G. J. (2000). A comparison of the STAI and CSAI-2 in five-day recalls of precompetition anxiety in collegiate track and field athletes. **Scandinavian Journal of Medicine and Science in Sports, 10**, 51-54. (Track and Field)

1598. Woodman, T., Albinson, J. G., & Hardy, L. (1997). An investigation of the zones of optimal functioning hypothesis within a multidimensional framework. **Journal of Sport & Exercise Psychology, 19**, 131-141. (Bowling)

Sport Anxiety Scale (SAS)

1599. Dunn, J. G. H., Dunn, J. C., Wilson, P. W., & Syrotuik, D. G. (2000). Reexamining the factorial composition and factor structure of the Sport Anxiety Scale. **Journal of Sport & Exercise Psychology, 22**, 183-193. (Psychometric, Various Sports)

1600. Giacobbi, P. R., & Weinberg, R. S. (2000). An examination of coping in sport: Individual trait anxiety differences and situational consistency. **The Sport Psychologist, 14**, 42-62. (Various Sports)

1601. Prapavessis, H., Cox, R. H., & Brooks, L. (1996). A test of Martens, Vealey and Burton's theory of competitive anxiety. **Australian Journal of Science and Medicine in Sport, 28**, 24-29. (Various Sports)

1602. Smith, R. E. (1989). Conceptual and statistical issues in research involving multidimensional anxiety scales. **Journal of Sport & Exercise Psychology, 11**, 452-457. (Psychometric)

1603. Smith, R. E., Ptacek, J. T., & Patterson, E. (2000). Moderator effects of cognitive and somatic trait and anxiety on the relation between life stress and physical injuries. **Anxiety, Stress and Coping, 13**, 269-288. (Dance, Injury)

1604. Smith, R. E., Smoll, F. L., & Schutz, R. W. (1990). Measurement and correlates of sport-specific cognitive and somatic trait anxiety: The Sport Anxiety Scale. **Anxiety Research, 24**, 263-280. (Psychometric)

1605. Voight, M. R., Callaghan, J. L., & Ryska, T. A. (2000). Relationship between goal orientations, self-confidence and multidimensional trait anxiety among Mexican-American female youth athletes. **Journal of Sport Behavior, 23**, 271-288. (Volleyball)

1606. White, S. A., & Zellner, S. R. (1996). The relationship between goal orientation, beliefs about the causes of sport success, and trait anxiety among high school, intercollegiate, and recreational sport participants. **The Sport Psychologist, 10**, 58-72. (Various Sports)

1607. Wilson, P. W., & Eklund, R. C. (1998). The relationship between competitive anxiety and self-presentational concerns. **Journal of Sport & Exercise Psychology, 20**, 81-97. (Various Sports)

Sport Competition Anxiety Test (SCAT)

1608. Abood, D. A., & Black, D. R. (2000). Health education prevention for eating disorders among college female athletes. **American Journal of Health Behavior, 24**, 209-219. (Various Sports)

1609. Albrecht, R. R., & Feltz D. L. (1987). Generality and specificity of attention related to competitive anxiety and sport performance. **Journal of Sport Psychology, 9**, 231-248. (Baseball, Softball)

1610. Andersen, M. B., & Williams, J. M. (1987). Gender role and sport competition anxiety: A re-examination. **Research Quarterly for Exercise and Sport, 58**, 52-56. (Exercise)

1611. Anshel, M. H. (1985). The effect of arousal on warm-up decrement. **Research Quarterly, 56**, 1-9. (Cycling)

1612. Armstrong, M., & Dowthwaite, P. (1984). An investigation into the anxiety levels of soccer players. **International Journal of Sport Management, 15**, 149-159. (Soccer)

1613. Ashley, F. (1989). Limited visibility dives and advanced Scuba divers' anxiety. **Journal of Applied Research in Coaching and Athletics, 4**, 88-93. (Scuba)

1614. Bakker, F. C., & Kayser, C. S. (1994). Effect of a self-help mental training programme. **International Journal of Sport Psychology, 25**, 158-175. (Field Hockey)

1615. Bergandi, T. A., Shryock, M. G., & Titus, T. G. (1990). The basketball concentration survey: Preliminary development and validation. **The Sport Psychologist, 4**, 119-129. (Basketball)

1616. Berry, T. R., & Howe, B. L. (2000). Risk factors for disordered eating in female university athletes. **Journal of Sport Behavior, 23**, 207-218. (Basketball, Field Hockey, Rowing, Soccer, Swimming)

1617. Betts, E. (1982). Relation of locus of control to aspiration level and to competitive anxiety. **Psychological Reports, 51**, 71-76. (Physical Education Class(es)

1618. Biddle, S. J. H., & Jamieson, K. I. (1988). Attribution dimensions: Conceptual clarification and moderator variables. **International Journal of Sport Psychology, 19**, 47-59. (Table Tennis)

1619. Blackwell, B., & McCullagh, P. (1990). The relationship of athletic injury to life stress, competitive anxiety, and coping resources. **Athletic Training, 25**, 23-27. (Football, Injury)

1620. Blais, M. R., & Vallerand R. J. (1986). Multimodal effects of electromyographic biofeedback: Looking at children's ability to control precompetitive anxiety. **Journal of Sport Psychology, 8**, 283-303. (Biofeedback, Psychometric)

1621. Brand, H. J., & Hanekom, J. D. M., & Scheepers, D. (1988). Internal consistency of the sport competition anxiety test. **Perceptual and Motor Skills, 67**, 441-442. (Psychometric)

1622. Brown, R. M., Hall, L. R., Holtzer, R., Brown, S. L., & Brown, N. L. (1997). Gender and video game performance. **Sex Roles, 36**, 793-812. (Motor Task)

1623. Brustad, R. J. (1988). Affective outcomes in competitive youth sport: The influence of intrapersonal and socialization factors. **Journal of Sport & Exercise Psychology, 10**, 307-321. (Basketball)

1624. Brustad, R. J., & Weiss, M. R. (1987). Competence perceptions and sources of worry in high, medium, and low competitive trait-anxious young athletes. **Journal of Sport Psychology, 9**, 97-105. (Baseball, Softball)

1625. Bull, S. J. (1989). The role of the sport psychology consultant: A case study of ultra- distance running. **The Sport Psychologist, 3**, 254-264. (Ultrarunning/Ultramarathon)

1626. Bull, S. J., (1991). Personal and situational influences on adherence to mental skills training. **Journal of Sport & Exercise Psychology, 13**, 121-132. (Various Sports)

1627. Burhans, R. S., Richman, C. L., & Bergey, D. B. (1988). Mental imagery training: Effects on running speed performance. **International Journal of Sport Psychology, 19**, 26-37. (Track and Field)

1628. Burke, K. L., Joyner, A. B., Pim, A., & Czech, D. R. (2000). An exploratory investigation of the perceptions of anxiety among basketball officials before, during, and after the contest. **Journal of Sport Behavior, 23**, 11. (Basketball, Sports Officials)

1629. Burke, S. T., & Jin, P. (1996). Predicting performance from a triathlon event. **Journal of Sport Behavior, 19**, 272-287. (Triathlon)

1630. Burton, D. (1989). Winning isn't everything: Examining the impact of performance goals on collegiate swimmers' cognitions and performance. **The Sport Psychologist, 3**, 105-132. (Swimming)

1631. Carron, A.V., & Robinson, T. T. (1982). Personal and situational factors associated with dropping out versus maintaining participation in competitive sport. **Journal of Sport Psychology, 4**, 364-378. (Football)

1632. Chartrand, J. M., Jowdy, D. P., & Danish, S. J. (1992). The psychological skills inventory for sports: Psychometric characteristics and applied implications. **Journal of Sport & Exercise Psychology, 14**, 405-413. (Psychometric)

1633. Cheatham, T., & Rosentswieg, J. (1982). Validation of the sport competition anxiety test. **Perceptual and Motor Skills, 55,** 1343-1346. (Psychometric, Softball)

1634. Colley, A., Roberts, N., & Chipps. A. (1985). Sex-role identity, personality and participation in team and individual sports by males and females. **International Journal of Sport Psychology, 16,** 103-112. (Various Sports)

1635. Cooley, E. J. (1987). Situational and trait determinants of competitive state anxiety. **Perceptual and Motor Skills, 64,** 767-773. (Tennis)

1636. Corcoran, K. J. (1989). Is competitive anxiety an observable behavior? A sociometric validity study of the SCAT. **Journal of Personality Assessment, 53**, 677-684. (Psychometric)

1637. Crocker, P. R. E. (1989). A follow-up of cognitive-affective stress management training. **Journal of Sport & Exercise Psychology, 11**, 236-242. (Volleyball)

1638. Crocker, P. R. E., Alderman, R. B., & Smith M. R. (1988). Cognitive-affective stress management training with high performance youth volleyball players: Effects on affect, cognition, and performance. **Journal of Sport & Exercise Psychology, 10**, 448-460. (Volleyball)

1639. Cunningham, G. B. (2000). Trait anxiety among students in a college activity class. **Perceptual and Motor Skills, 91**, 693-695. (Physical Education Class(es)

1640. Daw, J., & Burton, D. (1994). Evaluation of a comprehensive psychological skills training program for collegiate tennis players. **The Sport Psychologist, 8**, 37-57. (Tennis)

1641. Donzelli, G. J., Dugoni, B. L., & Johnson, J. E. (1990). Competitive state and competitive trait anxiety differences in non-elite runner. **Journal of Sport Behavior, 13**, 255-266. (Running)

1642. Duffy, L. J. & Hinwood, D. P. (1997). Home field advantage: Does anxiety contribute? **Perceptual and Motor Skills, 84**, 283-286. (Soccer)

1643. Ebbeck, V. (1994). Self-perception and motivational characteristics of tennis participants: The influence of age and skill. **Journal of Applied Sport Psychology, 6**, 71-86. (Tennis)

1644. Edison, T. A. (1997). Assessment of hearing-impaired athletes' anxiety and self- perceptions. **Perceptual and Motor Skills, 85**, 491-496. (Basketball)

1645. Elko, K. P., & Ostrow, A. C. (1991). Effects of a rational-emotive education program on heightened anxiety levels of female collegiate gymnasts. **The Sport Psychologist, 5**, 235-255. (Gymnastics)

1646. Elko, K. P., & Ostrow, A. C. (1992). The effects of three mental preparation strategies on strength performance of young and older adults. **Journal of Sport Behavior, 15**, 34-41. (Weight Training)

1647. Feher, P., Meyers, M. C., & Skelly, W. A. (1998). Psychological profile of rock climbers: State and trait attributes. **Journal of Sport Behavior, 21**, 167-180. (Rock Climbing)

1648. Feltz, D. L., Lirgg, C. D., & Albrecht, R. R. (1992). Psychological implications of competitive running in elite young distance runners: A longitudinal analysis. **The Sport Psychologist, 6**, 128-138. (Running)

1649. Finkenberg, M. E., DiNucci, J. M., McCune, E. D., & McCune, S. L. (1992). Analysis of the effect of competitive trait anxiety on performance in taekwondo competition. **Perceptual and Motor Skills, 75**, 239-243. (Martial Arts)

1650. Fisher, A. C., & Zwart, E. F. (1982). Psychological analysis of athletes' anxiety responses. **Journal of Sport Psychology, 4**, 139-158. (Basketball)

1651. Ford, S. K., & Summers, J. J. (1992). The factorial validity of the TAIS attentional-style subscales. **Journal of Sport & Exercise Psychology, 14**, 283-297. (Psychometric)

1652. Ford, I. W., Eklund, R. C., & Gordon, S. (2001). An examination of psychological variables moderating the relationship between life stress and injury time-loss among athletes of a high standard. **Journal of Sports Science, 18**, 301-312. (Injury, Various Sports)

1653. Frost, R. O., & Henderson, K. J. (1991). Perfectionism and reactions to athletic competition. **Journal of Sport & Exercise Psychology, 13**, 323-335. (Lacrosse, Rowing, Softball, Tennis, Track and Field)

1654. Gerson, R., & Deshaies, P. (1978). Competitive trait anxiety and performance as predictors of pre-competitive state anxiety. **International Journal of Sport Psychology, 9**, 16-26. (Softball)

1655. Gill, D. L. (1988). Gender differences in competitive orientation and sport participation. **International Journal of Sport Psychology, 19,** 145-159. (Various Sports)

1656. Gill, D. L., & Martens, R. (1977). The role of task type and success-failure in group competition. **International Journal of Sport Psychology, 8,** 160-177.

1657. Gill, D. L., Dzewaltowski, D. A., & Deeter, T. E. (1988). The relationship of competitiveness and achievement orientation to participation in sport and nonsport activities. **Journal of Sport & Exercise Psychology, 10,** 139-150. (Physical Education Class(es)

1658. Glenn, S. D., & Horn, T. S. (1993). Psychological and personal predictors of leadership behavior in female soccer athletes. **Journal of Applied Sport Psychology, 5,** 17-34. (Soccer)

1659. Gould, D., Petlichkoff, L., & Weinberg, R. S. (1984). Antecedents of, temporal changes in, and relationships between CSAI-2 subcomponents. **Journal of Sport Psychology, 6,** 289-304. (Volleyball, Wrestling)

1660. Gould, D., Eklund, R. C., Petlichkoff, L., Peterson, K., & Bump, L. (1991). Psychological predictors of state anxiety and performance in age-group wrestlers. **Pediatric Exercise Science, 3,** 198-208. (Wrestling)

1661. Gravelle, L., Searle, R., & St. Jean, P. (1982). Personality profiles of Canadian women's national volleyball team. **Volleyball Technical Journal, 7(**2), 13-17. (Volleyball)

1662. Halvari, H. (1996). Effects of mental practice on performance are moderated by cognitive anxiety as measured by the sport competition anxiety test. **Perceptual and Motor Skills, 83,** 1375-1383. (Physical Education Class(es)

1663. Halvari, H., & Gjesme, T. (1995). Trait and state anxiety before and after competitive performance. **Perceptual and Motor Skills, 81,** 1059-1074. (Motor Task)

1664. Hanson, S. J., McCullagh, P., & Tonymon, P. (1992). The relationship of personality characteristics, life stress, and coping resources to athletic injury. **Journal of Sport & Exercise Psychology, 14,** 262-272. (Injury, Running, Track and Field)

1665. Hanson, T. W., & Gould, D. (1988). Factors affecting the ability of coaches to estimate their athletes' trait and state anxiety levels. **The Sport Psychologist, 2,** 298-313. (Cross Country)

1666. Hassmen, P., Koivula, N., & Hansson, T. (1998). Precompetitive mood states and performance of elite male golfers: Do trait characteristics make a difference? **Perceptual and Motor Skills, 86,** 1443-1457. (Golf)

1667. Hellstedt, J. C. (1987). Sport psychology at a ski academy: Teaching mental skills to young athletes. **The Sport Psychologist, 1,** 56-68. (Skiing)

1668. Hisanaga, B., & Lanning, W. (1983). A study of the relation between the reduction of competition anxiety and an increase in athletic performance. **International Journal of Sport Management, 14,** 219-227. (Volleyball)

1669. Hume, P. A., Hopkins, W. G., Robinson, D. M., Robinson, S. M., & Hollings, S. C. (1993). Predictors of attainment in rhythmic sportive gymnastics. **Journal of Sports Medicine and Physical Fitness, 33,** 367-377. (Gymnastics)

1670. Jerome, G. J., & Williams, J. M. (2000). Intensity and interpretation of competitive state anxiety: Relationship to performance and repressive coping. **Journal of Applied Sport Psychology, 12,** 236-250. (Bowling)

1671. Jones, J. G. (1995). More than just a game: Research developments and issues in competitive anxiety in sport. **British Journal of Psychology, 86,** 449-478. (Review Article)

1672. Jones, J. G., Hanton, S., & Swain, A. (1994). Intensity and interpretation of anxiety symptoms in elite and non-elite sports performers. **Personality and Individual Differences, 17,** 657-663. (Swimming)

1673. Jones, J. G., Swain, A., & Cale, A. (1991). Gender differences in precompetition temporal patterning and antecedents of anxiety and self-confidence. **Journal of Sport & Exercise Psychology, 13,** 1-15. (Field Hockey, Netball, Rugby)

1674. Jones, J. G., Swain, A., & Hardy, L. (1993). Intensity and direction dimensions of competitive state anxiety and relationship with performance. **Journal of Sports Sciences, 11,** 525-532. (Gymnastics)

1675. Kang, L., Gill, D. L., Acevedo, E. O., & Deeter, T. E. (1990). Competitive orientations among athletes and nonathletes in Taiwan. **International Journal of Sport Psychology, 21,** 146-157. (Various Sports)

1676. Karteroliotis, C., & Gill, D. L. (1987). Temporal changes in psychological and physiological components of state anxiety. **Journal of Sport Psychology, 9,** 261-274. (Physical Education Class(es)

1677. Kelley, B. C., Eklund, R. C., & Ritter-Taylor, M. (1999). Stress and burnout among collegiate tennis coaches. **Journal of Sport & Exercise Psychology, 21,** 113-130. (Tennis)

1678. Kenow, L. J. & Williams, J. M. (1992). Relationship between anxiety, self-confidence, and evaluation of coaching behaviors. **The Sport Psychologist, 6,** 344-357. (Basketball, Coaching)

1679. Kenow, L., & Williams, J. M. (1999). Coach-athlete compatibility and athlete's perception of coaching behaviors. **Journal of Sport Behavior, 22,** 251-259. (Basketball, Coaching)

1680. Kerr, G. A., & Leith, L. (1993). Stress management and athletic performance. **The Sport Psychologist, 7,** 221-231. (Gymnastics)

1681. Kleine, D. (1990). Anxiety and sport performance: A meta-analysis. **Anxiety Research, 2,** 113-131. (Psychometric)

1682. Krane, V., Williams, J. M., & Feltz, D. L. (1992). Path analysis examining relationships among cognitive anxiety, somatic anxiety, state confidence, performance expectations, and golf performance. **Journal of Sport Behavior, 15,** 279-295. (Golf)

1683. Krotee, M. L. (1979). The effects of various physical activity situational settings on the anxiety level of children. **Journal of Sport Behavior, 4,** 158-164. (Running)

1684. Lavalee, L., & Flint, F. (1996). The relationship of stress, competitive anxiety, mood state, and social support to athletic injury. **Journal of Athletic Training, 31,** 296-299. (Football, Injury, Rugby)

1685. Lewthwaite, R. (1990). Threat perception in competitive trait anxiety: The endangerment of important goals. **Journal of Sport & Exercise Psychology, 12,** 280-300. (Soccer)

1686. Lewthwaite, R., & Scanlan, T. K. (1989). Predictors of competitive trait anxiety in male youth sport participants. **Medicine and Science in Sports and Exercise. 21,** 221-229. (Wrestling)

1687. Lohr, B. A. & Scogin, F. (1998). Effects of self-administered visuo-motor behavioral rehearsal on sport performance of collegiate athletes. **Journal of Sport Behavior, 21,** 206-221. (Various Sports)

1688. Man, F., Stuchlíková, I., & Kindlmann, P. (1995). Trait-state anxiety, worry, emotionality, and self-confidence in top-level soccer players. **The Sport Psychologist, 9,** 212-224. (Soccer)

1689. Marchant, D. B., Morris, T., & Andersen, M. B. (1998). Perceived importance of outcome as a contributing factor in competitive state anxiety. **Journal of Sport Behavior, 21,** 71-91. (Golf)

1690. Martens, R. (1977). **Sport Competition Anxiety Test**. Champaign, IL: Human Kinetics. (Test Manual)

1691. Martens, R., & Gill, D. L. (1976) State anxiety among successful and unsuccessful competitors who differ in competitive trait anxiety. **Research Quarterly, 47**, 698-708. (Physical Education Class(es)

1692. Martens, R., & Simon, J. A. (1976). Comparison of three predictors of state anxiety in competitive situations. **Research Quarterly, 47**, 381-387. (Basketball)

1693. Martens, R., Burton, D., Rivkin, F., & Simon, J. A. (1980). Reliability and validity of the Competitive State Anxiety Inventory (CSAI). In C. H. Nadeau, W. C. Halliwell, K. M. Newell, & G. C. Roberts (Eds.), **Psychology of motor behavior and sport-1979** (pp. 91-99). Champaign, IL: Human Kinetics. (Various Sports)

1694. Martens, R., Gill, D. L., & Scanlan, T. K. (1976). Competitive trait anxiety, success-failure and sex as determinants of motor performance. **Perceptual and Motor Skills, 43**, 1199-1208. (Exercise)

1695. Martin, J. J. & Gill, D. L. (1991). The relationships among competitive orientation, sport-confidence, self-efficacy, anxiety, and performance. **Journal of Sport & Exercise Psychology, 13**, 149-159. (Running)

1696. Martin, K. A., & Mack, D. (1996). Relationship between physical self-presentation and sport competition trait anxiety: A preliminary study. **Journal of Sport & Exercise Psychology, 18**, 75-82. (Exercise)

1697. Maynard I. W. & Howe, B. L. (1987). Interrelations of trait and state anxiety with game performance rugby players. **Perceptual and Motor Skills, 64**, 599-602. (Rugby)

1698. McKay, J. M., Selig, S. E., Carlson, J. S., & Morris, T. (1997). Psychophysiological stress in elite golfers during practice and competition. **Australian Journal of Science and Medicine in Sport, 29**, 55-61. (Golf)

1699. Miller, B. P. & Miller, A. J. (1985). Psychological correlates of success in elite sportswomen. **International Journal of Sport Psychology, 16**, 289-295. (Netball)

1700. Morgan, W. P. (1980). The trait psychology controversy. **Research Quarterly for Exercise and Sport, 51**, 50-76. (Review Article)

1701. Murphy, S. M., & Woolfolk, R. L. (1987). The effects of cognitive interventions on competitive anxiety and performance on a fine motor skill accuracy task. **International Journal of Sport Psychology, 18**, 152-166. (Golf)

1702. Nordell, K. A., & Sime, W. (1993). Competitive trait anxiety, state anxiety and perceptions of anxiety: Interrelationships in practice and in competition. **Journal of Swimming Research, 9** (Fall), 19-24. (Swimming)

1703. Ommundsen, Y., & Vaglum, P. (1991). Soccer competition anxiety and enjoyment in young boy players: The influence of perceived competence and significant others emotional involvement. **International Journal of Sport Psychology, 22**, 35-49. (Soccer)

1704. Owie, I. (1981). Influence of sex-role standards in sport competition anxiety. **International Journal of Sport Psychology, 12**, 289-292. (Exercise)

1705. Passer, M. W. (1983). Fear of failure, fear of evaluation, perceived competence, and self-esteem in competitive trait anxious students. **Journal of Sport Psychology, 5**, 172-188. (Various Sports)

1706. Peach, S. J. & Thomas, S. M. (1998). Ego threat and the development of competitive trait anxiety in elite junior British tennis players. **European Journal of Physical Education, 3**, 51-64. (Tennis)

1707. Pelham, T. W., & Holt, L. E. (1999). Competitive anxiety in elite and non-elite young male ice hockey players. **Clinical Kinesiology, 53**, 37-40. (Ice Hockey)

1708. Petrie, T. A. (1993). Coping skills, competitive trait anxiety, and playing status: Moderating effects of the life stress-injury relationship. **Journal of Sport & Exercise Psychology, 15**, 261-274. (Football, Injury)

1709. Petrie, T. A., & Falkstein, D. L. (1998). Methodological, measurement, and statistical issues in research on sport injury prediction. **Journal of Applied Sport Psychology, 10**, 26-45. (Injury)

1710. Petrie, T. A., & Russell, R. K. (1995). Academic and psychosocial antecedents of academic performance for minority and nonminority college football players. **Journal of Counseling and Development, 73**, 615-620. (Football)

1711. Petrie, T. A., & Stoever, S. (1997). Academic and nonacademic predictors of female student-athletes' academic performances. **Journal of College Student Development, 38**, 599-607. (Soccer, Volleyball)

1712. Poteet, D., & Weinberg, R. S. (1980). Competition trait anxiety, state anxiety, and performance. **Perceptual and Motor Skills, 50**, 651-654. (Weight Training)

1713. Power, S. L. (1986). Psychological assessment procedures of a track and field national event squad training weekend. In J. Watkins, T. Reilly, & L. Burwitz (Eds.), **Sports sciences**. New York: E & FN Spon. (Track and Field)

1714. Power, S. L. (1982). Analysis of anxiety levels in track and field athletes of varying ages and abilities. **International Journal of Sport Psychology, 13**, 258-267. (Track and Field)

1715. Prapavessis, H., & Grove, J. R. (1994). Personality variables as antecedents of precompetitive mood states. **International Journal of Sport Psychology, 25**, 81-99. (Shooting)

1716. Prapavessis, H., Grove, J. R., McNair, P. J., & Cable, N. T. (1992). Self-regulation training, state anxiety, and sport performance: A psychophysiological case study. **The Sport Psychologist, 6**, 213-229. (Shooting)

1717. Rainey, D. W., & Cunningham, H. (1988). Competitive trait anxiety in male and female college athletes. **Research Quarterly for Exercise and Sport, 59**, 244-247. (Various Sports)

1718. Rainey, D. W., Amunategui, F., Agocs, H., & Larick, J. (1992). Sensation seeking and competitive trait anxiety among college rodeo athletes. **Journal of Sport Behavior, 15**, 307-317. (Baseball, Hang Gliding, Rodeo, Wrestling)

1719. Rainey, D. W., Conklin, W. E., & Rainey, K. W. (1987). Competitive trait anxiety among male and female junior high school athletes. **International Journal of Sport Psychology, 18**, 171-179. (Various Sports)

1720. Richardson, P. A., Weinberg, R. S., Bruya, L., Baun, W., Jackson, A., Caton, I., & Bruya, L. (1980). Physical and psychological characteristics of young children in sports: A descriptive profile. **Physical Educator, 37**, 187-191. (Exercise)

1721. Riddick, C. C. (1984). Comparative psychological profiles of three groups of female collegians: Competitive swimmers, recreational swimmers, and inactive swimmers. **Journal of Sport Behavior, 7**, 160-174. (Swimming)

1722. Rupnow, A., & Ludwig, D. A. (1981). Psychometric note on the reliability of the sport competition anxiety test: Form C. **Research Quarterly for Exercise and Sport, 52**, 35-37. Physical Education Class(es)

1723. Ryska, T. A. (1993). Coping styles and response distortion on self-report inventories among high school athletes. **Journal of Psychology, 127**, 409-418. (Various Sports)

1724. Scanlan, T. K., & Passer, M. W. (1979). Factors influencing the competitive performance expectancies of young female athletes. **Journal of Sport Psychology, 1**, 212-220. (Soccer)

1725. Segal, J. D., & Weinberg, R. S. (1985) Sex, sex role orientation and competitive trait anxiety. **Journal of Sport Behavior, 7**, 153-159. (Physical Education Class(es)

1726. Smith, N. C., Burwitz, L., & Jakeman, P. (1988). Precompetitive anxiety and motor performance: A psychophysiological examination. **Journal of Sport Sciences, 6**, 115-130. (Exercise)

1727. Smith, T. (1983) Competition trait anxiety in youth sport: Differences according to age, sex, race, and playing status. **Perceptual and Motor Skills, 57**, 1235-1238. (Various Sports)

1728. Smith, T. (1983). Competitive trait anxiety in youth sport: Differences according to age, sex, race, and playing status. **Perceptual and Motor Skills, 57,** 1235-1238. (Baseball, Football, Softball, Volleyball)

1729. Sonstroem, R. J., & Bernardo, P. (1982). Intraindividual pregame state anxiety and basketball performance: A re-examination of the inverted-u curve. **Journal of Sport Psychology, 4,** 235-245. (Basketball)

1730. Summers, J. J., Miller, K., & Ford, S. K. (1991). Attentional style and basketball performance. **Journal of Sport & Exercise Psychology, 8,** 239-253. (Basketball)

1731. Swain, A., & Jones J. G. (1991). Gender role endorsement and competitive anxiety. **International Journal of Sport Psychology, 22,** 50-65. (Track and Field)

1732. Swain, A., & Jones, J. G. (1992). Relationships between sport achievement orientation and competitive state anxiety. **The Sport Psychologist, 6,** 42-54. (Track and Field)

1733. Thirer, J., & O'Donnell, L. A. (1980). Female intercollegiate athletes' trait-anxiety level and performance in a game. **Perceptual and Motor Skills, 50,** 18. (Badminton, Basketball, Softball, Track and Field)

1734. Trafton, T. A., Meyers, M. C., & Skelly, W. A. (1997). Psychological characteristics of the telemark skier. **Journal of Sport Behavior, 20,** 465-475. (Skiing)

1735. Tremayne, P., & Barry, R. J. (1990). Repression of anxiety and its effects on psychophysiological responses to stimuli in competitive gymnasts. **Journal of Sport & Exercise Psychology, 12,** 333-352. (Gymnastics)

1736. Wandzilak, T., Potter, G., & Lorentzen, D. (1982). Factors related to predictability of pre-game state anxiety. **International Journal of Sport Psychology, 13,** 31-42. (Volleyball)

1737. Wark, K. A., & Wittig, A. F. (1979). Sex role and sport competition anxiety. **Journal of Sport Psychology, 1,** 248-250. (Youth)

1738. Weinberg, R. S. (1979). Anxiety and motor performance: Drive theory vs. cognitive theory. **International Journal of Sport Psychology, 10,** 112-121. (Motor Task)

1739. Weinberg, R. S., & Genuchi, M. (1980). Relationship between competitive trait anxiety, state anxiety, and golf performance: A field study. **Journal of Sport Psychology, 2,** 148-154. (Golf)

1740. White, S. A. (1998). Adolescent goal profiles, perceptions of the parent-initiated motivational climate, and competitive trait anxiety. **The Sport Psychologist, 12,** 16-28. (Various Sports)

1741. Williams, D. A., & Jenkins, J. O. (1986). Role of competitive anxiety in the performance of black college basketball players. **Perceptual and Motor Skills, 63,** 847-853. (Basketball)

1742. Williams, J. M., & Andersen, M. B. (1998). Psychosocial antecedents of sport injury: Review and critique of the stress and injury model. **Journal of Applied Sport Psychology, 10,** 5-25. (Injury)

1743. Williams, J. M., & Krane, V. (1989). Response distortion on self-report questionnaires with female collegiate golfers. **The Sport Psychologist, 3,** 212-218. (Golf)

1744. Williams, J. M., & Krane, V. (1992). Coping styles and self-reported measures of state anxiety and self-confidence. **Journal of Applied Sport Psychology, 4,** 134-143. (Golf)

1745. Wilson, P. W. & Eklund, R. C. (1998). The relationship between competitive anxiety and self-presentational concerns. **Journal of Sport & Exercise Psychology, 20,** 81-97. (Various Sports)

1746. Wittig, A. F., Duncan, S. L., & Schurr, K. T. (1987). The relationship of gender, gender-role, endorsement and perceived physical self-efficacy to sport competition anxiety. **Journal of Sport Behavior, 11,** 192-199. (Exercise)

1747. Wong, E. H., & Bridges, L. J. (1994). Age related differences in inter- and intrapersonal variables related to motivation in a group sport setting. **Journal of Social Psychology, 134,** 497-509. (Soccer)

1748. Wong, E. H., & Bridges, L. J. (1995). A model of motivational orientation for youth sport: Some preliminary work. **Adolescence, 30,** 439-452. (Soccer)

1749. Wong, E. H., Lox, C. L., & Clark, S. E. (1993). Relationship between sports context, competitive trait anxiety, perceived ability, and self-presentation confidence. **Perceptual and Motor Skills, 76,** 847-850. (Various Sports)

1750. Xiao, M. & Zhu, S. (1997). Investigation and study on sports and competition trait anxiety in athletes of a Shanghai team. **Sports Science Research, 18,** 24-27. (Various Sports)

CHAPTER FOURTEEN
ATTRIBUTIONS

Attributional Style Questionnaire (ASQ)

1751. Corr, P. J., & Gray, J. A. (1996). Structure and validity of the attributional style questionnaire: A cross-sample comparison. **Journal of Psychology, 130,** 645-657. (Psychometric)

1752. Davis, H., & Zaichkowsky, L. D. (1998). Explanatory style among elite ice hockey athletes. **Perceptual and Motor Skills, 87,** 1075-1080. (Ice Hockey)

1753. Hale, B. D. (1993). Explanatory style as predictor of academic and athletic achievement in college athletes. **Journal of Sport Behavior, 16,** 63-75. (Psychometric, Various Sports)

1754. Hanrahan, S. J., & Grove, J. R. (1990). Further examination of the psychometric properties of the Sport Attributional Style Scale. **Journal of Sport Behavior, 13,** 183-193. (Psychometric)

1755. Higgins, N. C., Zumbo, B. D., & Hay, J. L. (1999). Construct validity of attributional style modeling context dependent item sets in the attributional style questionnaire. **Educational and Psychological Measurement, 59,** 804-820. (Psychometric)

1756 Hjelle, L., Belongia, C., & Nesser, J. (1996). Psychometric properties of the Life Orientation Test and Attributional Style Questionnaire. **Psychological Reports, 78,** 507-515. (Psychometric)

1757. Kendzierski, D., & Sheffield, A. (2000). Self-schema and attributions for an exercise lapse. **Basic and Applied Social Psychology, 22,** 1-8. (Exercise)

1758. Palmer, L. K. (1995). Effects of a walking program on attributional style, depression, and self-esteem in women. **Perceptual and Motor Skills, 81,** 891-898. (Exercise)

Revised Causal Dimension Scale I/II (CDS-I, CDS-II)

1759. Anshel, M. H., & Hoosima, D. E. (1989). The effect of positive and negative feedback on causal attributions and motor performance as a function of gender and athletic participation. **Journal of Sport Behavior, 12,** 119-130. (Motor Task)

1760. Bibik, J. M. (1999). Factors influencing college students' self-perceptions of competence in beginning physical education classes. **Journal of Teaching in Physical Education, 18,** 255-276. (Physical Education Class(es)

1761. Brewer, B. W., Cornelius, A. E., VanRaalte, J. L., Petitpas, A. J., Sklar, J. H., Pohlman, M. H., Krushell, R. J., & Ditmar, T. D. (2000). Attributions for recovery and adherence to rehabilitation following anterior cruciate ligament reconstruction: A prospective analysis. **Psychology and Health, 15,** 283-291. (Injury)

1762. Grove, J. R., & Hanrahan, S. J., & McInman, A. (1991). Success/failure bias in attributions across involvement categories in sport. **Personality and Social Psychology Bulletin, 17,** 93-97. (Basketball)

1763. Hamilton, P. R., & Jordan, J. S. (2000). Most successful and least successful performances: Perceptions of causal attributions in high school track athletes. **Journal of Sport Behavior, 23,** 245-254. (Track and Field)

1764. Mark, M. M., Mutrie, N., Brooks, D. R., & Harris, D. V. (1984). Causal attributions of winners and losers in individual competitive sports: Toward reformulation of the self-serving bias. **Journal of Sport Psychology, 6,** 184-196. (Squash)

1765. McAuley, E. (1991) Efficacy and attributional determinants of response to exercise participation. **Journal of Sport & Exercise Psychology, 13,** 382-393. (Exercise)

1766. McAuley, E., & Duncan, T. E. (1989). Causal attributions and affective reactions to disconfirming outcomes in motor performance. Journal **of Sport & Exercise Psychology,** 11, 187-200. (Motor Task)

1767. McAuley, E., & Duncan, T. E. (1990). The causal attribution process in sport and physical activity. In S. Graham & V. S. Folkes (Eds.), **Attribution theory: Applications in achievement, mental health, and interpersonal conflict** (pp. 37-52). Hillsdale, NJ: Lawrence Erlbaum. (Review Article)

1768. McAuley, E., & Duncan, T. E. (1990). Cognitive appraisal and affective reactions following physical achievement outcomes in motor performance. **Journal of Sport & Exercise Psychology, 12**, 425-426. (Gymnastics, Physical Education Class(es)

1769. McAuley, E., & Gross, J. B. (1983). Perceptions of causality in sport-An application of the Causal Dimension Scale. **Journal of Sport Psychology, 5**, 72-76. (Physical Education Class(es), Table Tennis)

1770. McAuley, E., & Shaffer, S. (1993). Affective responses to externally and personally controllable attributions. **Basic and Applied Social Psychology, 14**, 475-485. (College Students)

1771. McAuley, E., Duncan, T. E., & Russell, W. D. (1992). Measuring causal attributions: The revised Causal Dimension Scale (CDSII). **Personality and Social Psychology Bulletin, 18**, 566-573. (Psychometric)

1772. McAuley, E., Russell, R., & Gross, J. B. (1983). Affective consequences of winning and losing: An attributional analysis. **Journal of Sport Psychology, 5**, 278-287. (Physical Education Class(es)

1773. McAuley, E., Poag, K., Gleason, A., & Wraith, S. (1990). Attrition from exercise programs: Attributional and affective perspectives. **Journal of Social Behavior and Personality, 5**, 591-602. (Exercise)

1774. Morgan, L. K., Griffin, J., & Heyward, V. H. (1996). Ethnicity, gender, and experience effects on attributional dimensions. **The Sport Psychologist, 10**, 4-16. (Track and Field)

1775. Prapavessis, H., & Grove, J. R. (1994). Personality variables as antecedents of precompetitive mood states. **International Journal of Sport Psychology, 25**, 81-99. (Shooting)

1776. Rejeski, W. J., & Brawley, L. R. (1983). Attribution theory in sport: Current status and new perspectives. **Journal of Sport Psychology, 5,** 77-99. (Review Article)

1777. Robinson, D. W., & Howe, B L. (1987). Causal attribution and mood state relationships of soccer players in a sport achievement setting. **Journal of Sport Behavior, 10,** 137-146. (Soccer)

1778. Robinson, D. W., & Howe, B. L. (1989). Appraisal variable/affect relationships in youth sport: A test of Weiner's attributional model. **Journal of Sport & Exercise Psychology, 11,** 431-443. (Various Sports)

1779. Russell, W. D. (1982). The Causal Dimension Scale: A measure of how individuals perceive causes. **Journal of Personality and Social Psychology, 42,** 1137-1145. (Psychometric)

1780. Tubbs, M. E. & Jamesvalutis, M. (1992). Indirect measures of causal dimensions-Estimating the reliability of a composite of separate constructs. **Personality and Social Psychology Bulletin, 18,** 231-236. (Psychometric)

1781. Vallerand, R. J., & Richter, F. (1988). On the use of the Causal Dimension Scale in a field setting: A test with confirmatory factor analysis in success and failure conditions. **Journal of Personality and Social Psychology, 54,** 704-712. (Psychometric)

1782. Vlachopolous, S. P., Biddle, S. J. H., & Fox, K. R. (1996). A social-cognitive investigation into the mechanisms of affect generation in children's physical activity. **Journal of Sport & Exercise Psychology, 18,** 174-193. (Youth)

1783. Watkins, D., & Cheng, C. (1995). The revised Causal Dimension Scale-A confirmatory factor-analysis with Hong-Kong students. **British Journal of Educational Psychology, 65,** 249-252. (Psychometric)

1784. Watkins, D., Sachs, J., & Regmi, M. (1997). Confirmatory factor analysis of the revised Causal Dimension Scale: A Nepalese investigation. **Psychological Reports, 81,** 963-967. (Psychometric)

1785. Watt, S. E., & Martin, P. R. (1994). Effect of general self-efficacy expectancies on performance attributions. **Psychological Reports, 75**, 951-961. (Motor Task)

1786. White, S. A. (1993). The effect of gender and age on causal attributions of softball players. **International Journal of Sport Psychology, 24**, 49-58. (Softball)

CHAPTER FIFTEEN
GROUP COHESION AND SPORT LEADERSHIP

AUTHORS:
HOLLY CLIETT, LYDIA DUBUISSON, , JONATHAN CORNWELL, TODD MOORE, NOAH STEIN, & MARK WOOD

Group Environment Questionnaire (GEQ)

1787. Annesi, J. J. (1999). Effects of minimal group promotion on cohesion and exercise adherence. **Small Group Research, 30**, 542-557. (Exercise)

1788. Blanchard, C., Poon, P., Rodgers, W., & Pinel, B. (2000). Group Environment Questionnaire and its applicability in an exercise setting. **Small Group Research, 31**, 210-224. (Exercise)

1789. Brawley, L. R. (1990). Group cohesion: Status, problems, and future directions. **International Journal of Sport Psychology, 21**, 335-379. (Review Article)

1790. Brawley, L. R., Carron, A. V., & Widmeyer, W. N. (1987). Assessing the cohesion of teams: Validity of the Group Environment Questionnaire. **Journal of Sport Psychology, 9**, 275-294. (Psychometric)

1791. Brawley, L. S., Carron, A. V., & Widmeyer, W. N. (1988). Exploring the relationship between cohesion and group resistance to disruption. **Journal of Sport & Exercise Psychology, 10**, 199-213. (Basketball, Field Hockey, Ice Hockey, Soccer, Volleyball, Wrestling)

1792. Brawley, L. S., Carron, A. V., & Widmeyer, W. N. (1993). The influence of group and its cohesiveness on perceptions of group goal-related variables. **Journal of Sport & Exercise Psychology, 15**, 245-260. (Basketball, Ice Hockey, Swimming, Volleyball)

1793. Bray, C. D., & Whaley, D. E. (2001). Team cohesion, effort, and objective individual performance of high school basketball players. **The Sport Psychologist, 15,** 260-275. (Basketball)

1794. Carless, S. A. (2000). Cohesion: Conceptual and measurement issues - Reply. **Small Group Research, 31,** 107-118. (Review Article)

1795. Carron, A. V., & Brawley, L. R. (2000). Cohesion: Conceptual and measurement issues. **Small Group Research, 31,** 89-106. (Review Article)

1796. Carron, A. V., & Spink, K. S. (1992). Internal consistency of the Group Environment Questionnaire modified for an exercise setting. **Perceptual and Motor Skills, 74,** 304-306. (Exercise)

1797. Carron, A. V., & Spink, K. S. (1993). Team building in an exercise setting. **The Sport Psychologist, 7,** 8-18. (Exercise)

1798. Carron, A. V., & Spink, K. S. (1995). The group size-cohesion relationship in minimal groups. **Small Group Research, 26,** 86-105. (Exercise)

1799. Carron, A. V., Brawley, L. S., & Widmeyer, W. N. (1990). The impact of group size in an exercise setting. **Journal of Sport & Exercise Psychology, 12,** 276-287. (Exercise)

1800. Carron, A. V., Prapavessis, H., & Grove, J. R. (1994). Group effects and self-handicapping. **Journal of Sport & Exercise Psychology, 16,** 246-257. (Cricket, Rowing, Rugby, Water Polo)

1801. Carron, A. V., Widmeyer, W. N., & Brawley, L. R. (1985). The development of an instrument to assess cohesion in sport teams: The Group Environment Questionnaire. **Journal of Sport Psychology, 7,** 244-266. (Psychometric)

1802. Carron, A. V., Widmeyer, W. N., & Brawley, L. S. (1988). Group cohesion and individual adherence to physical activity. **Journal of Sport & Exercise Psychology, 10,** 127-138. (Various Sports)

1803. Chang, A., & Bordia, P. (2001). A multidimensional approach to the group cohesion-group performance relationship. **Small Group Research, 32**, 379-405. (College Students)

1804. Cogan, K. D., & Petrie, T. A. (1995). Sport consultation: An evaluation of a season-long intervention with female collegiate gymnasts. **The Sport Psychologist, 9**, 282-296. (Gymnastics)

1805. Colman, M. M., & Carron, A. V. (2000). The group norm for productivity in individual sport teams. **Journal of Sport & Exercise Psychology, 22**, S27-S28. (Rowing, Swimming, Track and Field, Wrestling)

1806. Colman, M. M., & Carron, A. V. Team social norms and social cohesiveness. **Journal of Sport & Exercise Psychology, 22**, S28. (Rowing, Swimming, Track and Field, Wrestling)

1807. Cota, A. A., Evans, C. R., Dion, K. L., Kilik, L., & Longman, R. S. (1995). The structure of group cohesion. **Personality and Social Psychology Bulletin, 21**, 572-580. (Various Sports)

1808. Courneya, K. S. (1995). Cohesion correlates with affect in structured exercise classes. **Perceptual and Motor Skills, 81**, 1021-1022. (Exercise)

1809. Dion, K. L., & Evans, C. R. (1992). On cohesiveness: Reply. **Small Group Research, 23**, 242-250. (Review Article)

1810. Eisler, L., & Spink, K. S. (1998). Effects of scoring configurations and task cohesion on perception of psychological momentum. **Journal of Sport & Exercise Psychology, 20**, 311-320. (Volleyball)

1811. Estabrooks, P. A., & Carron, A. V. (1999). The influence of the group with elderly exercisers. **Small Group Research, 30**, 438-452. (Exercise)

1812. Estabrooks, P. A., & Carron, A. V. (2000). Predicting scheduling self-efficacy in older adult exercisers: The role of task cohesion. **Journal of Aging and Physical Activity, 8**, 41-50. (Exercise)

1813. Evans, C. R., & Dion, K. L. (1991). Group cohesion and performance. **Small Group Research, 22**, 175-186. (Various Sports)

1814. Eys, M.A., & Carron, A.V. (2001). Role ambiguity, task cohesion, and task self-efficacy. **Small Group Research, 32**, 356-373. (Basketball)

1815. Gardner, D. E., Shields, D. L. L., Bredemeier, B. J. L., & Bostrom, A. (1996). The relationship between perceived coaching behaviors and team cohesion among baseball and softball players. **The Sport Psychologist, 10**, 367-381. (Baseball, Coaching, Softball)

1816. Granito, V. J., & Rainey, D. W. (1988). Differences in cohesion between high school and college football teams and starters and nonstarters. **Perceptual and Motor Skills, 66**, 471-477. (Football)

1817. Grieve, F. G., Whelan, J. P., & Meyers, A. W. (2000). An experimental examination of the cohesion-performance relationship on an interactive team. **Journal of Applied Sport Psychology, 12**, 219-235. (Basketball)

1818. Hausenblas, H. A., & Carron, A. V. (1996). Group cohesion and self-handicapping in female and male athletes. **Journal of Sport & Exercise Psychology, 18**, 132-143. (Various Sports)

1819. Henderson, J., Bourgeois, A. E., LeUnes, A., & Meyers, M. C. (1998). Group cohesiveness, mood disturbance, and stress in female basketball players. **Small Group Research, 29**, 212-225. (Basketball)

1820. Jacob, C. S., & Carron, A. V. (1998). The association between status and cohesion in sports teams. **Journal of Sports Sciences, 16**, 187-198. (Basketball, Field Hockey, Ice Hockey, Indoor Hockey, Soccer, Volleyball)

1821. Kim, M. S., & Sugiyama, Y. (1992). The relation of performance norms and cohesiveness for Japanese school athletic teams. **Perceptual and Motor Skills, 74**, 1096-1098. (Basketball, Martial Arts, Track and Field)

1822. Kozub, S. A., & Button, C. J. (2000). The influence of a competitive outcome on perceptions of cohesion in rugby and swimming teams. **International Journal of Sport Psychology, 31**, 82-95. (Rugby, Swimming)

1823. Kozub, S. A., & McDonnell, J. F. (2000). Exploring the relationship between cohesion and collective efficacy in rugby teams. **Journal of Sport Behavior, 23**, 120. (Rugby)

1824. Li, F., & Harmer, P. (1996). Confirmatory factor analysis of the Group Environment Questionnaire with an intercollegiate sample. **Journal of Sport & Exercise Psychology, 18**, 49-63. (Baseball, Psychometric, Softball)

1825. Losier, G. F., & Vallerand, R. J. (1995). Development and validation of an instrument to measure interpersonal relationships in sports: The Echelle-Des-Relations-Interpersonelles-Dans-le-Sport. **International Journal of Sport Psychology, 26**, 307-326. (Ice Hockey, Psychometric, Volleyball)

1826. Loughead, T. M., Colman, M. M., & Carron, A. V. (2001). Investigating the mediational relationship of leadership, class cohesion, and adherence in an exercise setting. **Small Group Research, 32**, 558-575. (Exercise)

1827. Lowther, J., & Lane, A. M. (2001). Relationships between mood, cohesion and performance among soccer players. **Journal of Sports Sciences, 19**. (Soccer)

1828. Matheson, H., Mathes, S., & Murray, M. (1995). Group cohesion of female intercollegiate coacting and interacting teams across a competitive season. **International Journal of Sport Psychology, 27**, 37-49. (Basketball, Gymnastics, Lacrosse, Swimming)

1829. Matheson, H., Mathes, S., & Murray, M. (1997). The effect of winning and losing on female interactive and coactive team cohesion. **Journal of Sport Behavior, 20**, 284-298. (Basketball, Gymnastics, Lacrosse, Swimming)

1830. McClure, B. A., & Foster, C. D. (1991). Group work as a method of promoting cohesiveness within a woman's gymnastics team. **Perceptual and Motor Skills, 73**, 307-313. Gymnastics)

1831. McCutcheon, L. E., & Ashe, D. (1999). Can individualists find satisfaction participating in interactive team sports? **Journal of Sport Behavior, 22**, 570-577. (Baseball, Basketball, Football)

1832. Meyer, B. B. (2000). The ropes and challenge course: A quasi-experimental examination. **Perceptual and Motor Skills, 90,** 1249-1257. (Leisure Activity, Tennis)

1833. Mroczkowska, H. (1997). Attributive reduction of failure-borne losses in view of team cohesion: Analogies and differences in individual versus team competition. **Biology of Sport, 14,** 325-332. (Various Sports)

1834. Mullen, B., & Copper, C. (1994). The relation between group cohesiveness and performance: An integration. **Psychological Bulletin, 115,** 21-227. (Review Article)

1835. Prapavessis, H., & Carron, A. V. (1996). The effect of group cohesion on competitive state anxiety. **Journal of Sport & Exercise Psychology, 18,** 64-74. (Basketball, Ice Hockey, Rugby, Soccer)

1836. Prapavessis, H., & Carron, A. V. (1997). Cohesion and work output. **Small Group Research, 28,** 294-301. (Basketball, Ice Hockey, Netball, Rugby, Soccer, Water Polo)

1837. Prapavessis, H., & Carron, A. V. (1997). Sacrifice, cohesion and conformity to norms in sports teams. **Group Dynamics, 1,** 231-240. (Cricket)

1838. Prapavessis, H., Carron, A. V., & Spink, K. S. (1996). Team building in sport. **International Journal of Sport Psychology, 27,** 269-285. (Soccer)

1839. Rainey, D. W., & Schweickert, G. J. (1988). An exploratory study of team cohesion before and after a spring trip. **The Sport Psychologist, 2,** 314-317. (Baseball)

1840. Remers, L., Widmeyer, W. N., Williams, J. M., & Myers, L. (1995). Possible mediators and moderators of the class-size member adherence relationship in exercise. **Journal of Applied Sport Psychology, 7,** 38-49. (Exercise)

1841. Salminen, S., & Luhtanen, P. (1998). Cohesion predicts success in junior ice hockey. **Perceptual and Motor Skills, 87,** 649-650. (Ice Hockey)

1842. Schutz, R. W., Eom, H. J., Smoll, F. L., & Smith, R. E. (1994). Examination of the factorial validity of the Group Environment Questionnaire. **Research Quarterly for Exercise and Sport, 65,** 226-236. (Psychometric, Various Sports)

1843. Shields, D. L. L., Gardner, D. E., Bredemeier, B. J. L., & Bostrom, A. (1995). Leadership, cohesion, and team norms regarding cheating and aggression. **Sociology of Sport Journal, 12,** 324-336. (Baseball, Softball)

1844. Shields, D. L. L., Gardner, D. E., Bredemeier, B. J. L., & Bostrom, A. (1997). The relationship between leadership behaviors and group cohesion in team sports. **Journal of Psychology, 13,** 196-210. (Baseball, Softball)

1845. Spink, K. S. (1990). Group cohesion and collective efficacy of volleyball teams. **Journal of Sport & Exercise Psychology, 12,** 301-311. (Volleyball)

1846. Spink, K. S. (1990). Collective efficacy in the sport setting. **International Journal of Sport Psychology, 21,** 380-395. (Ice Hockey, Volleyball)

1847. Spink, K. S. (1992). Group cohesion and starting status in successful and less successful elite volleyball teams. **Journal of Sports Sciences, 10,** 379-388. (Volleyball)

1848. Spink, K. S. (1995). Cohesion and intention to participate of female sport team athletes. **Journal of Sport & Exercise Psychology, 17,** 416-427. (Ringette)

1849. Spink, K. S., & Carron, A. V. (1992). Group cohesion and adherence in exercise classes. **Journal of Sport & Exercise Psychology, 14,** 78-86. (Exercise)

1850. Spink, K. S., & Carron, A. V. (1993). The effects of team building on the adherence patterns of female exercise participants. **Journal of Sport & Exercise Psychology, 15,** 39-49. (Exercise)

1851. Spink, K. S., & Carron, A. V. (1994). Group cohesion effects in exercise classes. **Small Group Research, 25,** 26-42. (Exercise)

1852. Sullivan, P. J., & Feltz, D. L. (2001). The relationship between intrateam conflict and cohesion within hockey teams. **Small Group Research, 32,** 342-355. (Ice Hockey)

1853. Westre, K. R., & Weiss, M. R. (1991). The relationship between perceived coaching behaviors and group cohesion in high school football teams. **The Sport Psychologist, 5**, 41-54. (Coaching, Football)

1854. Widmeyer, W. N., & Williams, J. M. (1991). Predicting cohesion in coacting teams. **Small Group Research, 22,** 548-557. (Golf)

1855. Widmeyer, W. N., Brawley, L. S., & Carron, A. V. (1985). **The measurement of cohesion in sports teams: The Group Environment Questionnaire.** London, Ontario: Sports Dynamics. (Test Manual)

1856. Widmeyer, W. N., Brawley, L. R., & Carron, A. V. (1990). The effects of group size in sport. **Journal of Sport & Exercise Psychology, 12**, 177-190. (Basketball)

1857. Widmeyer, W. N., Carron, A. V., & Brawley, L. S. (1993). Group cohesion in sport and exercise. In R. N. Singer, M. Murphey, and L. K. Tennant (Eds.), **Handbook of research in sport psychology** (pp. 672-692). New York: Macmillan. (Review Article)

1858. Widmeyer, W. N., Brawley, L. R., Carron, A V., & Hatfield, B. D. (1992). The measurement of cohesion in sport teams: The Group Environment Questionnaire. **Research Quarterly for Exercise and Sport, 57,** 347-349. (Psychometric)

1859. Williams, J. M., & Widmeyer, W. N. (1991). The cohesion-performance outcome relationship in a coacting sport. **Journal of Sport and Exercise Psychology, 13**, 364-371. (Golf)

1860. Wrisberg, C. A., & Draper, M. V. (1988). Sex, sex role orientation, and the cohesion of intercollegiate basketball teams. **Journal of Sport Behavior, 11**, 45-54. (Basketball)

Sports Cohesiveness Questionnaire (SCQ)

1861. Arnold, G. F., & Straub, W. F. (1973). Personality and group cohesiveness as determinants of success among interscholastic basketball teams. In I. D. Williams & L. M. Wankel (Eds.), **Proceedings of the fourth Canadian symposium on psycho-motor learning and sports psychology.** Ottawa: Fitness and Amateur Sports Directorate. (Basketball)

1862. Ball, J. R., & Carron, A. V. (1976). The influence of team cohesion and participation motivation upon performance success in intercollegiate ice hockey. **Canadian Journal of Applied Sports Sciences, 4**, 271-275. (Ice Hockey)

1863. Carron, A. V., & Chelladurai, P. (1981). The dynamics of group cohesion in sport. **Journal of Sport Psychology, 3**, 123-139. (Basketball, Volleyball, Wrestling)

1864. Gossett, D. M., & Widmeyer, W. N. (1981). Improving cohesion's prediction of performance outcome in sports. **Psychology of motor behavior and sport-1981.** Monterey, CA: North American Society for the Psychology of Sport and Physical Activity.

1865. Gruber, J. J., & Gray, G. R. (1981). Factor patterns of variables influencing cohesiveness at various levels of basketball competition. **Research Quarterly for Exercise and Sport, 52**, 19-30. (Basketball)

1866. Hacker, C. M., & Williams, J. M. (1981). Cohesion, satisfaction, and performance in intercollegiate field hockey: **Psychology of motor behavior and sport-1981.** Monterey, CA: North American Society for the Psychology of Sport and Physical Activity. (Field Hockey)

1867. Landers, D. M., & Crum, T. F. (1971). The effect of team success and formal structure on interpersonal relations and cohesiveness of baseball teams. **International Journal of Sport Psychology, 2**, 88-96. (Baseball)

1868. Landers, D. M., & Lueschen, G. (1974). Team performance outcome and the cohesiveness of competing coacting groups. **International Review of Sport Sociology, 9**, 57-69. (Bowling)

1869. Martens, R., & Peterson, J. A. (1971). Group cohesiveness as a determinant of success and member satisfaction in team performance. **International Review of Sport Sociology, 6,** 49-61. (Psychometric, Various Sports)

1870. Martens, R., Landers, D. M., & Loy, J. (1972). **Sport Cohesiveness Questionnaire.** Reston, VA: American Alliance for Health, Physical Education, Recreation and Dance. (Test Manual)

1871. Melnick, M. J., & Chemers, M. M. (1974). Effects of group structure on the success of basketball teams. **Research Quarterly, 45,** 1-8. (Basketball)

1872. Peterson, J. A., & Martens, R. (1972). Success and residential affiliation as determinants of team cohesiveness. **Research Quarterly, 43,** 62-76. (Basketball)

1873. Ruder, M. K., & Gill, D. L. (1982). Immediate effects of win-loss on perceptions of intramural and intercollegiate volleyball teams. **Journal of Sport Psychology, 4,** 227-234. (Intramural Sports, Volleyball)

1874. Widmeyer, W. N., & Martens, R. (1978). When cohesion predicts performance outcome in sport. **Research Quarterly, 49,** 372-380. (Basketball)

Leadership Scale for Sports (LSS)

1875. Bennett, G., & Maneval, M. (1998). Leadership styles of elite Dixie Youth baseball coaches. **Perceptual and Motor Skills, 87,** 754. (Baseball, Coaching)

1876. Brooks, D. D., Ziatz, D., Johnson, B., & Hollander, D. (2000). Leadership behavior and job responsibilities of NCAA Division 1A strength and conditioning coaches. **Journal of Strength and Conditioning, 14,** 483-492. (Coaching)

1877. Chelladurai, P. Leadership in sport. In J. M. Silva and R. S. Weinberg (Eds.), **Psychological foundations of sport** (pp. 329-339). Champaign, IL: Human Kinetics. (Review Article)

1878. Chelladurai, P. (1984). Discrepancy between the preferences and perceptions of leadership behavior and satisfaction of athletes in varying sports. **Journal of Sport Psychology, 6,** 27-41. (Basketball, Track and Field, Wrestling)

1879. Chelladurai, P. (1986). Applicability of the Leadership Scale for Sports to the Indian context. In J. Watkins, T. Reilly, and L. Burnitz (Eds.), **Sports science** (pp. 291-296). Glasgow, Scotland: Proceedings of the VIII Commonwealth and International Conference on Sport, Physical Education, Recreation and Health. (Psychometric)

1880. Chelladurai, P. (1990). Leadership in sports: A review. **International Journal of Sport Psychology, 21**, 328-354. (Various Sports)

1881. Chelladurai, P. (1993). Leadership. In R. N. Singer, M. Murphey, and L. K. Tennant (Eds.), **Handbook of research on sport psychology** (pp. 647-671). New York: Macmillan. (Review Article)

1882. Chelladurai, P., & Arnott, M. (1985). Decision styles in coaching: Preferences of basketball players. **Research Quarterly for Exercise and Sport, 56**, 15-24. (Basketball, Coaching)

1883. Chelladurai, P. & Carron, A. V. (1981). Applicability to youth sports of the Leadership Scale for Sports. **Perceptual and Motor Skills, 53**, 361-362. (Basketball, Wrestling)

1884. Chelladurai, P., & Carron, A. V. (1983). Athletic maturity and preferred leadership. **Journal of Sport Psychology, 5**, 371-380. (Basketball)

1885. Chelladurai, P., & Saleh, S. D. (1978). Preferred leadership in sports. **Canadian Journal of Sport Sciences, 3**, 85-92. (Psychometric)

1886. Chelladurai, P. & Saleh, S. D. (1980). Dimensions of leader behavior in sports: Development of a leadership scale. **Journal of Sport Psychology, 2**, 34-45. (Basketball, Rowing, Track and Field, Wrestling)

1887. Chelladurai, P., Haggerty, T. R., & Baxter, P. R. (1989). Decision style choices of university basketball coaches and players. **Journal of Sport & Exercise Psychology, 11**, 201-215. (Basketball)

1888. Chelladurai, P., Imamura, H., & Yamaguchi, Y. (1986). Subscale structure of the Leadership Scale for Sports in the Japanese context: A preliminary report. Kobe, Japan: **Proceedings of the FISU/CESU Conference** (pp. 372-389). (Psychometric)

1889. Chelladurai, P., Malloy, D., Imamura, H., & Yamaguchi, Y. (1987). A cross-cultural study of preferred leadership in sports. **Canadian Journal of Sport Sciences, 12**, 106-110. (Martial Arts)

1890. Chelladurai, P., Imamura, H., Yamaguchi, Y., Oinuma, Y., & Miyauchi, T. (1988). Sport leadership in a cross-national setting: The case of Japanese and Canadian university athletes. **Journal of Sport & Exercise Psychology, 10**, 374-389. (Various Sports)

1891. Dwyer, J. M., & Fischer, D. G. (1988). Psychometric properties of the coach's version of the Leadership Scale for Sports. **Perceptual and Motor Skills, 67**, 795-798. (Coaching, Psychometric, Wrestling)

1892. Dwyer, J. M., & Fischer, D. G. (1988). Leadership styles of wrestling coaches. **Perceptual and Motor Skills, 67**, 706. (Coaching, Wrestling)

1893. Dwyer, J. M., & Fischer, D. G. (1990). Wrestlers' perceptions of coaches' leadership as predictors of satisfaction with leadership. **Perceptual and Motor Skills, 71**, 511-517. (Coaching, Wrestling)

1894. Gardner, D. E., Shields, D. L. L., Bredemeier, B. J. L., & Bostrom, A. (1996). The relationship between perceived coaching behaviors and team cohesion among baseball and softball players. **The Sport Psychologist, 10**, 367-381. (Baseball, Coaching, Softball)

1895. Garland, D. J., & Barry, J. R. (1988). The effects of personality and perceived leadership behaviors on performance in collegiate football. **Psychological Record, 38**, 237-247. (Football)

1896. Garland, D. J., & Barry, J. R. (1990). Personality and leader behaviors in collegiate football: A multidimensional approach to performance. **Journal of Research in Personality, 24**, 355-370. (Football)

1897. Glenn, S. D., & Horn, T. S. (1993). Psychological and personal predictors of leadership behavior in female soccer athletes. **Journal of Applied Sport Psychology, 5**, 17-34. (Soccer)

1898. Gordon, S., (1988). Decision styles and coaching effectiveness in university soccer **Canadian Journal of Sport Sciences, 13**, 56-65. (Coaching, Soccer)

1899. Hastie, P. A. (1993). Coaching preferences of high school girl volleyball players. **Perceptual and Motor Skills, 77**, 1309-1310. (Coaching, Volleyball)

1900. Hastie, P. A. (1995). Factors affecting coaching preferences of secondary school volleyball players. **Perceptual and Motor Skills, 80**, 347-350. (Coaching, Volleyball)

1901. Horn, T. S., & Carron, A. V. (1985). Compatibility in coach-athlete relationships. **Journal of Sport Psychology, 7**, 137-149. (Basketball, Coaching, Swimming, Track and Field, Volleyball)

1902. Jambor, E. A., & Zhang, J. J. (1997). Investigating leadership, gender, and coaching levels using the Revised Leadership Scale for Sports. **Journal of Sport Behavior, 20**, 313-321. (Coaching)

1903. Junge, A, Dvorak, J., Rosch, D., Graf-Baumann, T., Chomiak, J., & Peterson, L. (2000). Psychological and sport-specific characteristics of football players. **American Journal of Sports Medicine, 28**, S22-S28. (Football)

1904. Martin, S. B., Jackson, A., Richardson, P. A. & Weiller, K. H. (1999). Coaching preferences of adolescent youths and their parents. **Journal of Applied Sport Psychology, 11**, 247-262. (Coaching, Various Sports)

1905. Prapavessis, H., & Gordon, S. (1991). Coach/player relationships in tennis. **Canadian Journal of Sport Sciences, 16**, 229-233. (Tennis)

1906. Reimer, H. A., & Chelladurai, P. (1995). Leadership and satisfaction in athletics. **Journal of Sport & Exercise Psychology, 17**, 276-293. (Football)

1907. Reimer, H. A., & Toon, K. (2001). Leadership and satisfaction in tennis: Examination of congruence, gender, and ability. **Research Quarterly for Exercise and Sport, 72,** 243-256. (Tennis)

1908. Robinson, T. T., & Carron, A. V. (1982). Personal and situational factors associated with dropping out versus maintaining participation in competitive sport. **Journal of Sport Psychology, 4,** 364-378. (Football)

1909. Salminen, S., & Liukkonen, J. (1994). The convergent and discriminant validity of the coach's version of the Leadership Scale for Sports. **International Journal of Sport Psychology, 25,** 119-127. (Psychometric)

1910. Salminen, S., & Liukkonen, J. (1996). Coach-athlete relationship and coaching behavior in training sessions. **International Journal of Sport Psychology, 27,** 59-67. (Coaching, Various Sports)

1911. Schliesman, E. S. (1987). Relationship between the congruence of preferred and actual leader behavior and subordinate satisfaction with leadership. **Journal of Sport Behavior, 10,** 157-166. (Track and Field)

1912. Serpa, S., Pataco, V., & Santos, F. (1991). Leadership patterns in handball international competition. **International Journal of Sport Psychology, 22,** 78-89. (Handball)

1913. Shields, D. L. L., Bredemeier, B. J. L., Gardner, D. E., & Bostrom, A. (1995). Leadership, cohesion, and team norms regarding cheating and aggression. **Sociology of Sport Journal, 12,** (Baseball, Softball)

1914. Shields, D. L. L., Gardner, D. E., Bredemeier, B. J. L., & Bostrom, A. (1997). The relationship between leadership behaviors and group cohesion in sports. **Journal of Psychology, 131,** 196-210. (Baseball, Softball)

1915. Summers, R. J. (1991). The association between athletes' perceptions of their abilities on the influence of coach technical-instruction. **Journal of Sport Behavior, 14,** 30-40. (Lacrosse)

1916. Terry, P. C. (1984). The coaching preferences of elite athletes competing at Universiade '83. **Canadian Journal of Sport Sciences, 9**, 201-208. (Coaching, Various Sports)

1917. Terry, P. C., & Howe, B. L. (1984). The coaching preferences of athletes. **Canadian Journal of Sport Sciences**, *9*, 188-193. (Coaching, Various Sports)

1918. Turman, P. D. (2001). Situational coaching styles: The impact of success and athlete maturity level on coaches' leadership styles over time. **Small Group Research, 32**, 576-594. (Coaching, Various Sports)

1919. Weiss, M. R., & Friedrichs, W. D. (1986). The influence of leader behaviors, coaches' attributes, and institutional variables on performance and satisfaction of collegiate basketball teams. **Journal of Sport Psychology, 8**, 332-346. (Basketball)

1920. Westre, K. R., & Weiss, M. R. (1991). The relationship between perceived coaching behaviors and group cohesion in high school football teams. **The Sport Psychologist, 5**, 41-54. (Coaching, Football)

1921. Zhang, J. J., Jensen, B. E., & Mann, B. L. (1997). Modification and revision of the Leadership Scale for Sports. **Journal of Sport Behavior, 20**, 105-122. (Coaching, Psychometric, Various Sports)

CHAPTER SIXTEEN
MENTAL SKILLS IN SPORT

Athletic Coping Skills Inventory (ACSI)

1922. Goudas, M., Theodorakis, Y., & Karamousalidis, G. (1998). Psychological skills in basketball: Preliminary study for development of a Greek form of the Athletic Coping Skills Inventory-28. **Perceptual and Motor Skills, 86**, 59-65. (Basketball)

1923. Junge, A., Dvorak, J., Rosch, D., Graf-Baumann, T., Chomiak, J., & Peterson, L. (2000). Psychological and sport-specific characteristics of football players. **American Journal of Sports Medicine, 28**, S22-S28. (Football)

1924. Petrie, T. A. (1993). Coping skills, competitive trait anxiety, and playing status: Moderating effects of the life stress-injury relationship. **Journal of Sport & Exercise Psychology, 15**, 261-274. (Football, Injury)

1925. Quinn, A. M., & Fallon, B. J. (1999). The changes in psychological characteristics and reactions of elite athletes from injury onset until full recovery. **Journal of Applied Sport Psychology, 11**, 210-229. (Injury)

1926. Smith, R. E., & Christensen, D. S. (1995). Psychological skills as predictors of performance and survival in professional baseball. **Journal of Sport & Exercise Psychology, 17**, 399-415. (Baseball)

1927. Smith, R. E., Schutz, R. W., Smoll, F. L., & Ptacek, J. T. (1995). Development and validation of a multidimensional measure of sport-specific psychological skills: The Athletic Coping Skills Inventory-28. **Journal of Sport & Exercise Psychology, 17**, 379-398. (Psychometric)

Athletic Motivation Inventory (AMI)

1928. Davis, H. (1991). Criterion validity of the Athletic Motivation Inventory: Issues in professional sport. **Journal of Applied Sport Psychology, 3**, 176-182. (Ice Hockey)

1929. Hammer, W. M., & Tutko, T. A. (1974). Validation of the Athletic Motivation Inventory. **International Journal of Sport Psychology, 5**, 3-12. (Psychometric)

1930. Horga, S., & Stimac, D. (1999). Why do children exercise? Evaluation of the motivation inventory. **Kinesiology, 31**, 61-67. (Exercise)

1931. Klonsky, B. G. (1991). Leaders' characteristics in same-sex sport groups: A study of interscholastic baseball and softball teams. **Perceptual and Motor Skills, 72**, 943-946. (Baseball, Softball)

1932. McClay, M. H., Appleby, D. C., & Plascak, F. D. (1989). Predicting injury in young cross country runners with the self-motivation inventory. **Sports Training, 1**, 191-195. (Cross Country, Injury)

1933. Morris, D. L. (1975). Socio-psychological study of highly skilled women field hockey players. **International Journal of Sport Psychology, 6**, 134-147. (Field Hockey)

1934. Ogilvie, B. C., & Tutko, T. A. (1971). Sport: If you want to build character, try something else. **Psychology Today, 5**, 61-63. (Review Article)

1935. Thomas, G. C., & Sinclair, G. D. (1977). The relationship between personality and performance of Canadian women intercollegiate basketball players. **Proceedings of the Ninth Canadian Psycho-Motor and Sport Psychology Symposium** (pp. 205-214). Banff, Canada. (Basketball)

Psychological Skills Inventory for Sports (PSIS)

1936. Chartrand, J. M., Jowdy, D. P., & Danish, S. J. (1992). The Psychological Skills Inventory for Sports: Psychometric characteristics and applied applications. **Journal of Sport & Exercise Psychology, 14**, 405-413. (Psychometric)

1937. Cox, R. H., & Davis, R. (1992). Psychological skills of elite wheelchair athletes. **Palaestra, 8**, 16-21. (Disabled Athletes, Various Sports)

1938. Cox, R. H. & Liu, Z. (1993). Psychological skills: A cross-cultural investigation. **International Journal of Sport Psychology, 24**, 326-340. (Basketball, Swimming, Track and Field, Volleyball)

1939. Cox, R. H. & Yoo, H. S. (1995). Playing position and psychological skill in American football. **Journal of Sport Behavior, 18**, 183-194. (Football)

1940. Cox, R. H., Liu, Z., & Qiu, Y. J. (1996). Psychological skills of elite Chinese athletes. **International Journal of Sport Psychology, 27**, 123-132. (Fencing, Gymnastics, Track and Field)

1941. Jopson, L., Henschen, K. P., & Schultz, B. (1989). Imagery and gymnastics. **Journal of Applied Research in Coaching and Athletics, 4**, 272-281. (Gymnastics)

1942. Mahoney, M. J. (1989). Psychological predictors of elite and non-elite performance in Olympic weight-lifting. **International Journal of Sport Psychology, 20**, 1-12. (Weightlifting)

1943. Mahoney, M. J., Gabriel, T. J., & Perkins, T. S. (1987). Psychological skills and exceptional athletic performance. **The Sport Psychologist, 1**, 181-199. (Various Sports)

1944. McIntyre, T., Mahoney, C. A., & Moran, A. (1998). Professional sport psychology in Ireland. **Irish Journal of Psychology, 19**, 504-518. (Various Sports)

1945. Meyers, M. C., LeUnes, A., & Bourgeois, A. E. (1996). Psychological skills assessment and athletic performance in collegiate rodeo athletes. **Journal of Sport Behavior, 19**, 132-146. (Rodeo)

1946. Meyers, M. C., Sterling, J. C., Treadwell, S., Bourgeois, A. E., & LeUnes, A. (1994). Mood and psychological skills of world-ranked female tennis players. **Journal of Sport Behavior, 17**, 156-165. (Tennis)

1947. Trafton, T. A., Meyers, M. C., & Skelly, W. A. (1997). Psychological characteristics of the telemark skier. **Journal of Sport Behaviour, 20**, 465-476. (Skiing)

1948. White, S. A. (1993). The relationship between psychological skills, experience, and practice commitment among collegiate male and female skiers. **The Sport Psychologist, 7,** 49-57. (Skiing)

1949. White, S. A., & Croce, R. V. (1992). Nordic disabled skiers and able-bodied skiers: An exploratory analysis of the Psychological Skills Inventory for Sport. **Clinical Kinesiology, 45,** 7-9. (Skiing)

Test of Performance Strategies (TOPS)

1950. Jackson, S. A., Thomas, P. R., Marsh, H. W., & Smethurst, C. J. (2001). Relationships between flow, self-confidence, psychological skills, and performance. **Journal of Applied Sport Psychology, 13,** 129-153. (Cycling, Orienteering, Surfing)

1951. Thomas, P. R., Murphy, S. M., & Hardy, L. (1999). Test of performance strategies: Development and preliminary validation of a comprehensive measure of athletes' psychological skills. **Journal of Sports Sciences, 17,** 697-711. (Various Sports)

CHAPTER SEVENTEEN

MOTIVATION

Willis Sport Motivational Scale

1952. Bourgeois, A. E., LeUnes, A., Burkett, S., Driggars-Bourgeois, T., Friend, J., & Meyers, M. C. (1995). Factors influencing intramural sport participation. **Journal of the National Intramural and Recreational Sports Association, 19**, (3), 44-48. (Intramural Sports)

1953. McElroy, M. A., & Willis, J. D. (1979). Women and the achievement conflict in sport: A preliminary study. **Journal of Sport Psychology, 1**, 241-247. (Psychometric, Various Sports)

1954. Prapavessis, H., & Grove, J. R. (1994). Personality variables as antecedents of precompetitive mood states. **International Journal of Sport Psychology, 25**, 81-99. (Shooting)

1955. Willis, J. D. (1982). Three scales to measure competition-related motives in sport. **Journal of Sport Psychology, 4**, 338-353. (Psychometric)

1956. Willis, J. D., & Layne, B. H. (1988). A validation study of sport-related motive scales. **Journal of Applied Research in Coaching and Athletics, 3**, 299-307. (Football, Psychometric)

CHAPTER EIGHTEEN

SELF-CONCEPT/SELF-CONFIDENCE/SELF-EFFICACY

Physical Self-Efficacy Scale (PSES)

1957. Cogan, K. D., Highlen, P. S., Petrie, T. A., Sherman, W. M., & Simonsen, J. (1991). Psychological and physiological effects of controlled intensive training and diet on collegiate rowers. **International Journal of Sport Psychology, 22,** 165-180. (Rowing)

1958. Duncan, T. E., & McAuley, E. (1987). Efficacy expectations and perceptions of causality in motor performance. **Journal of Sport Psychology, 9,** 385-393. (Motor Task, Physical Education Class(es)

1959. Focht, B. C., Bouchard, L. J., & Murphey, M. (2000). Influence of martial arts training on the perception of experimentally induced pressure pain and selected psychological responses. **Journal of Sport Behavior, 23,** 232-244. (Martial Arts)

1960. Gayton, W. F., Matthews, G. R., & Burchstead, G. N. (1986). An investigation of the validity of the physical self-efficacy scale in predicting marathon performance. **Perceptual and Motor Skills, 63,** 752-754. (Marathon)

1961. Kelley, M. P., Coursey, R. D., & Selby, P. M. (1997). Therapeutic adventures outdoors: A demonstration of benefits for people with mental illness. **Psychiatric Rehabilitation Journal, 20,** 61-73. (Adventure Activities, Leisure Activity)

1962. Matsudaira, M. (2000). Principal component analysis of Physical Self-Efficacy scale. **International Journal of Psychology, 35,** 251. (Psychometric)

1963. McAuley, E., & Gill, D. L. (1983). Reliability and validity of the Physical Self-Efficacy Scale in a competitive sport setting. **Journal of Sport Psychology, 5,** 410-418. (Gymnastics, Psychometric))

1964. Motl, R. W., & Conroy, D. E. (2000). Validity and factorial invariance of the social physique anxiety scale. **Medicine and Science in Sports and Exercise, 32**, 1007-1017. (Physical Education Class(es), Psychometric)

1965. Ryckman, R. M., & Hamel, J. (1993). Perceived physical ability differences in the participation motives of young athletes. **International Journal of Sport Psychology, 24**, 270-283. (Various Sports)

1966. Ryckman, R. M., Robbins, M. A., Thornton, B., & Cantrell, P. (1982). Development and validation of a physical self-efficacy scale. **Journal of Personality and Social Psychology, 42**, 891-900. (Psychometric)

1967. Thornton, B., Ryckman, R. M., Robbins, M. A., Donolli, J., & Biser, G. (1987). Relationship between perceived physical ability and indices of actual physical fitness. **Journal of Sport Psychology, 9**, 295-300. (Exercise)

1968. Williams, P. A., & Cash, T. F. (2001). Effects of a circuit weight training program on the body of images of college students. **International Journal of Eating Disorders, 30**, 75-82. (College Students, Exercise, Weightlifting)

1969. Wittig, A. F., Duncan, S. L., & Schurr, K. T. (1987). The relationship of gender, gender-role, endorsement and perceived physical self-efficacy to sport competition anxiety. **Journal of Sport Behavior, 10**, 192-199. ()

1970. Yeung, R. R., & Hemsley, D. R. (1997). Exercise behavior in an aerobics class: The impact of personality traits and efficacy cognitions. **Personality and Individual Differences, 23**, 425-431. (Exercise)

Physical Self-Perception Profile (PSPP)

1971. Asci, F. H., Asci, A. & Zorba, E. (1999). Cross-cultural validity and reliability of Physical Self-Perception Profile. **International Journal of Sport Psychology, 30**, 399-406. (Review Article)

1972. Asci, F. H., Kin, A., & Kosar, S. N. (1998). Effect of participation in an 8 week aerobic dance and step aerobics program on physical self-perception and body image satisfaction. **International Journal of Sport Psychology, 29**, 366-375. (Dance, Exercise)

1973. Crocker, P. R. E., Eklund, R. C., & Kowalski, K. C. (2000). Children's physical activity and physical self-perceptions. **Journal of Sports Sciences, 18**, 383-394. (Exercise)

1974. Diehl, N., Johnson, C. E., Rogers, R. L., & Petrie, T. A. (1998). Social physique anxiety and disordered eating: What's the connection? **Addictive Behaviors, 23**, 1-6. (College Students)

1975. Eapen, V., Naqvi, A., & Al-Dhaheri, A. S. (2000). Cross-cultural validation of Harter's Self-Perception Profile for Children in the United Arab Emirates. **Annals of Saudi Medicine,20**, 8-11. (Youth)

1976. Eklund, R. C., Whitehead, J. R. & Welk, G. J. (1997). Validity of the children and youth Physical Self-Perception Profile: A confirmatory factor analysis. **Research Quarterly for Exercise and Sport, 68**, 249-256. (Review Article).

1977. Fox, K. R. & Corbin C. B. (1989). The physical self-perception profile: Development and preliminary validation. **Journal of Sport & Exercise Psychology, 11**, 408-430. (Psychometric)

1978. Goni, A., & Zulaika, L. (2000). Relationship between physical education classes and the enhancement of fifth grade pupils' self-concept. **Perceptual and Motor Skills, 91**, 246-250. (Physical Education Class(es)

1979. Haggar, M., Ashford, B. & Stambulova, N. (1998). Russian and British children's physical self-perceptions and physical activity participation. **Pediatric Exercise Science, 10**, 137-152. (Exercise)

1980. Haggar, M., Ashford, B. & Stambulova, N. (1999). Physical self-perceptions: A cross-cultural assessment in Russian children. **European Journal of Physical Education, 2**, 228-245. (Review Article).

1981. Hayes, S. D., Crocker, P. R. E. & Kowalski, K. C. (1999). Gender differences in physical self-perceptions, global self-esteem and physical activity: Evaluation of the Physical Self-Perception Profile model. **Journal of Sport Behavior, 22,** 1-14. (Exercise)

1982. Janelle, C. M., Kiminski, T. W. & Murray, M. (1999). College football injuries: Physical self-perception as a potential predictor. **International Sports Journal, 3,** 93-102. (Football, Injury)

1983. Kowalski, N. P., Crocker, P. R. E., & Kowalski, K. C. (2001). Physical self and physical activity relationships in college women: Does social physique anxiety moderate effects? **Research Quarterly for Exercise and Sport, 72,** 55-62. (Exercise)

1984. Ninot, G., Bilard, J., Delignieres, D., & Sokolowski, M. (2000). Effects of integrated sport participation on perceived competence for adolescents with mental retardation. **Adapted Physical Education Quarterly, 17,** 208-221. (Basketball, Disabled Athlete, Exercise, Swimming)

1985. Ninot, G., Bilard, J., & Sokolowski, M. (2000). Athletic competition: A means of improving the self-image of the mentally retarded adolescent? **International Journal of Rehabilitation Research, 23,** 111-117. (Basketball, Disabled Athlete, Exercise, Swimming)

1986. Page, A., Ashford, B., Fox, K. R., & Biddle, S. J. H. (1993). Evidence of cross-cultural validity for the Physical Self-Perception Profile. **Personality and Individual Differences, 14,** 585-590. (Psychometric, Youth)

1987. Petrie, T. A., Diehl, N., Rogers, R. L., & Johnson, C. L. (1996). The Social Physique Anxiety Scale: Reliability and construct validity. **Journal of Sport & Exercise Psychology, 18,** 420-425. (College Students)

1988. Ransdell, L.B., Dratt, J., Kennedy, C., O'Neill, S., & DeVoe, D. (2001). Daughters and mothers exercising together (DAMET): A 12-week pilot project designed to improve physical self-perception and increase recreational physical activity. **Women and Health, 33,** 101-116. (Exercise)

1989. Raudsepp, L., Viira, R. & Liblik, R. (1999). Perceived physical competence and achievement goal orientations as related with physical activity of adolescents. **Acta-Kinesilogia Universitatis Tartuensis, 4**, 186-198. (Exercise)

1990. Smith, D. K., Hale, B. D. & Collins, D. (1998). Measurement of exercise dependence in bodybuilders. **Journal of Sports Medicine and Physical Fitness, 38**, 66-74. (Bodybuilding, Weight Training).

1991. Sonstroem, R. J. & Potts, S. A. (1996). Life adjustment correlates of physical self-concepts. **Medicine and Science in Sports and Exercise, 28**, 619-625. (Review Article)

1992. Sonstroem, R. J., Harlow, L. L. & Josephs, L. (1994). Exercise and self-esteem: Validity of model expansion and exercise associations. **Journal of Sport & Exercise Psychology, 16**, 29-42. (Exercise)

1993. Sonstroem, R. J., Speliotis, E. D. & Fava, J. L. (1992). Perceived physical competence in adults: An examination of the Physical Self-Perception Profile. **Journal of Sport & Exercise Psychology, 14**, 207-221. (Review Article)

1994. Spray, C. M. (2000). Predicting participation in noncompulsory physical education? Do goal perspectives matter? **Perceptual and Motor Skills, 90**, 1207-1215. (Physical Education Class(es)

1995. Welk, G. J., Corbin, C. B. & Lewis, L. A. (1995). Physical self-perceptions of high school athletes. **Pediatric Exercise Science, 7**, 152-161. (Various Sports)

1996. Welk, G. J., Corbin, C. B., Dowell, M. N. & Harris, H. (1997). The validity and reliability of two different versions of the Children and Youth Physical Self-Perception Profile. **Measurement in Physical Education and Exercise Science, 1**, 163-177. (Review Article).

1997. Whitehead, J. R. (1995). A study of children's physical self-perceptions using an adapted Physical Self-Perception Profile questionnaire. **Pediatric Exercise Science, 7**, 132-151. (Youth)

1998. Wittig, A. F., Duncan, S. L., & Schurr, K. T. (1988). The relationship of gender, gender-role, endorsement and perceived physical self-efficacy to sport competition anxiety. **Journal of Sport Behavior, 11**, 192-199. (Exercise)

Self-Perception Profile for Children/Adolescents

1999. Ebbeck, V., & Stuart, M. E. (1996). Predictors of self-esteem with youth basketball players. **Pediatric Exercise Science, 8**, 368-378. (Basketball)

2000. Ebbeck, V., & Weiss, M. R. (1998). Determinants of children's self-esteem: An examination of perceived competence and affect in sport. **Pediatric Exercise Science, 10**, 285-298. (Youth)

2001. Hagborg, W. J. (1993). The Rosenberg Self-Esteem Scale and Harter Self-Perception Profile for Adolescents: A concurrent validity study. **Psychology in the Schools, 30**, 132-136. (Psychometric)

2002. Harter, S. (1985). **Manual for the Self-Perception Profile for Children**. Denver, CO: University of Denver. (Test Manual)

2003. Hopper, C. (1988). Self-concept and motor performance of hearing impaired boys and girls. **Adapted Physical Activity Quarterly, 5**, 293-304. (Disabled Athletes, Motor Task)

2004. Mainano, C., Ninot, G., & Errais, B., (2001). Effects of alternated sport competition in perceived competence for adolescent males with mild to moderate mental retardation. **International Journal of Rehabilitation Research, 24**, 51-58. (Disabled Athletes)

2005. Mullan, E., Albinson, J. G., & Markland, D. (1997). Children's perceived physical competence at different categories of physical activity. **Pediatric Exercise Science 9**, 237-242. (Youth)

2006. Ninot, G., Bilard, J., Delignieres, D., & Sokolowski, M. (2000). Effects of integrated sport participation on perceived competence for adolescents with mental retardation. **Adapted Physical Activity Quarterly, 17**, 208-221. (Disabled Athletes)

2007. Ninot, G., Bilard, J., Sokolowski, M. (2000). Athletic competition: a means of improving the self-image of the mentally retarded adolescent? **International Journal of Rehabilitation Research, 23**, 111-117. (Mental Retardation)

2008. Van Veldhoven, N. H. M. J., Wijnroks, L., Bogaard, J. M. & Vermeer, A. (2000). Effects of an exercise program (PEP) for children with asthma: Results of a pilot study. **Pediatric Exercise Science, 12**, 244-257. (Exercise)

2009. Van Veldhoven, N. H. M. J., Vermeer, A., Bogaard, J. M., Hessels, M. G. P., Wijnroks, L., Colland, V. T., & van Essen-Zandvliet, E. E. M. (2001). Children with asthma and physical exercise: Effects of an exercise program. **Clinical Rehabilitation, 15**, 360-370. (Exercise)

2010. Wichstrom, L. (1995). Harter's Self-Perception Profile for Adolescents: Reliability, validity, and evaluation of the question format. **Journal of Personality Assessment, 65**, 100-116. (Psychometric)

State Self-Confidence Inventory (SSCI)

2011. Burke, S. T., & Jin, P. (1994). Predicting performance from a triathlon event. **Journal of Sport Behavior, 19**, 272-287. (Triathlon)

2012. Callow, N., & Hardy, L. (2001). Types of imagery associated with sport confidence in netball players of varying skill levels. **Journal of Applied Psychology, 13**, 1-17. (Netball)

2013. Gayton, W. F., & Nickless, C. J. (1987). An investigation of the validity of the train and state sport-confidence inventories in predicting marathon performance. **Perceptual and Motor Skills, 65**, 481-482. (Marathon)

2014. Leavitt, J., Young, J., & Connelly, D. (1989). The effects of videotape highlights on state self-confidence. **Journal of Applied Research in Coaching and Athletics, 4**, 225-232. (Volleyball)

2015. Magyar, T. M., & Duda, J. L., (2000). Confidence restoration following athletic injury. **The Sport Psychologist, 14**, 372-390. (Injury)

2016. Martin, J. J., & Gill, D. L. (1991). The relationships among competitive orientation, sport-confidence, self-efficacy, anxiety, and performance. **Journal of Sport & Exercise Psychology, 13,** 149-159. (Running)

2017. Ng, J. K., Cheung, S. Y., & Fung, L. (2001). Role of trait sport-confidence and state sport-confidence in affecting competitive track and field performances. **Journal of the International Council for Health, Physical Education, Recreation, Sport, and Dance, 37,** 35-38. (Track and Field)

2018. Quinn, A. M., & Fallon, B. J. (1999). The changes in psychological characteristics and reactions of elite athletes from injury onset until full recovery. **Journal of Applied Sport Psychology, 11,** 210-229. (Injury, Various Sports)

2019. Vealey, R. S. (1986). Conceptualization of sport-confidence and competitive orientation: Preliminary investigation and instrument development. **Journal of Sport Psychology, 8,** 221-246. (Various Sports)

2020. Vealey, R. S., & Campbell, J. L. (1988). Achievement goals of adolescent figure skaters: Impact on self-confidence, anxiety, and performance. **Journal of Adolescent Research, 3,** 227-243. (Figure Skating/Ice Skating)

Trait Self-Confidence Inventory (TSCI)

2021. Burke, S. T., & Jin, P. (1994). Predicting performance from a triathlon event. **Journal of Sport Behavior, 19,** 272-287. (Triathlon)

2022. Deeter, T. E. (1988). Does attitudinal commitment predict physical activity participation? **Journal of Sport Behavior, 11,** 177-192. (Exercise)

2023. Deeter, T. E. (1989). Development of a model of achievement behavior for physical activity. **Journal of Sport & Exercise Psychology, 11,** 13-25. (Physical Education Class(es), Various Sports)

2024. Deeter, T. E. (1990). Remodeling expectancy and value in physical activity. **Journal of Sport & Exercise Psychology, 12,** 86-91. (Physical Education Class(es)

2025. Gayton, W. F., & Nickless, C. J. (1987). An investigation of the validity of the train and state sport-confidence inventories in predicting marathon performance. **Perceptual and Motor Skills, 65**, 481-482. (Marathon)

2026. Martin, J. J. (1995). Competitive orientation, self-efficacy and goal importance in Filipino marathoners. **International Journal of Sport Psychology, 26**, 348-358. (Marathon)

2027. Martin, J. J., & Gill, D. L. (1991). The relationships among competitive orientation, sport-confidence, self-efficacy, anxiety, and performance. **Journal of Sport & Exercise Psychology, 13**, 149-159. (Running)

2028. Ng, J. K., Cheung, S. Y., & Fung, L. (2001). Role of trait sport-confidence and state sport-confidence in affecting competitive track and field performances. **Journal of the International Council for Health, Physical Education, Recreation, Sport, and Dance, 37**, 35-38. (Track and Field)

2029. Prapavessis, H., & Grove, J. R. (1994). Personality variables as antecedents of precompetitive mood states. **International Journal of Sport Psychology, 25**, 81-99. (Shooting)

2030. Sinclair, D. A., & Vealey, R. S. (1989). Effects of coaches' expectations and feedback on the self-perceptions of athletes. **Journal of Sport Behavior, 12**, 77-91. (Field Hockey)

2031. Solomon, G. B. (2001). Performance and personality impression cues as predictors of athletic performance: An extension of expectancy theory. **International Journal of Sport Psychology, 32**, 88-100. (Various Sports)

2032. Vealey, R. S. (1986). Conceptualization of sport-confidence and competitive orientation: Preliminary investigation and instrument development. **Journal of Sport Psychology, 8**, 221-246. (Various Sports)

2033. Vealey, R. S., & Campbell, J. L. (1988). Achievement goals of adolescent figure skaters: Impact on self-confidence, anxiety, and performance. **Journal of Adolescent Research, 3**, 227-243. (Figure Skating/Ice Skating)

2034. Voight, M. R., Callaghan, J. L., & Ryska, T. A. (2000). Relationship between goal orientations, self-confidence and multidimensional trait anxiety among Mexican-American female youth athletes. **Journal of Sport Behavior, 23**, 271-288. (Volleyball)

CHAPTER NINETEEN
MISCELLANEOUS SPORT INVENTORIES

Athletic Identity Measurement Scale (AIMS)

2035. Brewer, B. W., VanRaalte, J. L., & Linder, D. E. (1993). Athletic identity: Hercules' muscles or Achilles heel? **International Journal of Sport Psychology, 24,** 237-254. (College Students)

2036. Hale, B. D., James, B., & Stambulova, N. (1999). Determining the dimensionality of athletic identity: A "Herculean" cross-cultural undertaking. **International Journal of Sport Psychology, 30,** 83-100. (Various Sports)

2037. Horton, R. S., & Mack, D. (2000). Athletic identity in marathon runners: Functional focus or dysfunctional commitment? **Journal of Sport Behavior, 23,** 101-119. (Marathon)

2038. Lantz, C. D., & Schroeder, P. J. (1999). Endorsement of masculine and feminine gender roles: Differences between participation in and identification with the athletic role. **Journal of Sport Behavior, 22,** 545-557. (Physical Education Class(es), Various Sports)

2039. Martin, J. J. (1999). Predictors of social physique anxiety in adolescent swimmers with physical disabilities. **Adapted Physical Activity Quarterly, 16,** 75-85. (Disabled Athletes)

2040. Martin, J. J., & Adams-Mushett, C. (1995). Athletic identity and sport orientation of adolescent swimmers with disabilities. **Adapted Physical Activity Quarterly, 12,** 113-123. (Disabled Athletes)

2041. Martin, J. J., Eklund, R. C., & Adams-Mushett, C. (1997). Factor structure of the athletic identity measurement scale with athletes with disabilities. **Adapted Physical Activity Quarterly, 12,** 74-82. (Disabled Athletes, Psychometric)

2042. Martin, J. J., Adams-Mushett, C., & Eklund, R. C. (1994). Factor structure of the athletic identity measurement scale with adolescent swimmers with disabilities. **Brazilian International Journal of Adapted Physical Education Research, 1**, 87-99. (Disabled Athletes)

2043. Martin, J. J., Adams-Mushett, C., & Smith, K. L. (1995). Athletic identity and sport orientation of adolescent swimmers with disabilities. **Adapted Physical Activity Quarterly, 12**, 113-123. (Disabled Athletes, Swimming)

2044. Martin, J. J., Smith, K. L., & Adams-Mushett, C. (1995). Athletic identity and sport orientation of adolescent swimmers with disabilities. **Adapted Physical Education Quarterly, 12**, 113-123. (Disabled Athletes, Swimming)

2045. Smith, D. K., Hale, B. D., & Collins, D. (1998). Measurement of exercise dependence in bodybuilders. **Journal of Sports Medicine and Physical Fitness, 38**, 66-74. (Bodybuilding)

2046. Wiechman, S. A., & Williams, J. M. (1997). Relation of athletic identity to injury and mood disturbance. **Journal of Sport Behavior, 20**, 199-210. (Injury)

Attitudes Toward Physical Activity Scale (ATPA)

2047. Alderman, R. B. (1970). A sociopsychological assessment of attitude toward physical activity in champion athletes. **Research Quarterly, 41**, 1-9. (Various Sports)

2048. Brustad, R. J. (1991). Children's perspective on exercise and physical activity: Measurement issues and concerns. **Journal of School Health, 61**, 228-230. (Exercise)

2049. Cooper, M., Sherrill, C., & Marshall, D. (1986). Attitudes toward physical activity of elite cerebral palsied athletes. **Adapted Physical Activity Quarterly, 3**, 14-21. (Disabled Athletes)

2050. Corbin, C. B. (1976). Attitudes toward physical activity of champion women basketball players. **International Journal of Sport Psychology, 7**, 14-21. (Basketball)

2051. Finkenberg, M. E. (1991). Sex and ethnicity as factors for participation in physical activity. **International Journal of Physical Education, 28**, 23-26. (Exercise)

2052. Godin, G., & Shephard, R. J. (1986). Importance of type of attitude to the study of exercise-behavior. **Psychological Reports, 58,** 991-1000. (Exercise)

2053. Kenyon, G. S. (1968). A conceptual model for characterizing physical activity. **Research Quarterly, 39,** 96-105. (Psychometric)

2054. Kenyon, G. S. (1968). Six scales for assessing attitude toward physical activity. **Research Quarterly, 39,** 566-574. (Psychometric)

2055. McCready, M. L., & Long, B. C. (1985). Locus of control, attitudes toward physical activity, and exercise adherence. **Journal of Sport Psychology, 7**, 346-359. (Exercise)

2056. Pistacchio, T., Weinberg, R. S., & Jackson, A. (1989). The development of a psychobiologic profile of individuals who experience and those who do not experience exercise related mood enhancement. **Journal of Sport Behavior, 12**, 151-166. (Exercise)

2057. Rees, C. R., Andres, F. F., & Howell, F. M. (1986). On the trail of the "turkey trotters": The effect of previous sport involvement and attitudes on commitment to and skill in running. **Sociology of Sport Journal, 3**, 134-143. (Running)

2058. Reid, B. M., & Hay, D. (1979) Some behavioral characteristics of rugby and association footballers. **International Journal of Sport Psychology, 10**, 239-251. (Football, Rugby)

2059. Sidney, K. H., Niinimaa, V., & Shephard, R. J. (1983). Attitudes towards exercise and sports: Sex and age differences, and changes with endurance training. **Journal of Sports Sciences**, 1, 195-210. (Exercise)

2060. Simon, J. A., & Smoll, F. L. (1974). Instrument for assessing children's attitudes toward physical activity. **Research Quarterly, 45**, 407-415. (Exercise)

2061. Theodorakis, Y., Doganis, G., Bagiatis, K., & Gouthas, M. (1991). Preliminary study of the ability of reasoned action model in predicting exercise behavior of young children. **Perceptual and Motor Skills, 72,** 51-58. (Exercise)

2062. Williams, L. R. T., & Coldicott, A. G. (1982). High school students: Their self-esteem and attitudes toward physical activity. **New Zealand Journal of Health, Physical Education and Recreation, 15,** 62-65. (Exercise)

2063. Zaichkowsky, L. D.. (1978). Factorial validity of Kenyon's attitude toward physical activity inventory. **Canadian Journal of Applied Sport Sciences, 3,** 144-146. (Psychometric)

Competitive Orientation Inventory (COI)

2064. Gill, D. L., & Dzewaltowski, D. A. (1988). Competitive orientations among intercollegiate athletes: Is winning the only thing? **The Sport Psychologist, 2,** 212-221. (Various Sports)

2065. Gill, D. L., Kelley, B. C., Martin, J. J., & Caruso, C. M. (1991). A comparison of competitive-orientation measures. **Journal of Sport & Exercise Psychology, 13,** 266-280. (Various Sports)

2066. Martin, J. J., & Gill, D. L. (1991). The relationships among competitive orientation, sport-confidence, self-efficacy, anxiety, and performance. **Journal of Sport & Exercise Psychology, 13,** 149-159. (Running)

2067. Vealey, R. S. (1986). Conceptualization of sport-confidence and competitive orientation: Preliminary investigation and instrument development. **Journal of Sport Psychology, 8,** 221-246. (Various Sports)

2068. Vealey, R. S. (1988). Sport-confidence and competitive orientation: An addendum on scoring procedures and gender differences. **Journal of Sport & Exercise Psychology, 10,** 471-478. (Gymnastics, Psychometric)

2069. Vealey, R. S., & Campbell, J. L. (1988). Achievement goals of adolescent figure skaters: Impact on self-confidence, anxiety, and performance. **Journal of Adolescent Research, 3,** 227-243. (Figure Skating/Ice Skating)

Flow State Scale

2070. Doganis, G., Iosifidou, P., & Vlachopolous. S. P. (2000). Factor structure and internal consistency of the Greek version of the Flow State Scale. **Perceptual and Motor Skills, 91,** 1231-1240. (Handball, Psychometric, Volleyball)

2071. Jackson, S. A., & Marsh, H. W. (1996). Development and validation of a scale to measure optimal experience: The Flow State Scale. **Journal of Sport & Exercise Psychology, 18,** 17-35. (Psychometric)

2072. Jackson, S. A., Thomas, P. R., Marsh, H. W., & Smethurst, C. J. (2001). Relationships between flow, self-concept, psychological skills, and performance. **Journal of Applied Sport Psychology, 13,** 129-153. (Cycling, Orienteering, Surfing)

2073. Kowal, J., Fortier, M. (1999). Motivational determinants of flow: Contributions from self-determination theory. **Journal of Social Psychology, 139,** 355-368. (Swimming)

2074. Pates, J., & Maynard, I. W. (2000). Effects of hypnosis on flow states and golf performance. **Perceptual and Motor Skills, 91,** 1057-1075. (Golf)

2075. Vlachopolous, S. P., Karageorghis, C. I., & Terry, P. C. (2000). Hierarchical confirmatory factor analysis of the Flow State Scale in exercise. **Journal of Sports Sciences, 18,** 815-823.(Psychometric)

2076. Wiggins, M. S., & Freeman, P. (2000). Anxiety and flow: Examination of anxiety direction and the flow experience. **International Sports Journal, 4,** 78-87. (Volleyball)

Life Events Survey for Collegiate Athletes (LESCA)

2077. Andersen, M. B., & Williams, J. M. (1999). Athletic injury, psychosocial factors, and perceptual changes during stress. **Journal of Sports Sciences, 17,** 735-741. (Injury, Various Sports)

2078. Brewer, B. W., & Petrie, T. A. (1995). A comparison between injured and uninjured football players on selected psychosocial variables. **The Academic Athletic Journal**, Spring, 11-18. (Football, Injury)

2079. Gunnoe, A. J., Horodyski, M., Tennant, L. K., & Murphey, M. (2001). The effect of life events on incidence of injury in high school football players. **Journal of Athletic Training, 36**, 150-155. (Football, Injury)

2080. Petrie, T. A. (1992). Psychosocial antecedents of athletic injury: The effects of life stress and social support on female collegiate gymnasts. **Behavioral Medicine, 18**, 127-137. (Gymnastics, Injury)

2081. Petrie, T. A. (1993). Racial differences in the prediction of college football players' academic performance. **Journal of College Student Development, 34**, 418-421. (Football)

2082. Petrie, T. A.. (1993). The moderating effects of social support and playing status on the life stress-injury relationship. **Journal of Applied Sport Psychology, 5**, 1-16. (Football, Injury)

2083. Petrie, T. A. (1993). Coping skills, competitive trait anxiety, and playing status: Moderating effects of the life stress-injury relationship. **Journal of Sport & Exercise Psychology, 15**, 261-274. (Football, Injury)

2084. Petrie, T. A. (1995). Academic and psychosocial antecedents of academic performance for minority and nonminority college football players. **Journal of Counseling and Development, 73**, 615-620. (Football)

2085. Petrie, T. A., & Stoever, S. (1997). Academic and nonacademic predictors of female student-athletes' academic performances. **Journal of College Student Development, 38**, 599-607. (Soccer, Volleyball)

2086. Petrie, T. A., Andersen, M., & Williams, J. M. (1996). Gender differences in the prediction of college student-athletes' academic performances. **College Student Affairs Journal, 16**, 63-70. (Various Sports)

Motivation Of Marathoners Scale (MOMS)

2087. Masters, K. S., & Ogles, B. M. (1995). An investigation of the different motivations of marathon runners with varying degrees of experience. **Journal of Sport Behavior, 18,** 69-79. (Marathon, Running)

2088. Masters, K. S., Ogles, B. M., & Jolton, J. A. (1993). The development of an instrument to measure motivation for marathon running: The motivations of marathoners scales (MOMS). **Research Quarterly for Exercise and Sport, 64,** 134-143. (Marathon, Psychometric)

2089. Ogles, B. M., & Masters, K. S. (2000). Older vs. younger adult male marathon runners: Participative motives and training habits. **Journal of Sport Behavior, 23,** 130-143. (Marathon, Running)

2090. Ogles, B. M., Masters, K. S., & Richardson, S. A. (1995). Obligatory running and gender: An analysis of participative motives and training habits. **International Journal of Sport and Exercise, 26,** 233-248. (Running)

Negative Addiction Scale

2091. Estok, P. J., & Rudy, E. B. (1986). Physical, psychosocial, menstrual changes/risks, and addiction in female marathon and nonmarathon runners. **Health Care for Women International, 7,** 187-202. (Marathon, Running)

2092. Furst, D. M., & Germone, K. (1993). Negative addiction in male and female runners and exercisers. **Perceptual and Motor Skills, 77,** 192-194. (Exercise, Running)

2093. Hailey, B. J., & Bailey, L. A. (1982). Negative addiction in runners: A quantitative approach. **Journal of Sport Behavior, 5,** 150-154. (Running)

2094. Kirkby, R. J., & Adams, J. (1996). Exercise dependence: The relationship between two measures. **Perceptual and Motor Skills, 82,** 366. (Exercise)

2095. Leedy, M. G. (2000). Commitment to distance running: Coping mechanism or addiction? **Journal of Sport Behavior, 23,** 255-270. (Marathon, Running)

2096. Mathers, S., & Walker, M. B. (1999). Extraversion and exercise addiction. **Journal of Psychology, 133,** 125-128. (Exercise)

2097. Pierce, E. F., Daleng, M. L., & McGowan, R. W. (1993). Scores on exercise dependence among dancers. **Perceptual and Motor Skills, 76,** 531-535. (Dance, Field Hockey, Running)

2098. Rudy, E. B., & Estok, P. J. (1989). Measurement and significance of negative addiction in runners. **Western Journal of Nursing Research, 11,** 548-558. (Running)

2099. Rudy, E. B., & Estok, P. J. (1990). Running addiction and dyadic adjustment. **Research in Nursing and Health, 13,** 219-225. (Running)

2100. Sachs, M. L., & Pargman, D. (1979). Running addiction: A depth interview examination. **Journal of Sport Behavior, 2,** 143-155. (Running)

2101. Salokun, S. O., & Toriola, A. L. (1985). Personality characteristics of sprinters, basketball, soccer, and field hockey players. **Journal of Sports Medicine, 25,** 222-226. (Basketball, Field Hockey, Soccer, Track and Field)

2102. Thaxton, L. (1982). Physiological and psychological effects of short-term exercise addiction on habitual runners. **Journal of Sport Psychology, 4,** 73-80. (Running)

2103. Thornton, E. W., & Scott, S. E. (1995). Motivation in the committed runner: Correlations between self-report scales and behavior. **Health Promotion International, 10,** 177-184. (Running)

Physical Activity Enjoyment Scale (PACES)

2104. Crocker, P. R. E., Bouffard, M., & Gessaroli, M. E. (1995). Measuring enjoyment in youth sport settings: A confirmatory factor analysis of the Physical Activity Enjoyment Scale. **Journal of Sport & Exercise Psychology, 17,** 200-205. (Psychometric)

2105. Kendzierski, D., & DeCarlo, K. J. (1991). Physical Activity Enjoyment Scale: Two validation studies. **Journal of Sport & Exercise Psychology, 13**, 50-64. (Psychometric)

2106. Motl, R. W., Berger, B. G., & Leuschen, P. S. (2000). The role of enjoyment in the exercise-mood relationship. **International Journal of Sport Psychology, 31**, 347-363. ((Rock Climbing)

Recovery-Stress-Questionnaire for Athletes (RESTQ-Sport)

2107. Kellman, M., & Gunther, K. D. (2000). Changes in stress and recovery in elite rowers during preparation for the Olympic Games. **Medicine and Science in Sports and Exercise, 32**, 676-683. (Rowing)

2108. Kellman, M., Alternburg, D., Lormes, W., & Steinacker, J. M. (2001). Assessing stress and recovery during preparation for the world championships in rowing. **The Sport Psychologist, 15**, 151-167. (Rowing)

Scale of Children's Action Tendencies in Sport (SCATS)

2109. Braathen, E. T., & Svebak, S. (1994). EMG response patterns and motivational styles as predictors of performance and discontinuation in explosive and endurance sports among talented teenage athletes. **Personality and Individual Differences, 17**, 545-556. (Various Sports)

2110. Bredemeier, B. J. L. (1994). Children's moral reasoning and their assertiveness, aggressive, and submissive tendencies in sport and daily life. **Journal of Sport & Exercise Psychology, 16**, 1-14. (Youth)

2111. Deluty, R. H. (1979). Children's action tendency scale: A self-report measure of aggressiveness, assertiveness, and submissive tendencies in children. **Journal of Consulting and Clinical Psychology, 47**, 1061-1071. (Psychometric)

2112. Katzenellenbogen, E. H. (1990). Physical education as non-formal schooling: An educational opportunity for interpersonal relationships. **S. A. Journal for Research in Sport, Physical Education, and Recreation, 13**, 11-29. (Physical Education Class(es)

Social Physique Anxiety Scale (SPAS)

2113. Conroy, D. E., Motl, R. W., & Hall, E. G. (2000). Progress toward construct validity of the Self-Presentation in Exercise Questionnaire (SPEQ). **Journal of Sport & Exercise Psychology, 22**, 21-38. (Exercise)

2114. Cox, L. M., Lantz, C. D., & Mayhew, J. L. (1997). The role of social physique anxiety and other variables in predicting eating behaviors in college students. **International Journal of Sport Nutrition, 7**, 310-317. (College Students)

2115. Crawford, S., & Eklund, R. C. (1994). Social physique anxiety, reasons for exercise, and attitudes toward exercise settings. **Journal of Sport & Exercise Psychology, 16**, 70-82. (Exercise)

2116. Diehl, N., Johnson, C. E., Rogers, R. L., & Petrie, T. A. (1998). Social physique anxiety and disordered eating: What's the connection? **Addictive Behaviors, 23**, 1-6. (College Students)

2117. Eklund, R. C. (1998). With regard to the Social Physique Anxiety Scale (conceptually speaking). **Journal of Sport & Exercise Psychology, 20**, 225-227. (Review Article)

2118. Eklund, R. C., & Crawford, S. (1994). Active women, social physique anxiety, and exercise. **Journal of Sport & Exercise Psychology, 16**, 431-448. (Exercise)

2119. Eklund, R. C., Kelley, B. C., & Wilson, P. W. (1997). The Social Physique Anxiety Scale: Men, women, and the effects of modifying item 2. **Journal of Sport & Exercise Psychology, 19**, 188-196. (Psychometric)

2120. Eklund, R. C., Mack, D., & Hart, E. A. (1996). Factorial validity of the Social Physique Anxiety Scale for females. **Journal of Sport & Exercise Psychology, 18**, 281-295. (Psychometric)

2121. Finkenberg, M. E., DiNucci, J. M., & McCune, S. L. (1998). Commitment to physical activity and anxiety about physique among college women. **Perceptual and Motor Skills, 87**, 1393-1394. (Exercise)

2122. Frederick, C. M., & Morrison, C. S. (1996). Social physique anxiety: Personality constructs, motivations, exercise attitudes, and behaviors. **Perceptual and Motor Skills, 82**, 963-972. (Exercise)

2123. Frederick, C. M., & Morrison, C. S. (1998). A mediational model of social physique anxiety and eating disordered behaviors. **Perceptual and Motor Skills, 86**, 139-145. (College Students)

2124. Hart, E. A., Leary, M. R., & Rejeski, W. J. (1989). The measurement of social physique anxiety. **Journal of Sport & Exercise Psychology, 11**, 94-104. (Physical Education Class(es), Psychometric)

2125. Hurst, R., Hale, B. D., Smith, D. K., & Collins, D. (2000). Exercise dependence, social physique anxiety, and social support in experienced and inexperienced bodybuilders and weightlifters. **British Journal of Sports Medicine, 34**, 431-435. (Bodybuilding, Weightlifting)

2126. Isogai, H., Brewer, B. W., Cornelius, A. E., Komiya, S., Tokunaga, M., & Tokushima, S. (2001). Cross-cultural validation of the Social Physique Anxiety Scale. **International Journal of Sport Psychology, 32**, 76-87. (Physical Education Class(es)

2127. Kowalski, N. P., Crocker, P. R. E., Kowalski, K. C. (2001). Physical self and physical activity relationships in college women: Does social physique anxiety moderate effects? **Research Quarterly for Exercise and Sport, 72**, 55-62. (College Students, Exercise)

2128. Krane, V., Stiles-Shipley, J. A., Waldron, J., & Michalenok, J. (2001). Relationships among body satisfaction, social physique anxiety, and eating behaviors in female athletes and exercisers. **Journal of Sport Behavior, 24**, 247-264. (Exercise, Various Athletes)

2129. Lantz, C. D., Hardy, C. J., & Ainsworth, B. E. (1997). Social physique anxiety and perceived exercise behavior. **Journal of Sport Behavior, 20**, 83-93. (Exercise)

2130. Martin, K. A., Rejeski, W. J., Leary, M. R., McAuley, E., & Bane, S. (1997). Is the Social Physique Anxiety Scale really multidimensional? Conceptual and statistical arguments for a unidimensional model. **Journal of Sport & Exercise Psychology, 19**, 359-367. (Psychometric)

2131. McAuley, E., & Burman, G. (1993). The Social Physique Anxiety Scale: Construct validity in adolescent females. **Medicine and Science in Sports and Exercise, 25**, 1049-1053. (Psychometric)

2132. Motl, R. W., & Conroy, D. E. (2000). Validity and factorial invariance of the Social Physique Anxiety Scale. **Medicine and Science in Sports and Exercise, 32**, 1007-1017. (Physical Education Class(es), Psychometric)

2133. Nevill, A. M., Lane, A. M., Kilgour, L. J., Bowes, N., & Whyte, G.P. (2001). Stability of psychometric questionnaires. **Journal of Sports Sciences, 19**, 273-278. (Psychometric)

2134. Petrie, T. A., Diehl, N., Rogers, R. L., & Johnson, C. L. (1996). The Social Physique Anxiety Scale: Reliability and construct validity. **Journal of Sport & Exercise Psychology, 18**,
(Psychometric)

2135. Reel, J. J., & Gill, D. L. (1996). Psychosocial factors related to eating disorders among high school and college female cheerleaders. **The Sport Psychologist, 10**, 195-206. (Cheerleading)

2136. Smith, A. L., & Etzbach, M. E. (2001). Factorial validity and invariance of the Social Physique Anxiety Scale in female and male young adolescents. **Journal of Sport & Exercise Psychology, 23,** S35-S36. (Psychometric)

2137. Spink, K. S. (1992). Relation of anxiety about social physique to location of participation in physical activity. **Perceptual and Motor Skills, 74,** 1075-1078. (Exercise)

2138. Williams, P. A., & Cash, T. F. (2001). Effects of a circuit weight training program on the body of images of college students. **International Journal of Eating Disorders, 30,** 75-82. (College Students, Exercise, Weightlifting)

2139. Yin, Z. N. (2001). Examining the validity of the Social Physique Anxiety Scale. **Journal of Sport & Exercise Psychology, 23,** S44-S45. (Psychometric)

Sport Orientation Questionnaire (SOQ)

2140. Braathen, E. T., & Svebak, S. (1994). EMG response patterns and motivational styles as predictors of performance and discontinuation in explosive and endurance sports among talented teenage athletes. **Personality and Individual Differences, 17,** 545-556. (Various Sports)

2141. Deeter, T. E. (1988). Does attitudinal commitment predict physical activity participation? **Journal of Sport Behavior, 11,** 177-192. (Exercise)

2142. Deeter, T. E. (1989). The development of a model of achievement behavior for physical activity. **Journal of Sport & Exercise Psychology, 11,** 13-25. (Physical Education Class(es), Various Sports)

2143. Deeter, T. E. (1990). Remodeling expectancy and value in physical activity. **Journal of Sport & Exercise Psychology, 12,** 86-91. (Physical Education Class(es)

2144. Finkenberg, M. E., Moode, F. M., & DiNucci, J. M. (1998). Analysis of sport orientation of female collegiate athletes. **Perceptual and Motor Skills, 86,** 647-650. (Basketball, Softball, Volleyball)

2145. Gill, D. L., & Deeter, T. E. (1988). Development of the Sport Orientation Questionnaire. **Research Quarterly for Exercise and Sport, 59**, 191-202. (Psychometric)

2146. Gill, D. L., Dzewaltowski, D. A., & Deeter, T. E. (1988). The relationship of competitiveness and achievement orientation to participation in sport and nonsport activities. **Journal of Sport & Exercise Psychology, 10**, 139-150. (Physical Education Class(es)

2147. Hellandsig, E. T. (1998). Motivational predictors of high performance and discontinuation in different types of sports among talented teenage athletes. **International Journal of Sport Psychology, 29**, 27-44. (Various Sports)

2148. Jones, J. G., & Swain, A. (1992). Intensity and direction as dimensions of competitive state anxiety and relationships with competitiveness. **Perceptual and Motor Skills, 74**, 467-472. (Various Sports)

2149. Lerner, B. S., & Locke, E. A. (1995). The effects of goal-setting, self-efficacy, competition, and personal traits on the performance of an endurance task. **Journal of Sport & Exercise Psychology, 17**, 138-152. (Physical Education Class(es)

2150. Marsh, H. W. (1994). Sport motivation orientations: Beware of jingle-jangle fallacies. **Journal of Sport & Exercise Psychology, 16**, 365-380. (Youth)

2151. Martin, J. J., Smith, K. L., & Adams-Mushett, C. (1999). Athletic identity and sport orientation of adolescent swimmers with disabilities. **Adapted Physical Education Quarterly, 12**, 113-123. (Disabled Athletes, Swimming)

2152. Meyer, B. B. (2000). The ropes and challenge course: A quasi-experimental examination. **Perceptual and Motor Skills, 90**, 1249-1257. (Tennis)

2153. Prapavessis, H., & Grove, J. R. (1994). Personality variables as antecedents of precompetitive mood states. **International Journal of Sport Psychology, 25**, 81-99. (Shooting)

2154. Skordilis, E. K., Koutsouki, D., Asonitou, K., Evans, E., Jensen, B., & Wall, K. (2001). Sport orientations and goal perspectives of wheelchair athletes. **Adapted Physical Education Quarterly, 18**, 304-315. (Disabled Athletes, Marathon, Basketball)

2155. Zoerink, D. A., & Wilson, J. (1995). The competitive disposition: Views of athletes with mental retardation. **Adapted Physical Education Quarterly, 12**, 34-42. (Disabled Athletes, Various Sports)

Sports Inventory for Pain (SIP)

2156. Bartholomew, J. B., Brewer, B. W., VanRaalte, J. L., Linder, D. E., Cornelius, A. E., & Bart, S. M. (1998). A psychometric evaluation of the sports inventory for pain. **The Sport Psychologist, 12**, 29-39. (Psychometric)

2157. Bartholomew, J. B., Edwards, S. M., Brewer, B. W., VanRaalte, J. L., & Linder, D. E. (1998). The sports inventory for pain: A confirmatory factor analysis. **Research Quarterly for Exercise and Sport, 69**, 24-29. (Psychometric)

2158. Encarnacion, M. L., Meyers, M. C., Ryan, N. D., & Pease, D. G. (2000). Pain coping styles of ballet performers. **Journal of Sport Behavior, 23**, 20-32. (Dance)

2159. Leddy, M. H., Lambert, M. J., & Ogles, B. M. (1994). Psychological consequences of athletic injury among high-level competitors. **Research Quarterly for Exercise and Sport, 65**, 347-354. (Injury, Various Sports)

2160. Meyers, M. C., Bourgeois, A. E., & LeUnes A. (2001). Pain coping responses of athletes involved in high contact, high injury-potential sport. **International Journal of Sport Psychology, 32**, 29-42. (Injury, Rodeo)

2161. Meyers, M. C., Bourgeois, A. E., Stewart, S., & LeUnes, A. (1992). Predicting pain response in athletes: Development and assessment of the sports inventory for pain. **Journal of Sport & Exercise Psychology, 14**, 249-261. (Psychometric)

2162. Nichols, D. S., & Glenn, T. M. (1994). Effects of aerobic exercise on pain perception, affect, and level of disability in individuals with fibromyalgia. **Physical Therapy, 74**, 327-332. (Exercise)

Task and Ego Orientation in Sport Questionnaire (TEOSQ)

2163. Balaguer, I., Duda, J. L., & Crespo, M. (1999). Motivational climate and goal orientations as predictors of perceptions of improvement, satisfaction and coach ratings among tennis players. **Scandinavian Journal of Medicine and Science in Sports, 9**, 381-388. (Tennis)

2164. Biddle, S. J. H., Akande, A., Vlachopoulos, S. P., & Fox, K. R. (1996). Toward an understanding of children's motivation for physical activity: Achievement goal orientations, beliefs about sport success, and sport emotion in Zimbabwean children. **Psychology and Health, 12**, 49-55. (Youth)

2165. Boyd, M., & Callaghan, J. (1994). Task and ego goal perspectives in organized youth sport. **International Journal of Sport Psychology, 25**, 411-424. (Baseball)

2166. Chi, L., & Duda, J. L. (1995). Multi-sample confirmatory factor analysis of the task and ego orientation in sport questionnaire. **Research Quarterly for Exercise and Sport, 66**, 91-98. (Psychometric)

2167. Duda, J. L. (1989). The relationship between task orientation and ego orientation and the perceived purpose of sport among male and female high school athletes. **Journal of Sport & Exercise Psychology, 11**, 318-335. (Various Sports)

2168. Duda, J. L. (1992). Motivation in sport settings: A goal perspective. In G. Roberts (Ed.), **Motivation in sport and exercise** (pp. 57-91). Champaign, IL: Human Kinetics. (Review Article)

2169. Duda, J. L. (1993). Goals: A social cognitive approach to the study of achievement motivation in sport. In. R. N. Singer, M. Murphy, & L. K. Tennant (Eds.), **Handbook of research in sport psychology** (p. 421-436). St. Louis, MO: Macmillan. (Review Article)

2170. Duda, J. L. (1996). Maximizing motivation in sport and physical education among children and adolescents: The case for greater task involvement. **Quest, 48**, 290-302. (Review Article)

2171. Duda, J. L., & Hom, H. L. (1993). Interdependencies between the perceived and self-reported goal orientations of young athletes and their parents. **Pediatric Exercise Science, 5**, 234-241. (Basketball)

2172. Duda, J. L., & Huston, L. (1995). The relationship of goal orientation and degree of competitive sport participation in the endorsement of aggressive acts in American football. In R. Vanfraechem-Raway & Y. vanden Auweele (Eds.), **IXth European Congress on Sport Psychology Proceedings** (pp. 655-662). Brussels, Belgium. (Football)

2173. Duda, J. L., & Nicholls, J. G. (1989). **The Task and Ego Orientation Questionnaire: Psychometric properties.** Unpublished manuscript. (Psychometric, Test Manual)

2174. Duda, J. L., & Nicholls, J. G. (1992). Dimensions of achievement motivation in schoolwork and sport. **Journal of Educational Psychology, 84**, 290-299. (Youth)

2175. Duda, J. L., & White, S. A. (1992). Goal orientations and beliefs about the causes of sport success among elite skiers. **The Sport Psychologist, 6**, 334-343. (Skiing)

2176. Duda, J. L. & Whitehead, J. R. (1998). Measurement of goal perspectives in the physical domain. In J. L. Duda (Ed.), **Advances in sport and exercise psychology measurement** (pp. 21-48). Morgantown, WV: Fitness Information Technology. (Review Article)

2177. Duda, J. L., Fox, K. R., Biddle, S. J. H., & Armstrong, N. (1992). Children's achievement goals and beliefs about success in sport. **British Journal of Educational Psychology, 62**, 313-323. (Youth)

2178. Duda, J. L., Olson, L. K., & Templin, T. J. (1991). The relationship of task and ego orientation to sportsmanship attitudes and the perceived legitimacy of injurious acts. **Research Quarterly for Exercise and Sport, 62**, 79-87. (Basketball)

2179. Duda, J. L., Chi, L., Newton, M. L., Walling, M. D., & Catley, D. (1995). Task and ego orientation and intrinsic motivation in sport. **International Journal of Sport Psychology, 26**, 40-63. (Tennis)

2180. Dunn, J. C. (2000). Goal orientations, perceptions of the motivational climate, and perceived competence of children with movement difficulties. **Adapted Physical Activity Quarterly, 17**, 1-19. (Disabled Athletes, Youth)

2181. Ebbeck, V., & Becker, S. L. (1994). Psychosocial predictors of goal orientations in youth soccer. **Research Quarterly for Exercise and Sport, 65**, 355-362. (Soccer)

2182. Ferrer-Caja, E., & Weiss, M. R. (2000). Predictors of intrinsic motivation among adolescent students in physical education. **Research Quarterly for Exercise and Sport, 71**, 267-279. (Physical Education Class(es)

2183. Fox, K. R., Goudas, M., Biddle, S. J. H., Duda, J. L., & Armstrong, N. (1994). Children's task and ego profiles in sport. **British Journal of Educational Psychology, 64**, 253-261. (Youth)

2184. Georgiadis, M., Biddle, S. J. H., & vanden Auweele, Y. (2001). Cognitive, emotional, and behavioural connotations of task and ego goal orientation profiles: An ideographic approach using hierarchical class analysis. **International Journal of Sport Psychology, 32**, 1-20. (Cricket)

2185. Givvin, K. B., (2001). Goal orientations of adolescents, coaches, and parents: Is there a convergence of beliefs? **Journal of Early Adolescence, 21**, 227-247. (Swimming)

2186. Goudas, M., Biddle, S. J. H., & Fox, K. R. (1994). Perceived locus of causality, goal orientations, and perceived competence in school physical-education classes. **British Journal of Educational Psychology, 64**, 453-463. (Physical Education Class(es)

2187. Guinn, B., Vincent, V., Semper, T., & Jorgensen, L. (2000). Activity involvement, goal perspective, and self-esteem among Mexican American adolescents. **Research Quarterly for Exercise and Sport, 71**, 308-311. (Physical Education Class(es)

2188. Hall, H. K., & Kerr, A. W. (1997). Motivational antecedents of precompetitive anxiety in youth sport. **The Sport Psychologist, 11**, 24-42. (Fencing)

2189. Harwood, C. G., Hardy, L., & Swain, A. (2000). Achievement goals in sport: A critique of conceptual and measurement issues. **Journal of Sport & Exercise Psychology, 22**, 235-255. (Review Article)

2190. Hatzigeorgiadis, A., & Biddle, S. J. H. (1999). The effects of goal orientation and perceived competence on cognitive interference during tennis and snooker performance. **Journal of Sport Behavior, 22**, 479-501. (Snooker, Tennis)

2191. Hodge, K., & Petlichkoff, L. (2000). Goal profiles in sport motivation: A cluster analysis. **Journal of Sport & Exercise Psychology, 22**, 256-272. (Psychometric, Rugby)

2192. Kim, B. J., & Gill, D. L. (1997). A cross-cultural extension of goal perspective theory to Korean youth sport. **Journal of Sport & Exercise Psychology, 19**, 142-155. (Various Sports, Youth)

2193. King, L. A., & Williams, T. A. (1997). Goal orientation and performance in martial arts. **Journal of Sport Behavior, 20**, 397-411. (Martial Arts)

2194. Li, F., Harmer, P., & Acock, A. (1996). The task and ego orientation in sport questionnaire: Construct equivalence and mean differences across gender. **Research Quarterly for Exercise and Sport, 67,** 228-238. (Psychometric)

2195. Li, F., Harmer, P., Chi, L., & Vongjaturapat, N. (1996). Cross-cultural validation of the task and ego orientation in sport questionnaire. **Journal of Sport & Exercise Psychology, 18**, 392-407. (Psychometric)

2196. Li, F., Duncan, T. E., Duncan, S. C., Harmer, P., & Acock, A. (1998). Testing the task and ego orientation in sport questionnaire (TEOSQ) measurement model with incomplete data: An application of maximum likelihood-based estimation procedures. **Measurement in Physical Education and Exercise Science, 2**, 1-19. (Psychometric)

2197. Li, F., Harmer, P., Acock, A., Vongjaturapat, N., & Boonverabut, S. (1997). Testing the cross-cultural validity of TEOSQ and its factor covariance and mean structures across gender. **International Journal of Sport Psychology, 28**, 271-286. (Various Sports)

2198. Li, F. Z., Harmer, P., Duncan, T. E., Duncan, S. C., Acock, A., & Yamamoto, T. (1998). Confirmatory factor analysis of the Task and Ego Orientation in Sport Questionnaire with cross-validation. **Research Quarterly for Exercise and Sport, 69**, 276-283. (Physical Education Class(es), Psychometric)

2199. Magyar, T. M., & Duda, J. L., (2000). Confidence restoration following athletic injury. **The Sport Psychologist, 14**, 372-390. (Injury)

2200. Martinek, T. J., & Williams, L. (1997). Goal orientation and task persistence in learned helpless and mastery oriented students in middle school physical education classes. **International Sports Journal, 1**, 63-76. (Physical Education Class(es)

2201. Newton, M. L., & Duda, J. L. (1993). Elite adolescent athletes achievement goals and beliefs concerning success in tennis. **Journal of Sport & Exercise Psychology, 15**, 437-448. (Tennis)

2202. Ntoumanis, N., & Biddle, S. J. H. (1998). The relationship between achievement goal profile groups and perceptions of motivational climates in sport. **Scandinavian Journal of Medicine and Science in Sports, 8,** 120-124. (Basketball, Ice Hockey, Netball, Rugby, Soccer, Volleyball)

2203. Ryska, T. A., & Blasdel, T., (2001). The role of sport motivation on academic strategy use among high school athletes. **Journal of Sport & Exercise Psychology, 23,** S31-S31. (Various Sports)

2204. Ryska, T. A., & Kazen, T., (2000). The effect of acculturation on dispositional goal perspectives among Hispanic adolescent athletes. **International Journal of Psychology, 35,** 76-76. (Various Sports)

2205. Ryska, T. A., & Schuetz, L. (2001) Testing the factor structure and invariance of the TEOSQ among culturally diverse athletes. **Journal of Sport & Exercise Psychology, 23,** S31-S31. (Various Sports)

2206. Ryska, T. A., & Yin, Z. N. (1999). Dispositional and situational goal orientation as discriminators among recreational and competitive league athletes. **Journal of Social Psychology, 139,** 335-342. (Soccer)

2207. Skordilis, E. K., Koutsouki, D., Asonitou, K., Evans, E., Jensen, B., & Wall, K. (2001). Sport orientations and goal perspectives of wheelchair athletes. **Adapted Physical Education Quarterly, 18,** 304-315. (Basketball, Disabled Athletes, Marathon)

2208. Solomon, G. A., & Boone, J. (1993). The impact of student goal orientation in physical-education classes. **Research Quarterly for Exercise and Sport, 64,** 418-424. (Physical Education Class(es)

2209. Spray, C. M. (2000). Predicting participation in noncompulsory physical education: Do goal perspectives matter? **Perceptual and Motor Skills, 90,** 1207-1215. (Physical Education Class(es)

2210. Stein, G. L., Kimiecik, J. C., Daniels, J., & Jackson, S. A. (1995). Psychological antecedents of flow in recreational sport. **Personality and Social Psychology Bulletin, 21,** 125-135. (Basketball, Golf, Tennis)

2211. Steinberg, G., Grieve, F. G., & Glass, B. (2001). Achievement goals across the lifespan. **Journal of Sport Behavior, 24**, 298-306. (Various Sports)

2212. Stephens, D. E. (1998). The relationship of goal orientation and perceived ability to enjoyment and value in youth sport. **Pediatric Exercise Science, 10**, 236-247. (Soccer)

2213. Stephens, D. E. (2000). Predictors of likelihood to aggress in youth soccer: Examination of coed and all-girls teams. **Journal of Sport Behavior, 23**, 311-325. (Soccer)

2214. Stephens, D. E. (2001). Predictors of aggressive tendencies in girls' basketball: An examination of beginning and advanced participants in a summer skills camp. **Research Quarterly for Exercise and Sport, 72**, 257-266. (Basketball)

2215. Stephens, D. E., & Bredemeier, B. J. L. (1996). Moral atmosphere and judgments about aggression in girls' soccer: Relationships among moral and motivational variables. **Journal of Sport & Exercise Psychology, 18**, 158-173. (Soccer)

2216. Stephens, D. E., & Kavanagh, B. (1997). Predictors of aggression and cheating in youth ice hockey. **Journal of Sport & Exercise Psychology, 19** (Supplement), S110. (Ice Hockey)

2217. Stephens, D. E., Janz, K. E., & Mahoney, L. T. (2000). Goal orientation and ratings of perceived exertion in graded exercise testing of adolescents. **Perceptual and Motor Skills, 90**, 813-822. (Exercise)

2218. Swain, A. (1996). Social loafing and identifiability: The mediating role of achievement goal orientations. **Research Quarterly for Exercise and Sport, 67**, 337-344. (Physical Education Class(es)

2219. Swain, A., & Harwood, C.G. (1996). Antecedents of state goals in age-group swimmers: An interactionist perspective. **Journal of Sports Sciences, 14**, 111-124. (Swimming)

2220. Tenenbaum, G., Spence, R., & Christensen, S. (1999). The effect of goal difficulty and goal orientation on running performance in young females. **Australian Journal of Psychology, 51**, 6-11. (Running)

2221. Van-Yperen, N. W., & Duda, J. L. (1999). Goal orientations, beliefs about success, and performance improvement among young elite Dutch soccer players. **Scandinavian Journal of Medicine and Science in Sports, 9**, 358-364. (Soccer)

2222. Viira, R., & Raudsepp, L. (2000). Achievement goal orientations, beliefs about sport success and sport emotions as related to moderate to vigorous physical activity of adolescents. **Psychology and Health, 15**, 625-633. (Youth)

2223. Voight, M. R., Callaghan, J. L., & Ryska, T. A. (2000). Relationship between goal orientations, self-confidence and multidimensional trait anxiety among Mexican-American female youth athletes. **Journal of Sport Behavior, 23**, 271-288. (Volleyball)

2224. Walling, M. D. & Duda, J. L. (1995). Goals and their associations with beliefs about success in and perceptions of the purposes of physical education. **Journal of Teaching of Physical Education, 14**, 140-156. (Physical Education Class(es)

2225. White, S. A. (1996). Goal orientation and perceptions of the motivational climate initiated by parents. **Pediatric Exercise Science, 8**, 122-129. (Volleyball)

2226. White, S. A. (1998). Adolescent goal profiles, perceptions of the parent-initiated motivational climate, and competitive trait anxiety. **The Sport Psychologist, 12**, 16-28. (Various Sports)

2227. White, S. A. (1998). Young adolescents' task and ego goal orientation profiles and purposes of sport. **International Sports Journal, 2**, 18-27. (Volleyball)

2228. White, S. A., & Duda, J. L. (1993). Dimensions of goals and beliefs among adolescent athletes with physical disabilities. **Adapted Physical Activity Quarterly, 10**, 125-136. (Disabled Athletes)

2229. White, S. A., & Duda, J. L. (1994). The relationship of gender, level of sport involvement, and participation motivation to task and ego orientation. **International Journal of Sport Psychology, 25**, 4-18. (Psychometric, Various Sports)

2230. White, S. A., & Zellner, S.R. (1996). The relationship between goal orientation, beliefs about the causes of sport success, and trait anxiety among high school, intercollegiate, and recreational sport participants. **The Sport Psychologist, 10**, 58-72. (Various Sports)

2231. Williams, L. (1994). Goal orientations and athletes' preferences for competence information sources. **Journal of Sport & Exercise Psychology, 16**, 416-430. (Various Sports)

Test of Attentional and Interpersonal Style (TAIS)

2232. Albrecht, R. R., & Feltz, D. L. (1987). Generality and specificity of attention related to competitive anxiety and sport performance. **Journal of Sport Psychology, 9**, 231-248. (Baseball, Softball)

2233. Bergandi, T. A., Shryock, M. G., & Titus, T. G. (1990). The basketball concentration survey: Preliminary development and validation. **The Sport Psychologist, 4**, 119-129. (Basketball)

2234. Bergandi, T. A., & Wittig, A. F. (1988). Attentional style as a predictor of athletic injury. **International Journal of Sport Psychology, 19**, 226-235. (Injury, Various Sports)

2235. Bird, E. I. (1987). Psychophysiological processes during rifle shooting. **International Journal of Sport Psychology, 18**, 9-18. (Shooting)

2236. Bond, J. W., Miller, B. P., & Chrisfield, P. M. (1988). Psychological prediction of injury in elite swimmers. **International Journal of Sports Medicine, 9**, 345-348. (Injury, Swimming)

2237. Bond, J. W., & Sargent, G. (1995). Concentration skills in sport: An applied perspective. In T. Morris & J. Summers, J. (Eds.), **Sport psychology: Theory, applications, and issues**. (pp. 386-419). Brisbane, John Wiley. (Review Article)

2238. Cote, J., Salmela, J., & Papathanasopoulu, K. P. (1992). Effects of progressive exercise on attentional focus. **Perceptual and Motor Skills, 75**, 351-354, (Cycling).

2239. Dewey, D., Brawley, L. R., & Allard, F. (1989). Do the TAIS attentional-style scales predict how visual information is processed? **Journal of Sport & Exercise Psychology, 11**, 171-186. (Various Sports)

2240. Ford, S. K., & Summers, J. J. (1992). The factorial validity of the TAIS attentional style subscales. **Journal of Sport & Exercise Psychology, 14**, 283-297. (Psychometric)

2241. Hinton-Bayre, A. D., & Hanrahan, S. J. (1999). Sensation seeking, physical self -concept and attentional style in elite springboard and platform divers. **Journal of Human Movement Studies, 37**, 183-203. (Gymnastics)

2242. Maynard, I. W., & Howe, B. L. (1989). Attentional styles in rugby players. **Perceptual and Motor Skills, 69**, 283-289. (Rugby)

2243. McGowan, R. W., Talton, B. J., & Tobacyk, J. J. (1990). Attentional style and powerlifting performance. **Perceptual and Motor Skills, 70**, 1253-1257. (Weightlifting)

2244. Molander, B., & Backman, L. (1994). Attention and performance in miniature golf across life-span. **Journal of Gerontology, 49**, 35-41. (Golf)

2245. Nideffer, R. M. (1976). Test of attentional and interpersonal style. **Journal of Personality and Social Psychology, 34**, 394-404. (Review Article)

2246. Nideffer, R. M. (1987). Issues in the use of psychological tests in applied settings. **The Sport Psychologist, 1**, 18-28. (Diving)

2247. Nideffer, R. M. (1989). Anxiety, attention, and performance in sports: Theoretical and practical considerations. In D. Hackfort and C. D. Spielberger (Eds.), **Anxiety in sports: An international perspective**. (pp. 117-136). New York, New York: Hemisphere Publishing Company. (Various Sports)

2248. Nideffer, R. M. (1989). Attention control training. **Tasmanian Coach, 6,** 2-5. (Review Article)

2249. Nideffer, R. M. (1990). Use of the Test of Attentional and Interpersonal Style (TAIS) in sport. **The Sport Psychologist, 4,** 285-300. (Various Sports)

2250. Owen, H., & Lanning, W. (1982). The effects of three treatment methods upon anxiety and inappropriate attentional style among high school athletes. **International Journal of Sport Psychology, 13,** 154-162. (Various Sports)

2251. Power, S. L. (1986). Psychological assessment procedures of a track and field national event squad training weekend. In J. Watkins, T. Reilly, & L. Burwitz (Eds.), **Sports science**. New York: E & FN Spon. (Track and Field)

2252. Reis, J., & Bird, A. M. (1982). Cue processing as a function of breadth of attention. **Journal of Sport Psychology, 4,** 64-72. (Various Sports)

2253. Roeder, L. M., & Aufsesser, P. M. (1986). Selected attentional and interpersonal characteristics of wheelchair athletes. **Palaestra, 2**(2), 28-32, 43, 44. (Disabled Athletes)

2254. Savoy, C. (1993). A yearly mental training program for a college basketball player. **The Sport Psychologist, 7,** 173-190. (Basketball)

2255. Slogrove, C. L., Buys, F. J., & Foxcroft, C. D. (1989). Anxiety and attentional styles of women's field hockey teams. **Journal for Research in Sport, Physical Education and Recreation, 12,** 49-56. (Field Hockey)

2256. Solomon, R., Solomon, J., Micheli, L. J., Saunders, J. J., & Zurakowski, D. (2001). A personality profile of professional and conservatory student dancers. **Medical Problems of Performing Artists, 16,** 85-93. (Dance)

2257. Summers, J. J., & Ford, S. K. (1990). The Test of Attentional and Interpersonal Style: An evaluation. **International Journal of Sport Psychology, 21**, 102-111. (Psychometric)

2258. Summers, J. J., Miller, K., & Ford, S. K. (1991). Attentional style and basketball performance. **Journal of Sport & Exercise Psychology, 13**, 239-253. (Basketball)

2259. Terreni, L., Raffagnino, R., & Celesti, A. (1994). Trap shoot. **Movimento, 10** (2), 67-68. (Shooting)

2260. Vallerand, R. J. (1983). Attention and decision-making: A test of the predictive validity of the test of attention and interpersonal style (TAIS) in a sport setting. **Journal of Sport Psychology, 5**, 449-459. (Psychometric)

2261. Van Schoyck, S. R., & Grasha, A. F. (1981). Attentional style variations and athletic ability: The advantages of a sports-specific test. **Journal of Sport Psychology, 3**, 149-165. (Psychometric)

2262. Wilson, V. E., & Kerr, G. A. (1991). Attentional style and basketball shooting. **Perceptual and Motor Skills, 73**, 1025-1026. (Basketball)

2263. Wilson, V. E., Ainsworth, M., & Bird, E. I. (1985). Assessment of attentional abilities in male volleyball athletes. **International Journal of Sport Psychology, 16**, 296-306. (Volleyball)

2264. Ziegler, S. G. (1994). The effects of attentional shift training on the execution of soccer skills: A preliminary investigation. **Journal of Applied Behavior Analysis, 27**, 545-552. (Soccer).

SECTION FOUR

<u>MEASURES OF RESPONSE TENDENCIES</u>

The popularity of psychological assessment within sport and exercise psychology has grown considerably over the past several decades. At the same time, there has been an increasing awareness that the assessment devices are susceptible to a variety of response sets on the part of subjects being tested. One of these response sets is known as social desirability; that is, the tendency on the part of subjects to respond in socially desirable ways as opposed to responding in a completely honest fashion. Some of this socially desirable responding is probably subconscious. In other cases, the subject may be trying to project a more positive image to the sport psychologist administering the test. This latter situation is most likely to arise if an athlete feels that the test results will affect his or her selection to, or retention on, a team. A number of studies have tried to control for these response problems by administering tests of social desirability, the most popular of these being the Marlowe-Crowne Scale of Social Desirability.

CHAPTER TWENTY

Marlowe-Crowne Scale of Social Desirability

2265. Ballard, R. (1992). Short forms of the Marlowe-Crowne Social Desirability Scale. **Psychological Reports, 71**, 1155-1160. (Psychometric)

2266. Ballard, R., Crino, M. D., & Rubenfeld, S. (1988). Social desirability response bias and the Marlowe-Crowne Social Desirability Scale. **Psychological Reports, 63**, 227-237. (Psychometric)

2267. Dunn, E. C., Smith, R. E., & Smoll, F. L. (2001). Do sport-specific stressors predict athletic injury? **Journal of Science and Medicine in Sport, 4,** 283-291. (Injury)

2268. Fischer, D. G., & Fick, C. (1993). Measuring social desirability: Short forms of the Marlowe-Crowne Social Desirability Scale. **Educational and Psychological Measurement, 53**, 417-424. (Psychometric)

2269. Fraboni, M. A., & Cooper, D. (1989). Further validation of 3 short forms of the Marlowe-Crowne Scale of Social Desirability. **Psychological Reports, 65,** 595-600. (Psychometric)

2270. Goss, J. D. (1994). Hardiness and mood disturbances in swimmers while overtraining. **Journal of Sport & Exercise Psychology, 16,** 135-149. (Overtraining, Steroids/Drugs)

2271. Haase, A. M., Prapavessis, H., & Owens, R. G. (1999). Perfectionism and eating attitudes in competitive rowers: Moderating effects of body mass, weight classification and gender. **Psychology and Health, 14,** 643-657. (Rowing)

2272. Long, B. C., & Haney, C. J. (1986). Enhancing physical activity in sedentary women: Information, locus of control, and attitudes. **Journal of Sport Psychology, 8**, 8-24. (Exercise)

2273. Loo, R., & Thorpe, K. (2000). Confirmatory factor analyses of the full and short versions of the Marlowe-Crowne Desirability Scale. **Journal of Social Psychology, 140**, 628-635. (Psychometric)

2274. Markland, D., & Hardy, L. (1993). The Exercise Motivations Inventory: Preliminary development and validity of a measure of individual reasons for participation in regular physical exercise. **Personality and Individual Differences, 15**, 289-296. (Exercise)

2275. McCready, M. L., & Long, B. C. (1985). Locus of control, attitudes toward physical activity, and exercise adherence. **Journal of Sport Psychology, 7**, 346-359. (Exercise)

2276. McDonald, S., & Hardy, C. J. (1990). Affective response patterns of the injured athlete: An exploratory analysis. **The Sport Psychologist, 4**, 261-274. (Injury)

2277. Milburn, T. W., Bell, N., & Koeske, G. F. (1970). Effect of censure or praise and evaluative dependence on performance in a free-learning task. **Journal of Personality and Social Psychology, 15**, 43-47. (Motor Task)

2278. Motl, R. W., & Conroy, D. E. (2000). Validity and factorial invariance of the social physique anxiety scale. **Medicine and Science in Sports and Exercise, 32**, 1007-1017. (Psychometric)

2279. Persson, C. V. (1988). **The adaptation and validation of a sport-specific measure of locus of control**. (Microform Publications), University of Oregon: College of Human Development and Performance. (Various Sports)

2280. Prapavessis, H., Cox, R. H., & Brooks, L. (1996). A test of Martens, Vealey and Burton's theory of competitive anxiety. **Australian Journal of Science and Medicine and Sport, 28**, 24-29. (Various Sports)

2281. Ryska, T. A. (1993). Coping styles and response distortion on self-report inventories among high school athletes. **The Journal of Psychology, 127**, 409-418. (Various Sports)

2282. Simons, C. W., & Birkimer, J. C. (1988). An exploration of factors predicting the effects of aerobic conditioning on mood state. **Journal of Psychosomatic Research, 32**, 63-75. (Exercise)

2283. Smith, D. K., Hale, B. D., & Collins, D. (1998). Measurement of exercise dependence in bodybuilders. **Journal of Applied Sport Psychology, 4**, 134-143. (Bodybuilding)

2284. Voight, M. R., Callaghan, J. L., & Ryska, T. A. (2000). Relationship between goal orientations, self-confidence and multidimensional trait anxiety among Mexican-American female youth athletes. **Journal of Sport Behavior, 23**, 271-288. (Volleyball)

2285. Whitehead, J. R., & Corbin, C. B. (1988). Multidimensional scales for the measurement of locus of control of reinforcements for physical fitness behaviors. **Research Quarterly for Exercise and Sport, 59,** 108-117. (Exercise)

2286. Wichstrom, L. (1995). Harter's Self-Perception Profile for Adolescents: Reliability, validity, and evaluation of the question format. **Journal of Personality Assessment, 65**, 100-116. (Psychometric)

2287. Williams, J. M., & Krane, V. (1992). Coping styles and self-reported measures of state anxiety and self-confidence. **Journal of Applied Sport Psychology, 4,** 134-143. (Golf)

CHAPTER TWENTY-ONE
LIST OF SPORTS

A

Abseiling: 1343

Adventure Activities: 607, 653, 1961

Aerobatics: 392

Archery: 452, 1333

Automobile Racing: 279, 280, 281, 382, 383, 384, 473, 474, 475, 662, 681, 686, 1486

B

Badminton: 433, 516, 722, 1388, 1460, 1733

Baseball: 192, 200, 233, 284, 388, 455, 512, 513, 672, 946, 1061, 1420, 1426, 1465, 1609, 1624, 1718, 1728, 1815, 1824, 1831, 1839, 1843, 1844, 1867, 1875, 1894, 1913, 1914, 1926, 1931, 2165, 2232

Basketball: 23, 31, 41, 209, 410, 445, 446, 453, 478, 489, 492, 507, 513, 517, 537, 568, 580, 624, 638, 640, 641, 698, 717, 737, 741, 745, 849, 912, 974, 976, 980, 1113, 1132, 1153, 1211, 1233, 1253, 1275, 1317, 1396, 1417, 1418, 1426, 1430, 1437, 1445, 1446, 1447, 1456, 1472, 1493, 1502, 1503, 1505, 1536, 1539, 1541, 1542, 1544, 1552, 1555, 1556, 1557, 1563, 1567, 1569, 1579, 1583, 1615, 1616, 1623, 1628, 1644, 1650, 1678, 1679, 1692, 1729, 1730, 1733, 1741, 1762, 1791, 1792, 1793, 1814, 1817, 1819, 1820, 1821, 1828, 1829, 1831, 1835, 1836, 1856, 1860, 1861, 1863, 1865, 1871, 1872, 1874, 1878, 1882, 1883, 1884, 1886, 1887, 1901, 1919, 1922, 1935, 1938, 1984, 1985, 1999, 2050, 2101, 2144, 2154 2171, 2178, 2202, 2207, 2210, 2214, 2233, 2254, 2258, 2262

Bodybuilding: 87, 150, 286, 322, 323, 447, 606, 943, 948, 1103, 1245, 1299, 1990, 2045, 2125, 2283

Bowling: 1274, 1487, 1598, 1670, 1868

C

Cheerleading: 134, 1462, 2135

Cricket: 211, 1202, 1494, 1500, 1535, 1577, 1800, 1837, 2184

Cross Country: 168, 452, 478, 1477, 1479, 1569, 1665, 1932

Cycling: 156, 326, 758, 835, 879, 951, 963, 1000, 1006, 1031, 1059, 1060, 1119, 1164, 1267, 1438, 1478, 1611, 1950, 2072, 2238

D

Dance: 60, 64, 70, 73, 88, 99, 102, 110, 111, 113, 115, 122, 136, 154, 249, 402, 591, 594, 603, 612, 1043, 1051, 1076, 1603, 1972, 2097, 2158, 2256

Decathlon: 198

Disabled Athletes: 541, 550, 551, 552, 553, 554, 565, 598, 619, 629, 636, 898, 899, 900, 949, 959, 975, 976, 986, 987, 994, 1061, 1062, 1063, 1064, 1130, 1131, 1132, 1299, 1316, 1317, 1339, 1348, 1374, 1436, 1542, 1937, 2003, 2004, 2006, 2039, 2040, 2041, 2042, 2043, 2044, 2049, 2151, 2154, 2155, 2180, 2207, 2228, 2253

Dog Sled Racing: 300

Duathlon: 1516

E

Equestrian Sports: 598, 1080

Exercise: 82, 92, 94, 95, 98, 101, 121, 125, 129, 135, 139, 157, 158, 162, 164, 165, 166, 167, 169, 170, 171, 172, 174, 175, 178, 190, 212, 235, 238, 239, 240, 248, 251, 254, 266, 92, 293, 307, 308, 312, 328, 335, 340, 342, 354, 358, 359, 360, 365, 366, 373, 394, 398, 405, 419, 421, 430, 444, 451, 468, 470, 518, 519, 522, 529, 539, 559, 560, 561, 563, 564, 567, 569, 590, 599, 600, 601, 602, 620, 627, 637, 641, 682, 699 706, 707, 710, 718, 719, 721, 725, 727, 728, 729, 733, 739, 740, 749, 750, 751, 757, 759, 760, 761, 762, 763, 764, 766, 768, 771, 773,

G

H

I

L

M

Marathon: 129, 136, 140, 182, 347, 471, 662, 925, 953, 970, 1088, 1244, 1246, 1960, 2013, 2025, 2026, 2037, 2087, 2088, 2089, 2091, 2095, 2154, 2207

Martial Arts: 338, 404, 438, 452, 482, 500, 584, 605, 648, 897, 998, 1039, 1068, 1070, 1072, 1106, 1207, 1212, 1226, 1289, 1295, 1297, 1335, 1336, 1360, 1410, 1439, 1452, 1461, 1531, 1532, 1572, 1587, 1649, 1821, 1889, 1959, 2193

Motorcross: 1285, 1286

Mountain Climbing: 431, 440, 476, 486, 506, 645, 649, 652, 662, 686, 687, 1352

N

Netball: 1085, 1218, 1351, 1455, 1489, 1497, 1673, 1699, 1836, 2012, 2202

O

Orienteering: 1950, 2072

P

Parasailing: 648

R

Racquetball: 722

Rock Climbing: 232, 315, 332, 352, 665, 673, 674, 679, 802, 936, 1104, 1176, 1528, 1647, 2106

Rodeo: 343, 672, 1067, 1079, 1082, 1083, 1158, 1718, 1945, 2160

Roller Skating: 1581

Rowing: 112, 149, 305, 348, 389, 452, 487, 526, 568, 647, 745, 769, 858, 880, 909, 964, 1007, 1093, 1154, 1203, 1204, 1206, 1215, 1218, 1355, 1616, 1653, 1800, 1805, 1806, 1886, 1957, 2107, 2108, 2271

S

T

U

V

Volleyball: 176, 234, 277, 341, 367, 717, 741, 1115, 1243, 1294, 1302, 1380, 1421, 1442, 1443, 1446, 1447, 1448, 1449, 1450, 1467, 1536, 1552, 1591, 1605, 1637, 1638, 1659, 1661, 1668, 1711, 1728, 1736, 1791, 1792, 1810, 1820, 1825, 1845, 1846, 1847, 1863, 1873, 1899, 1900, 1901, 1938, 2014, 2034, 2070, 2076, 2085, 2144, 2202, 2223, 2225, 2227, 2263, 2284

W

Weightlifting: 92, 129, 130, 150, 197, 297, 447, 611, 716, 881, 927, 965, 1056, 1163, 1311, 1942, 1968, 2125, 2138, 2243

Wrestling: 62, 149, 346, 396, 446, 463, 479, 510, 513, 672, 851, 1108, 1177, 1178, 1394, 1395, 1467, 1471, 1518, 1558, 1580, 1659, 1660, 1686, 1718, 1791, 1805. 1806, 1863, 1878, 1883, 1886, 1891, 1892, 1893

Y

Yoga: 295, 870, 871

SPORT-RELATED TOPICS

Athletic Training: 29

Biofeedback: 159, 166, 184, 228, 1265, 1620

Coaching: 23, 24, 28, 31, 32, 33, 36, 37, 38, 39, 47, 48, 50, 624, 1063, 1502, 1503, 1678, 1679, 1815, 1853, 1875, 1876, 1878, 1882, 1891, 1892, 1893, 1894, 1898, 1899, 1900, 1901, 1902, 1904, 1910, 1916, 1917, 1918, 1920, 1921

College Students: 51, 61, 82, 93, 103, 285, 573, 583, 660, 1466, 1770, 1803, 1968, 1974, 1987, 2035, 2114, 2116, 2123, 2127, 2138

Health Behavior: 753

Injury: 187, 198, 258, 339, 534, 576, 613, 615, 643. 890, 1012, 1040, 1066, 1074, 1083, 1092, 1100, 1149, 1184, 1185, 1186, 1187, 1269, 1337, 1507, 1603,

1619, 1652, 1664, 1684, 1708, 1709, 1742, 1761, 1924, 1925, 1932, 1982, 2015, 2018, 2046, 2077, 2078, 2079, 2080, 2082, 2083, 2159, 2160, 2199, 2234, 2236, 2267, 2276

Leisure Activity: 21, 30, 201, 202, 203, 226, 260, 269, 329, 401, 409, 462, 558, 614, 653, 705, 712, 811, 820, 823, 843, 1292, 1408, 1832, 1961

Motor Task: 195, 196, 199, 204, 250, 432, 697, 894, 1293, 1303, 1310, 1312, 1321, 1369, 1622, 1663, 1738, 1759, 1766, 1785, 1958, 2003, 2277

Physical Education Class(es): 13, 19, 25, 229, 288, 290, 387, 426, 434, 498, 503, 575, 581, 618, 675, 802, 1283, 1412, 1501, 1538, 1617, 1639, 1657, 1662, 1676, 1691, 1722, 1725, 1760, 1768, 1772, 1958, 1964, 1978, 1994, 2023, 2024, 2038, 2112, 2124, 2126, 2132, 2142, 2143, 2146, 2149, 2182, 2186, 2187, 2198, 2200, 2208, 2209, 2218, 2224

Psychometric: 1, 2, 4, 6, 7, 8, 9, 11, 12, 18, 22, 27, 42, 43, 44, 45, 49, 55, 56, 57, 65, 67, 74, 77, 78, 109, 116, 133, 137, 142, 152, 154, 160, 177, 179, 193, 208, 214, 215, 218, 220, 222, 223, 230, 237, 242, 246, 247, 255, 261, 264, 267, 268, 301, 304, 316, 317, 318, 324, 357, 372, 379, 403, 411, 412, 417, 418, 423, 424, 425, 429, 442, 459, 461, 530, 532, 533, 536, 538, 542, 543, 544, 545, 546, 555, 556, 557, 571, 574, 577, 578, 581, 587, 597, 609, 642, 654, 657, 666, 669, 676, 680, 683, 691, 692, 694, 695, 696, 701, 709, 714, 723, 726, 730, 731, 735, 744, 747, 748, 754, 755, 758, 765, 767, 770, 772, 777, 779, 781, 785, 788, 789, 790, 791, 793, 795, 797, 798, 799, 800, 801, 803, 804, 805, 809, 810, 815, 816, 817, 839, 842, 844, 845, 846, 848, 850, 855, 863, 864, 865, 886, 887, 888, 889, 902, 907, 914, 924, 929, 938, 960, 961, 968, 977, 995, 996, 997, 998, 1001, 1005, 1020, 1025, 1026, 1027, 1028, 1029, 1030, 1031, 1032, 1033, 1034, 1042, 1045, 1084, 1087, 1118, 1129, 1136, 1152, 1159, 1160, 1161, 1170, 1172, 1173, 1174, 1196, 1198, 1210, 1214, 1217, 1227, 1228, 1232, 1235, 1256, 1265, 1282, 1324, 1334, 1342, 1347, 1389, 1440, 1459, 1463, 1506, 1517, 1522, 1599, 1602, 1604, 1620, 1621, 1632, 1633, 1636, 1651, 1681, 1722, 1751, 1753, 1754, 1755, 1756, 1771, 1779, 1780, 1781, 1783, 1784, 1790, 1801, 1824, 1825, 1842, 1858, 1869,

1879, 1885, 1888, 1891, 1909, 1921, 1927, 1929, 1936, 1951, 1953, 1955, 1956, 1962, 1963, 1964, 1966, 1977, 1986, 2001, 2010, 2041, 2053, 2054, 2063, 2068, 2070, 2071, 2075, 2088, 2104, 2105, 2111, 2119, 2120, 2124, 2130, 2131, 2132, 2133, 2134, 2136, 2139, 2145, 2156, 2157, 2161, 2166, 2173, 2191, 2194, 2195, 2196, 2198, 2229, 2240, 2257, 2260, 2261, 2265, 2266, 2268, 2269, 2273, 2278, 2286

Review Article: 52, 58, 66, 71, 89, 100, 106, 108, 117, 123, 143, 185, 206, 207, 228, 243, 314, 336, 369, 376, 380, 390, 400, 414, 416, 420, 435, 457, 465, 477, 485, 592, 593, 604, 608, 610, 616, 617, 622, 626, 635, 689, 690, 752, 767, 778, 787, 878, 896, 915, 1004, 1019, 1043, 1046, 1047, 1089, 1090, 1141, 1151, 1165, 1205, 1208, 1209, 1236, 1320, 1324, 1329, 1342, 1434, 1435, 1488, 1540, 1562, 1570, 1671, 1700, 1767, 1776, 1789, 1794, 1795, 1809, 1834, 1857, 1877, 1881, 1934, 1971, 1977, 1980, 1991, 1993, 1996, 2117, 2168, 2169, 2170, 2176, 2189, 2237, 2245, 2248

Sport Employees: 34

Sports Fans: 10, 337, 1233, 1585

Sports Officials: 40, 41, 46, 537, 580, 1430, 1628

Steroids/Drugs: 575, 859, 861, 867, 868, 869, 871, 872, 875, 895, 903, 920, 931, 940, 957, 958, 983, 1095, 1096, 1103, 1121, 1123, 1124, 1145, 1152, 1155, 1156, 1166, 1245, 2270

Test Manual: 5, 105, 107, 275, 374, 406, 436, 437, 688, 732, 756, 829, 838, 853, 1077, 1400, 1473, 1499, 1690, 1855, 1870, 2002, 2173

Various Sports: 26, 47, 59, 76, 81, 83, 84, 86, 88, 96, 97, 99, 102, 104, 121, 122, 131, 132, 144, 145, 146, 147, 151, 155, 186, 189, 194, 203, 205, 210, 217, 221, 241, 253, 270, 271, 272, 273, 274, 276, 278, 289, 303, 309, 310, 311, 325, 334, 353, 370, 371, 378, 381, 385, 386, 395, 397, 399, 427, 439, 443, 449, 450, 460, 464, 480, 484, 488, 490, 496, 497, 500, 502, 508, 520, 523, 525, 531, 534, 535, 548, 549, 562, 566, 572, 575, 576, 588, 615, 623, 625, 634, 644, 650, 651, 655, 656, 658, 663, 664, 670, 677, 678, 693, 700, 702, 704, 715, 720, 724, 734, 743,

746, 808, 847, 852, 1116, 1181, 1197, 1278, 1337, 1349, 1362, 1367, 1415, 1440, 1444, 1483, 1522, 1546, 1561, 1593, 1599, 1600, 1601, 1606, 1607, 1608, 1626, 1634, 1652, 1655, 1675, 1687, 1693, 1705, 1717, 1719, 1723, 1727, 1740, 1745, 1749, 1750, 1753, 1778, 1802, 1807, 1813, 1818, 1833, 1842, 1869, 1880, 1890, 1904, 1910, 1916, 1917, 1918, 1921, 1937, 1943, 1944, 1951, 1953, 1965, 1995, 2018, 2019, 2023, 2031, 2032, 2036, 2038, 2047, 2064, 2065, 2067, 2077, 2086, 2109, 2140, 2142, 2147, 2148, 2155, 2159, 2167, 2192, 2197, 2203, 2204, 2205, 2211, 2226, 2229, 2230, 2231, 2234, 2239, 2247, 2249, 2250, 2252, 2279, 2280, 2281

Youth: 256, 578, 738, 1265, 1737, 1782, 1975, 1986, 1997, 2000, 2005, 2110, 2150, 2164, 2174, 2177, 2180, 2183, 2192, 2222

CHAPTER TWENTY-TWO
<u>LIST OF AUTHORS</u>
A

Abadie. B. R., 1257

Abdelkader, M. S., 426

Abood, D. A., 86, 566, 1608

Abrams, P., 561

Abulafia, J., 324, 654

Acevedo, E. O., 29, 1675

Acock, A., 2194, 2196, 2197, 2198

Adame, D. D., 249

Adams, A. J., 269

Adams, I. C., 426

Adams, J., 2094

Adams-Mushett, C., 2040, 2041, 2042, 2043, 2044, 2151

Adamson, D. R., 1585

Agarwal, V., 433

Agocs, H., 672, 1158, 1718

Aguglia, E., 176

Aheng, R., 367

Ahnberg, J. L., 772

Ainsworth, B. E., 2129

Ainsworth, M., 1243, 2263

Akande, A., 2164

Alattar, M. M., 1197

Albinson, J. G., 84, 155, 588, 1598, 2005

Albrecht, R. R., 855, 1420, 1609, 1648, 2232

Alderman, R. B., 1450, 1638, 2047

Al-Dhaheri, A. S., 1975

Alexander, J. F., 1108

Alexander, V., 1421

Ali, A., 1136

Allard, F., 2239

Allemann, Y., 90

Allen, M., 856

Allen, R., 1309

Allen, T. W., 809, 810

Allender, J., 85, 225, 364, 408, 742, 794, 1250

Alpert, B., 175

Al-Sabhan, K., 57

Al-Shamari, S., 57

Al-Shehri, S., 57

Al-Subaie, A., 57

Altenburg, D., 1007

Amber, D., 567

Amunategui, F., 672, 1158, 1718

Amusa, L. O., 427

Anders, B., 1017

Andersen, M. B., 693, 1059. 1060, 1412, 1521, 1610, 1689, 1742, 2077, 2086

Anderson, C. A., 6, 823

Anderson, K. B., 6

Anderson, S. C., 260

Anderson, S. L., 87

Andersson, G., 530, 765

Andre, T., 743

Andres, F. F., 940, 2057

Andrykowski, M A., 914

Annesi, J. J., 857, 1258, 1259, 1422, 1423, 1787

Anshel, M. H., 250, 537, 580, 858, 1260, 1611, 1759

Ansorge, C. J., 216, 283, 603

Antill, J. K., 694

Appelbaum, M. C., 768

Appleby, D. C., 1932

Arabatzis, K., 1171

Arai, Y., 292

Araujo, J., 1086, 1224

Archer, J., 1

Argyle, M., 329

Arheart, K., 175

Armatas, C., 139

Armer, J. M., 164

Armstrong, L., 47

Armstrong, M., 1424, 1612

Armstrong, N., 2177, 2183

Arnett, J., 642

Arnold, G. F., 1861

Arnott, M., 1882

Arroll, B., 1189

Asci, A., 1971

Asci, F. H., 1971, 1972

Ashe, D., 1831

Ashford, B., 1979, 1980, 1986

Ashley, C. D., 88

Ashley, F., 1613

Ashley, M., 397

Ashton, M. K., 1388

Bell, G., 991

Bell, N., 2277

Belongia, C., 536, 1756

Bem, S. L., 18, 177, 695, 696, 709

Benedict, G. J., 560

Bennett, G., 1875

Ben-Porath, Y., 1045

Benson, H., 892

Benson, J. E., 90

Bentler, P. M., 680

Benton, D., 1222

Benzi, M., 401

Berenson, G. S., 268

Bergandi, T. A., 1615, 2233, 2234

Berger, B. G., 295, 296, 352, 710, 796, 866, 867, 868, 869, 870, 871, 872, 873
874, 875, 876, 877, 878, 879, 945, 1076, 1104, 1145, 1263, 1264, 1414, 2106

Bergey, D. B., 1627

Berglund, B., 880

Berkhoff, F., 782

Bernardo, P., 1396, 1729

Berry, D. T. R., 418

Berry, M., 1164

Berry, T. R., 568, 1616

Berryman-Miller, S., 591

Bertinetti, J. F., 592

Best, D. L., 749, 751

Betts, E., 1617

Betts, W., 229

Bezjak, J. E., 178

C

Callaghan, J. L., 1605, 2034, 2165, 2223, 2284

Callies, A., 300

Callister, R., 1106, 1289, 1452, 1531

Callow, N., 2012

Camacho, T. C., 174

Campbell, E., 898, 899, 1436

Campbell, J. B., 647

Campbell, J. L., 1582, 2020, 2033, 2069

Campbell, T., 701, 744

Canabal, M. Y., 900, 1061

Candas, B., 451

Cantrell, P., 1966

Capel, S. A., 23

Carda, R. D., 1319

Caregaro, L., 101

Carless, S. A., 1794

Carlisle, C. S., 498

Carlson, J. S., 1699

Carlson, N., 1157

Carlton, E. B., 234

Carney, R. M., 801, 809, 810

Caro, L., 979

Caron, S. L., 702

Carr, R. J., 434

Carroll, D., 567, 1343

Carroll, J. M., 848

Carron, A. V., 213, 1216, 1218, 1544, 1575, 1631, 1790, 1791, 1792, 1795, 1796, 1797, 1798, 1799, 1800, 1801, 1802, 1805, 1806, 1811, 1812, 1814, 1818, 1820,

Delaney, D., 166, 167, 1331

Delignieres, D., 707, 1283, 1984, 2006

Delk, J. L., 375

Delmonte, M. M., 799

Deluty, R. H., 2111

DeMarco, P., 1284

DeMers, G., 920

DeMoja, C. A., 1284, 1285, 1286

DeMoja, G., 1285, 1286

Denisoff, E., 816

Desertrain, G. S., 23

Deshaies, P., 1654

DeSouza, M. J., 120, 780

Deuser, W. E., 6

DeVaney, S., 921

DeVoe, D., 1988

Dewey, D., 2239

Dewey, T., 1075

Diamond, P., 451

DiCarlo, S., 627

Dickinson, A., 653

Diehl, N., 51, 61, 573, 1974, 1987, 2116, 2134

Dienstbier, R., 1427

DiGiuseppe, R. A., 189

DiGregorio, M. P., 825

Dill, K. E., 6

Dillon, C., 979

DiLorenzo, T. M., 602, 771, 922, 1287

Dimeo, F. C., 923

Dimitriou, L. A., 1004

DiNucci, J. M., 607, 1462, 1649, 2121, 2144

Dion, K. L., 1807, 1809, 1813

Dishman, R. K., 161, 162, 1148, 1288

Ditmar, T. D., 1761

Dixon, R. S., 259

Doan, B. T. T., 825

Dobson, K. S., 772

Dodge, C. S., 803

Doganis, G., 190, 2061, 2070

Dolphin, C., 452, 1000

Donolli, J., 1967

Donzelli, G. J., 1641

Doody, S. G., 1415

Doraiswamy, M., 766, 768

Dorr, T., 104

Dowell, L., 12

Dowell, M. N., 1996

Downes, J. W., 1197

Downes, M., 1017

Downs, W. R., 785

Dowthwaite, P., 1424, 1612

Doyle, J., 924

Dozois, D. J. A., 772

Draper, M. V., 741, 1860

Dratt, J., 1988

Dreiling, A. M., 1319

Drewnowski, A., 62

Driessens, M., 1107

Driggars-Bourgeois, T., 884, 1952

Driver, H. S., 894

Droppleman, L., 1077

Dube, M., 543, 544, 545, 546

Duche, P., 1294

Duda, J. L., 1533, 1570, 2015, 2163, 2166, 2167, 2168, 2169, 2170, 2171, 2172, 2173, 2174, 2175, 2176, 2177, 2178, 2179, 2183, 2199, 2201, 2221, 2224, 2228, 2229

Dudley, G., 1106, 1289, 1452, 1531

Duffy, L. J., 1642

Dugmore, D., 782

Dugoni, B. L., 1641

Duignan, P., 703

Duncan, C., 966

Duncan, S. C., 2196, 2198

Duncan, S. L., 740, 1746, 1969, 1998

Duncan, T. E., 1766, 1767, 1768, 1771, 1958, 2196, 2198

Dunn, E. C., 2267

Dunn, J. C., 1599, 2180

Dunn, J. G. H., 1599

Dunnagan, T., 1162

Durr, K. R., 1453

Durtschi, S., 925

Dvorak, J., 1903, 1923

Dworkin, R. H., 376

Dwyer, J. M., 1891, 1892, 1893

Dyer, J., 926, 927

Dzewaltowski, D. A., 959, 1016, 1438, 1657, 2064, 2146

E

Ferrand, C., 1295, 1461

Ferrando, A., 297, 881

Ferreira, R., 1293

Ferrer-Caja, E., 2182

Ferring, D., 574

Fetscher, S., 923

Fick, C., 2268

Figone, A. J., 455

Filaire, E., 1294, 1295, 1461

Filipp, S. H., 574

Fillingim, R., 937, 1169

Fillion, L., 938

Finer, E., 863

Fink, W., 989

Finkenberg, M. E., 605, 606, 607, 1462, 1649, 2051, 2121, 2144

Finn, J. A., 191

Firth, S., 1035, 1038

Fischer, D. G., 1891, 1892, 1893, 2268

Fisher, A. C., 1252, 1253, 1650

Fisher, M., 575

Fleck, S. J., 1106, 1531

Fletcher, R., 276

Flint, F., 1040, 1685

Flood, M., 1254

Flor, K. K., 26

Flory, J. D., 826, 939

Flynn, M. G., 831, 940, 1096

Focht, B. C., 941, 1296, 1959

Fogarty, G. J., 1578

G

Gansneder, B., 1429

Gappmaier, E., 1134

Garbin, M. G., 767

Garbutt, G., 1231

Gardner, D. E., 1815, 1843, 1844, 1894, 1913, 1914

Garfinkel, P. E., 65, 67, 106, 110, 111, 1136

Garl, T., 1153

Garland, D. J., 456, 1895, 1896

Garner, D. M., 65, 66, 67, 105, 106, 107, 108, 109, 110, 111

Garrett, J., 661

Garza, D. L., 1464

Gat, I., 951

Gates, R. D., 1233

Gates, W., 935, 1059, 1060

Gathright, T., 845

Gaudieri, S., 947

Gaulin, P., 543, 544, 545, 546

Gauvin, L., 1199

Gayton, W. F., 1960, 2013, 2025

Gebhardt, S. M., 1365

Gellen, M. I., 608, 610

Gemar, J. A., 1301

Gench, B., 551, 552, 553, 1064

Genuchi, M., 1739

George, D. M., 493

George, T. R., 1465

Georgiadis, M., 2184

Germone, K., 2092

Geron, E., 378

Gerson, R., 1654

Gessaroli, M. E., 2104

Gettman, L. R., 161

Getty, D., 1239

Giacobbi, P. R., 1600

Gibson, B. J., 457

Gilbert, D. G., 791, 1174

Gilchrist, H., 653

Gill, A., 1451

Gill, D. L., 134, 1302, 1346, 1438, 1466, 1484, 1501, 1523, 1655, 1656, 1657, 1675, 1676, 1691, 1694, 1695, 1873, 1963, 2016, 2027, 2064, 2065, 2066, 2135, 2145, 2146, 2192

Gillaspy, J. A., 701, 744

Gilliland, K., 194

Gilstrap, T., 541, 552, 553

Ginn, E. M., 982

Girandola, R., 322, 943, 1299

Gitlin, L., 1005

Givvin, K. B., 2185

Gjesme, T., 1312, 1663

Glass, B., 2211

Glazer, A., 952

Gleason, A., 1773

Gleim, G. W., 1043, 1051

Glenn, S. D., 1658, 1897

Glenn, T. M., 2162

Glicksohn, J., 324, 654

Glover, T. L., 1160

Godin, G., 2052

H

Jacobsen, B. S., 837

Jacomb, P. A., 846

Jaggli, N., 705

Jakeman, P., 1726

Jambor, E. A., 256, 1485, 1902

James, B., 2036

Jamesvalutis, M., 1780

Jamieson, K. I., 1618

Janelle, C. M., 1271, 1486, 1982

Janz, K. E., 2217

Jawad, A., 1147

Jean-Louis, G., 997

Jeffrey, A. C., 1159, 1160

Jenkins, C., 979

Jenkins, J. O., 1741

Jensen, B., 2154, 2207

Jensen, B. E., 1921

Jerome, G. J., 1487, 1671

Jerome, W. C., 471

Jevne, R., 81

Jin, P., 998, 1273, 1431, 1629, 2011, 2021

Joesting, J., 472, 812, 999

Johnsgard, K., 279, 280, 281, 382, 383, 384, 473, 474, 475

Johnson, A., 1000

Johnson, B., 1876

Johnson, C. E., 51, 61, 573, 1974, 2116

Johnson, C. L., 1987, 2134

Johnson, J. E., 1641

Johnson, M., 1171

Kowal, D. M., 335, 1015, 1328

Kowal, J., 2073

Kowalski, K. C., 1973, 1981, 1983, 2127

Kowalski, N. P., 1985, 2127

Kozub, S. A., 1822, 1823

Kraemer, R., 1016

Kraft, M., 670

Krahenbuhl, G. S., 1240, 1241

Krane, V., 121, 1421, 1508, 1509, 1510, 1511, 1512, 1513, 1594, 1595, 1682, 1743, 1744, 2128, 2287

Kraus, A., 787

Kreider, R. B., 1017

Krishnan, K. R., 766, 768, 783

Kroll, W., 386, 479, 480, 481, 1329

Krotee, M. L., 1330, 1683

Krushell, R. J., 1761

Kubitz, K. A., 757, 1366

Kudar, K., 600, 601

Kulhavy, R. W., 482

Kulkarni, P., 893

Kumar, A., 205

Kumaraiah, V., 215, 357, 805, 1389

Kunce, J., 637, 1238, 1411

Kurian, M., 482

Kurtzman, F. D., 122

Kusulas, J. W., 538

Kyllo, L., 1170

L

M

Maksud, M., 935

Malkin, M. J., 667

Mall, N. N., 345

Mallet, C. J., 1519

Malloy, D., 1889

Malloy, G. N., 487

Malone, C., 1429

Malumphy, T. M., 488

Man, F., 1345, 1520, 1688

Man, R., 875

Maneval, M., 1875

Mann, B. L., 1921

Manore, M., 58, 89

Manuel, G. M., 825, 833

Marceau, R., 1161

Marcellini, A., 707, 1283

Marcenaro, M., 442

Marchant, D. B., 1521, 1689

Marcotte, D., 833

Marigliano, V., 1368

Marisi, D. Q., 1542

Mark, M. M., 1764

Markland, D., 2005, 2274

Markoff, R., 1057

Marks, A. D., 138

Maroulakis, E., 1058

Marsh, H. W., 616, 716, 1950, 2071, 2072, 2150

Marshall, D., 2049

Marshall, G. N., 538

Myers, L., 1840

Myung Woo, H., 1360, 1532

N

Naessens, G., 1107

Nagle, F. J., 1108

Nagy, S., 240, 1109

Nahakian-Nelms, M., 87

Nakagawa, K., 1125

Nakano, K., 9

Napolitano, M. A., 80, 768, 783

Naqvi, A., 1975

Naruse, K., 821, 1361

Nash, J., 136, 706

Nasser, M., 74

Nation, J. R., 14, 15, 16, 188, 236, 916, 1048, 1049, 1110, 1111, 1112

Naylor, S., 1434

Needels, T. L., 882, 883, 1266

Nelson, D., 614

Nelson, D. O., 492

Nemeroff, C. J., 245

Nesser, J., 536, 1756

Nesti, A. S., 1517

Nettleton, B., 299

Neufeld, P. S., 158

Nevill, A. M., 905, 906, 907, 1248, 2133

Newby, R. W., 1113, 1114, 1115, 1180

Newcomb, M. D., 680

Newcombe, P. A., 353, 1116, 1362

O

P

Petlichkoff, L., 1467, 1469, 1471, 1659, 1660, 2191

Petrak, B., 494

Petrie, T. A., 51, 53, 54, 61, 131, 231, 570, 573, 585, 769, 909, 1269, 1441, 1708, 1709, 1710, 1711, 1804, 1924, 1957, 1974, 1987, 2078, 2080, 2081, 2082, 2083, 2084, 2085, 2086, 2216, 2134

Petruzello, S. J., 763, 1291, 1366, 1371

Pfleger, B., 1197

Phelan, J. G., 209

Phillips, D. A., 498

Picard, C. L., 76, 132

Piedmont, R. L., 422, 1372

Pierce, C., 300

Pierce, E. F., 1071, 1072, 1074, 1075, 1135, 2097

Piercy, M., 1163

Piering, P. N., 1353

Pim, A., 1430, 1628

Pinel, B., 1788

Pinhas, L., 1136

Pink, M. J., 1218

Pistacchio, T., 171, 1137, 2056

Pittenger, D. J., 416

Pivik, R. T., 359

Pizza, F., 940

Plake, B., 1427

Plante, T. G., 825, 832, 833

Plascak, F. D., 1932

Plummer, O. K., 620

Poag, K., 1773

Poe, C., 428

Pratz, O., 152

Price, A. A., 1133

Price, J. H., 169, 173

Privette, G., 912

Prochaska, J., 1118

Pronk, N., 1146, 1147

Prusaczyk, W., 1148

Prussin, R., 786

Przybeck, T. R., 1198

Ptacek, J. T., 1603, 1927

Puckett, J. R., 562

Pugh, S. F., 129, 973

Pugliese, M., 401

Puleo, E., 892

Putnam, B. A., 622

Pyecha, J., 500

Q

Qiu, Y. J., 367, 1940

Quarterman, J., 453

Quigley, T., 37, 38

Quinn, A. M., 1149, 1925, 2018

R

Rabinowitz, E., 667

Rabinowitz, S., 172

Raciti, M. C., 77, 133

Radell, S. A., 249

Raedeke, T. D., 39, 1547

Rafeld, J., 1512

Raffagnino, R., 2259

Raglin, J. S., 1095, 1096, 1121, 1122, 1123, 1124, 1150, 1151, 1152, 1153, 1154, 1155, 1156, 1157, 1270, 1313 1326, 1364, 1378, 1379, 1380, 1381, 1382, 1407, 1413, 1548, 1597

Rainbolt, W., 550, 900

Rainey, D. W., 40, 41, 672, 1158, 1717, 1718, 1719, 1816, 1839

Rainey, K. W., 1719

Ramel, W., 793

Rampazzo, M., 486

Randle, S., 1549

Ransdell, L. B., 1988

Rasch, P. J., 396

Rasmussen, P. R., 1159, 1160

Ratliff, W. R., 1067

Ratusny, D., 312

Rauch, T., 1176, 1219, 1220

Raudsepp, L., 1989, 2222

Rawson, H. E., 656

Reardon, J. P., 611

Rechnitzer, P. A., 468

Reddon, J., 1161

Reed, C., 1444

Reel, J. J., 134, 2135

Rees, C. R., 2057

Reeves, D. L., 834

Regmi, M., 1784

Rehm, M., 915

Rehor, P. R., 1162

Reid, B. M., 356, 2058

Reilley, R. R., 398

Reilly, T., 1078, 1163, 1383, 1385

Reimer, H. A., 1906, 1907

Reis, J., 2252

Reitano, M., 1284

Rejeski, W. J., 749, 750, 751, 758, 830, 835, 1164, 1384, 1776, 2124, 2130

Remers, L., 1840

Renfrow, N. E., 430, 501

Renger, R., 1165

Renneckar, C. A., 502

Restorick, L., 706

Reus, V., 966

Reznikoff, M., 181

Rhind, S., 782

Ribak, J., 172

Rich, E. L., 752

Richalet, J. P., 1352

Richards, G. E., 616

Richards, L. A., 129

Richardson, M., 88

Richardson, P. A., 200, 563, 1720, 1904

Richardson, S. A., 2090

Richert, A. J., 135

Richir, K., 552, 553

Richman, C. L., 1627

Richter, F., 1781

Richter, P., 787

Riddick, C. C., 17, 1166, 1721

Ridgway, M. E., 548

Rimm, H., 773, 1290

Rinehardt, F., 1016

Rippe, J. M., 892

Rippon, C., 136

Ritter, E., 297, 881

Ritter-Taylor, M., 32, 1435, 1677

Rivkin, F., 1522, 1693

Robazza, C., 1550

Robb, M., 1443, 1444, 1445, 1446, 1447, 1552

Robbins, M. A., 1966, 1967

Roberts, L., 342

Roberts, N., 186, 303, 704, 1278, 1634

Robertson, K., 1385

Robertson, P. G., 396

Robinson, B. E., 788

Robinson, D. M., 1669

Robinson, D. W., 763, 1167, 1777, 1778

Robinson, J. B., 88

Robinson, S. M., 1669

Robinson, T. L., 1366

Robinson, T. T., 1631, 1908

Rockert, W., 110

Rodger, J. S. E., 1514

Rodgers, B., 846

Rodgers, W., 1788

Rodin, J., 72, 118

Rodrigo, G., 1386, 1551

Rodriguez-Zayas, J., 940

Rodzilsky, D., 564

Roeder, L. M., 2253

Roemmich, J., 990

Rogers, R. L., 51, 61, 573, 1974, 1987, 2116, 2134

Rohack, J., 1146, 1147

Ronan, K. R., 662

Ronzoni, S., 1368

Rosch, D., 1903, 1923

Rosen, J. C., 75, 78, 126, 137, 582, 784

Rosen, L. W., 66, 108

Rosentsweig, J., 1633

Rosnet, E., 1352

Ross, K. G., 659

Rossi, B., 674

Roswal, G., 976, 987, 994, 1317

Roth, D., 937, 955, 1168, 1169

Roth, W. T., 298, 646, 1268

Rotstein, P., 378

Rowland, G. L., 675, 676

Rowley, A., 1170

Rubenfeld, S., 2266

Ruble, A. E., 142

Ruble, V., 410, 415

Ruby, B. C., 915

Rucinski, A., 79

Rudisill, M. E., 256, 1487, 1588

Ruder, M. K., 1873

Rudestam, K. E., 679

Rudolph, K. D., 845

S

Sees, K., 966

Sefton, J. M., 1584

Segal, J. D., 728, 1725

Segebartt, K., 1171

Segerstrom, S. C., 1172

Segger, J. F., 614

Selby, P. M., 1961

Selig, S. E., 1698

Semper, T., 2187

Senkfor, A. J., 807, 1393

Seraganian, P., 1199

Serfass, R. C., 1108

Serpa, S., 1912

Sewell, D. F., 1517, 1560

Sforzo, G. A., 831

Shacham, S., 1173

Shaffer, D. R., 752

Shaffer, S., 1770

Shapiro, J. E., 243

Sharp, M. W., 398

Sharpe, J. P., 791, 1174

Sharpley, C. F., 626

Shaw, C. N., 432

Shaw, J., 758, 1384

Shea, C. H., 204

Sheffield, A., 1757

Shek, P. N., 782

Shephard, R. J., 254, 782, 1230, 2052, 2059

Sheppard, S., 746

Sherman, C., 139

Sherman, C. A., 214, 242

Sherman, W. M., 769, 909, 1957

Sherrill, C., 252, 541, 550, 551, 552, 553, 554, 900, 1064, 1131, 1132, 2049

Shevlin, M. E., 316, 587

Shields, D. L. L., 1815, 1843, 1844, 1894, 1913, 1914

Shifren, K., 358, 729, 753

Shimomitsu, T., 82, 1065

Shin, Y. H., 1175

Shiraki, H., 1405

Shisslak, C. M., 85, 225, 364, 408, 742, 794, 1250

Short, M. A., 627

Shows, D., 607

Shryock, M. G., 1615, 2233

Shukitt-Hale, B., 1176

Shultz, B. B., 510, 1069, 1178, 1394, 1395

Sidney, K. H., 2059

Siegel, A. J., 140

Silberg, N. T., 78, 137

Silliman, L., 551, 554

Silva, J. M., 463, 510, 1177, 1178, 1394, 1395

Sime, W., 1427, 1534, 1537, 1702

Simini, G., 486

Simon, J. A., 1469, 1522, 1561, 1692, 1693, 2060

Simons, C. W., 266, 1179, 2282

Simonsen, J., 769, 909, 1957

Simpson-Housley, P., 221

Simpson, S., 1113, 1114, 1115, 1180

Sinclair, D. A., 2030

Sinclair, E. D., 511

Sinclair, G. D., 517, 1935

Singer, R. N., 284, 512, 1486, 1570

Singh, A. P., 496

Singh, R. B., 496

Singh, U. B., 496

Sinyor, D., 836

Sisley, B. L., 23

Skelly, W. A., 232, 244, 315, 361, 936, 1225, 1647, 1734, 1947

Skinner, C. S., 158

Skirka, N., 1181

Sklar, J. H., 1761

Sklov, M. C., 268

Skordilis, E. K., 2154, 2207

Skowron, E. A., 141

Slack, T., 37, 38

Slade, A., 1212, 1572

Slanger, E., 679

Slaven, L., 1182, 1183

Slay, H. A., 80

Slenker, S. E., 173

Slogrove, C. L., 2255

Slusher, H., 399, 513

Small, L., 625

Smethurst, C. J., 1460, 1950, 2072

Smith, A. L., 2136

Smith, A. M., 1100, 1184, 1185, 1186, 1187

Smith, B. D., 2

Smith, D. K., 1990, 2045, 2125, 2283

Thomas, P. R., 1578, 1950, 1951, 2072

Thomas, S. M., 1706

Thomas, S., 1230

Thomas, T. R., 860, 1223, 1224, 1261

Thompson, A., 835, 1164

Thompson, B., 701, 744

Thompson, C., 860

Thompson, J. K., 130

Thompson, M., 1073

Thorland, W., 603

Thornton, B., 1966, 1967

Thornton, E. W., 2103

Thorpe, J. A., 288

Thorpe, K., 2273

Thuot, S. M., 1579

Tibbs, J., 73

Tiggeman, M., 235

Tinsley, E. G., 735

Tinsley, H. E., 617

Titus, T. G., 1615, 2233

Tobacyk, J. J., 2243

Tokunaga, M., 2126

Tokushima, S., 2126

Tolson, H., 1083

Toner, B. B., 1136

Tonymon, P., 198, 1412, 1664

Toon, K., 1907

Toriola, A. L., 507, 2101

Torki, M. A., 682

MELLEN STUDIES IN PSYCHOLOGY